MY FIRST 18 YEARS

BORN IN
1983
FROM 1983 TO 2000

© 2024 TDM Publishing. Rights reserved.

My First 18 Years is a brand of TDM Publishing.
The image, brand and logos are protected and owned by TDM Publishing.

www.mijneerste18jaar.nl
info@mijneerste18jaar.nl

My First 18 Years idea and concept: Thars Duijnstee.
Research and text: Lucinda Gosling, Stephen Barnard, Jeffrey Roozeboom, Katherine Alcock.
Composition and image editing: Jeffrey Roozeboom.
Design: Ferry Geutjes, Boudewijn van der Plas, Jeffrey Roozeboom.
Proofreading: Alison Griffiths.

Every effort has been made to trace the rights holders of all images. If you believe an image has been incorrectly credited, please contact the publisher.

No part of this publication may be reproduced, stored in or introduced to an automated data-file, or made public, in any form or by electronic, digital, mechanical, photocopying, recording or any other means, without the prior written consent of the publisher.

Photos: Sound & Vision, National Archives, Getty images, Mary Evans Picture Library, Shutterstock, BNNVARA, AVROTROS, Veronica, KRO-NCRV, KIPPA, *Mijn eerste 18 jaar* archives.

In writing this series, the authors drew from the following sources: view from 1963-1999, NTS / NOS Annual Review, nueens.nl, vandaagindegeschiedenis.nl, beleven.org, IMDb, Wikipedia, Eye Filmmuseum, Rollingstone.com, image & sound, National Archives, Onthisday.com, Parlement.com. *Complete Book of UK Hit Singles, First Hits 1949-1959* (Boxtree Books), Billboard Books, *Reader's Digest* Music series 1950s-1970s, British Library Newspaper Archive, rogerebert.com

Thanks to: Spotify, Rick Versteeg, Rik Booltink.

The Top 10 list for each year is compiled by Stephen Barnard and is a personal selection of best-selling hits, radio favourites and lesser-known tracks that reflect the popular artists and styles of each year. Some are universally regarded classics, others will be less remembered yet are equally emblematic of the tastes of that year. Each list should provoke many 'Ah yes!' moments, particularly those almost forgotten treasures that are rarely heard even as 'golden oldies' yet tickled the ears in their day.

How to use Spotify playlists:

1. Open Spotify.
2. Click search (the magnifying glass in the image).
3. Click scan (the camera in the picture).
4. Point your camera at the Spotify code in the book.
5. After that, you can play the selected list.

ISBN 978 94 9331 792 5
NUR: 400

1983

MY FIRST 18 YEARS

SPORT

Dev digs deep
In the Cricket World Cup at the Nevill Ground, Tunbridge Wells, India's Kapil Dev gives an incredible individual performance during a group match against Zimbabwe. India have just 17 for 5 when Dev smashes a breathtaking 175 runs off 138 balls; an innings that includes sixteen boundaries and six sixes. Buoyed up by his brilliant performance, India proceed to defeat England and Australia, to reach the final at Lord's where they topple the mighty West Indies by 43 runs.

Corbiere a winner
Corbiere wins the Grand National on 9th April, the first winner of the legendary steeplechase to be trained by a woman, Jenny Pitman.

World Championships in Helsinki
British athletes prove their worth on the world stage at the World Athletics Championship in Helsinki which has its final day on 14th August. Steve Cram emerges from the shadow of Ovett and Coe to take gold in the 1500m, while Daley Thompson seals victory in the decathlon. Elsewhere, American multi-discipline maestro Carl Lewis (photo) wins gold in the 100m, long jump and 4 x 100m relay.

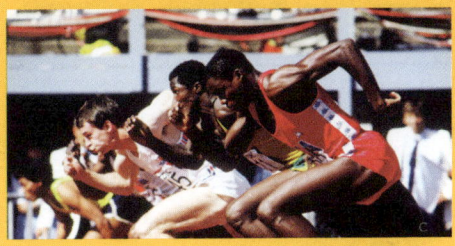

Jennings reaches 1,000 goal
Arsenal and Northern Ireland goalkeeper Pat Jennings becomes the first footballer in the English league to make one thousand senior appearances, at a match against West Bromwich Albion on 26th February, which, fortunately, is goalless!

England defeat the All Blacks
The All Blacks' rugby union tour of England and Scotland reaches its climax at Twickenham on 19th November, when a New Zealand team depleted of more experienced members, but still dangerous, meet England, who have not beaten them on home turf since 1936. In a rough match, beset by injury on both sides, England manage to hold off New Zealand to seal a 15-9 win, thanks in part to a try from Maurice Colclough.

8 JAN 1983
Margaret Thatcher arrives in the Falkland Islands for a four-day visit to British troops.

15 FEB 1983
The Austin Metro is Britain's best-selling car.

15 MAR 1983
The Budget raises tax thresholds, effectively cutting taxes by £2 billion.

1983

DOMESTIC NEWS

Police drown in Blackpool
5th January 1983 Tragedy strikes Blackpool as three members of the police force, two men and a woman, drown whilst attempting to rescue a man from the sea. The man had gone into the water after his Jack Russell terrier and cannot be saved despite best efforts.

Shooting of Stephen Waldorf
14th January 1983 26-year-old Stephen Waldorf is shot and seriously injured by armed policemen whilst travelling through London in the passenger seat of a friend's car. The police had mistaken Waldorf for an escaped prisoner, David Martin, who would be rearrested two weeks later.

Muswell Hill murderer
11th February 1983 Dennis Nielson is arrested and charged with murder after human remains are discovered at his Muswell Hill flat. As the investigation progresses, he is revealed to have murdered at least twelve young men and boys since 1978.

New £1 coin
21st April 1983 A new £1 coin is introduced to replace the £1 note, a feature of the British currency since 1797. The new coin features the Queen's portrait on the front, and a different reverse image is issued every year, starting with the royal coat of arms, and followed by emblems reflecting the different nations of the UK.

British Airways S-61 crash
16th July 1983 A British Airways helicopter flight is downed in heavy fog over the Celtic Sea. Twenty people on board are killed, while six are rescued by a lifeboat.

Maze Prison escape
25th September 1983 20 guards are injured, and one dies of a heart attack, when 38 IRA prisoners escape from HM Prison Maze in Northern Ireland. The prisoners escape using guns, smuggled into the prison, to hijack a lorry in what becomes the biggest prison break in British history.

DO YOU REMEMBER THIS?

Double deck cassette recorder

Seatbelts mandatory
31st January 1983 The wearing of seatbelts becomes mandatory across the UK. Seat belts have been essential safety components in cars since 1972, but compliance has been low. This next step of legislation leads to a 30% reduction in fatal injuries of front seat passengers.

23 APR 1983
The People's March for Jobs sets off from Glasgow, reaching London in early June.

11 MAY 1983
Aberdeen win the European Cup Winner's cup against Real Madrid 2-1.

23 JUN 1983
Monty Python's *The Meaning of Life* is released, the final film for the Python gang.

1983

ROYALTY & POLITICS

Thrust 2 land speed record
4th October 1983 Scottish entrepreneur Richard Noble breaks the land speed record in jet-powered car Thrust 2. Racing over a course in the Black Rock Desert in Nevada, he sets a speed of 634.051 miles per hour.

Thatcher wins second term in office
On June 10th, the Conservatives win a landslide victory in the General Election, with a 144 majority. The decisive victory leads to the resignation of Labour leader Michael Foot and the SDP's Roy Jenkins. On 2nd October, Labour elects 41-year-old Welsh left-winger Neil Kinnock as party leader, with the more moderate Roy Hattersley as deputy leader.

Brink's-Mat robbery
26th November 1983 A robbery at Heathrow International Trading Estate sees six thieves break into the Brink's-Mat warehouse. Described as the 'crime of the century', the men make away with 6,800 gold bars, diamonds, and cash, in total worth nearly £26 million. Whilst two men are arrested and convicted, most of the stolen goods are never recovered.

Tory scandal - Cecil Parkinson resigns
Cecil Parkinson, Secretary for Trade and Industry and mastermind of the Tory election campaign, admits to his long-term affair with his former secretary, who is pregnant with his child. Parkinson announces he will not be resigning, and has decided to stay with his wife. But Sara Keays gives an interview to *The Times*, and her revelations force Parkinson, Mrs Thatcher's golden boy (photo), to resign in disgrace. He is replaced by Norman Tebbit.

Harrods bombing
17th December 1983 A car bomb planted by the Provisional IRA explodes outside Harrods department store in London. Despite a warning being received, the area is not evacuated in time and six people are killed alongside 90 injured. Eight days later, on Christmas Day, another bomb explodes on Oxford Street with no casualties.

26 JUL 1983
Mother of 10, Victoria Gillick, loses a court case against the DHSS to prevent the distribution of contraceptives to under-16s.

1 AUG 1983
Sales of new cars receive a boost as A-prefix car registration plates are introduced.

5 SEP 1983
Adventure cartoon *He-Man and the Masters of the Universe* has its world premiere on Children's ITV.

1983

Queen presents honour
The Queen presents the Order of Merit to Mother Teresa of Calcutta in a ceremony in the grounds of the Presidential Palace in New Delhi.

FOREIGN NEWS

Switched on
1st January 1983 A switch is turned at the American Advanced Research Projects Agency. The switch marks the beginning of the internet as we know it.

Black holes
1st January 1983 Scientists discovered the first black hole - formed when a star implodes at the end of its existence - in 1971. Now an article appears about a second black hole, 170,000 light-years from Earth. It is smaller than Scotland, but weighs ten times as much as the Sun.

Fake Hitler diaries
30th January 1983 Fifty years after Adolf Hitler came to power, 62 of his diaries are found in Germany. The Führer describes his experiences from 1932 until the day before his death. Then master forger Konrad Kujau confesses that he wrote the diaries himself and that he received 2.5 million marks from the Der Stern journalist who supposedly 'discovered' them. The blunder marks a new low in European journalism.

Ice cold
21st July 1983 At the Vostok station in Antarctica, in the middle of the polar cap, the polar station measures a temperature of -89.2°C. It is the lowest reliably measured temperature ever recorded on Earth.

Korean Air Flight 007
1st September 1983 When Korean Air Flight 007 en route from New York to Seoul ends up in a restricted part of Soviet airspace due to a navigation error, the Boeing 747 is shot down 55 kilometres from Moneron Island. All 269 people on board are killed. It is another low point in the Cold War and sends a shiver across the world.

---

27 OCT 1983
A memorial service is held for much-loved actor and raconteur David Niven who had died on 30th July.

18 NOV 1983
Janet Walton from Liverpool gives birth to six baby girls after taking fertility drugs. The sextuplets become national celebrities.

3 DEC 1983
As part of an ongoing peace campaign, women protestors break into RAF Greenham Common in Berkshire.

1983

Word and Lotus 1-2-3
1st October 1983 Microsoft releases the first version of the word processing programme Word, which allows computer users to format typed text with line breaks and bold and italic letters. Multi-Tool Word, as it is called, comes free with *PC World magazine*. Users find the interface strange and WordStar and WordPerfect prove more popular. How different things will be with Lotus 1-2-3, now ready for launch. Many businesses buy the IBM computer specifically for it, to create clear spreadsheets, graphs and databases.

US invades Grenada
25th October 1983 The Caribbean island of Grenada, a member of the British Commonweath, is invaded by US forces aiming to prevent communist rule there. For virtually the only time in Ronald Reagan's presidency, Margaret Thatcher expresses private disapproval of US action, especially over the fact that the UK was not consulted.

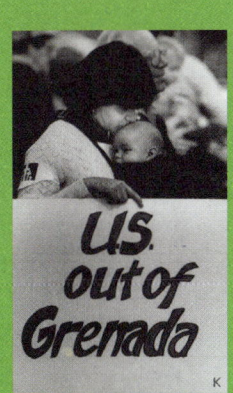

Nuclear false alarms
As cruise missiles arrive in Europe for stationing in NATO countries, two major nuclear scares bring the world momentarily to the brink of catastrophe. On 26th September, Soviet officer Stanislav Petrov correctly identifies a warning of a US missIle attack as a false alarm. On 7th November, a NATO exercise is misinterpreted by Soviet officials as cover for a nuclear attack and Warsaw Pact forces are placed on full alert. The danger passes with the conclusion of the exercise four days later.

ENTERTAINMENT

The Roly Polys
Dance troupe The Roly Polys, seven generously proportioned ladies, led by 4' 11" Mo Moreland, tap and shimmy their way onto screens for the first time on *The Les Dawson Show* on 15th January.

The Machine Gunners
The first episode of the TV adaptation of Robert Westall's 1975 Carnegie medal-winning children's novel, *The Machine Gunners*, is aired on 23rd February. The Second World War drama set in a north-east coastal town in February 1941 centres on Chas McGill and his friends who discover a crashed German plane, complete with machine gun and ammunition.

Home video surges
New figures show that 10% of UK households now own a video recorder - and that the vast majority of those prefer VHS to Betamax, its technically superior but more expensive rival format. Home video is a revolutionary new medium that enables recording and playback of television programmes, gives users the opportunity to make videos of their own, and makes movies old and new available for home viewing. By the end of the decade, more than half of households in the UK will own a VCR.

1983

Let's act
Nagisa Oshima's *Merry Christmas, Mr. Lawrence* is released on 25th August. Based on Laurens van der Post's memoirs about his experiences in a Japanese POW camp in Java during the Second World War, Bowie is the rebellious Major Jack Culliers opposite Tom Conti and Ryuichi Sakamoto. Oshima cast Bowie in the role after seeing him perform in the play *The Elephant Man* on Broadway in 1980.

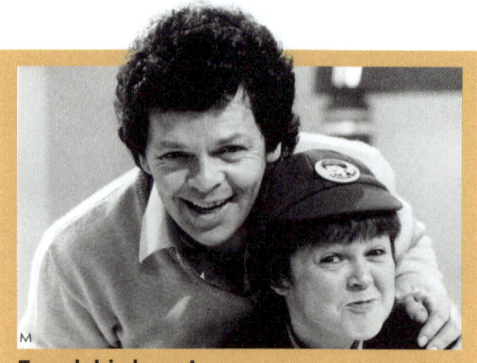

Fan-dabi-dozee!
After years on the cabaret circuit, Wee Jimmy Krankie and his sensible, grown-up sidekick, Ian Krankie, have become TV favourites through appearances on *Crackerjack*. Their star has risen to such heights that they get their own show this year; *The Krankies Klub* begins on BBC1 on 10th September. Much loved by a generation of kids, who adore cheeky Jimmy Krankie's mischievous antics and his catchphrase, 'Fan-dabi-dozee', the eventual realisation that Jimmy is in real life Janette Krankie, a woman in her thirties who is married to Ian, comes as a shock, second only to finding out Father Christmas doesn't really exist.

Wake up and smell... a rat?
Early risers can enjoy telly with their cornflakes from 17th January, when *Breakfast Time* launches on BBC1. Hot on its heels is ITV's morning offering, *TV-am*, beginning on 1st February. *TV-am*'s early weeks are beset by problems and viewing figures flag but the introduction of puppet rodent Roland Rat on 1st April helps to revive its fortunes.

Corrie love triangle
Coronation Street fans are gripped during its 21st February episode when Ken Barlow discovers his wife Deirdre has been having an affair with Mike Baldwin who Ken describes as a 'spiv' and 'little creep'. It's an emotional scene full of high drama with the usually mild-mannered Ken losing his cool and almost throttling Deirdre when Mike arrives at their door.

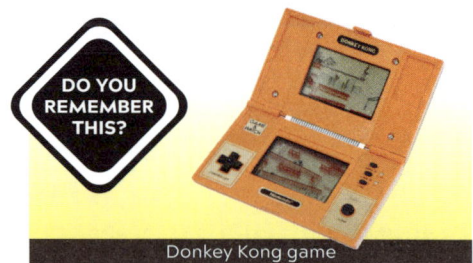

Do you remember this?

Donkey Kong game

The Dark Crystal
Chief Muppeteer Jim Henson taps into the vogue for fantasy films, working with Frank Oz on *The Dark Crystal*, first shown in UK cinemas on 17th February. Five years in the making, it is essentially a tale of good versus evil, with the vulture-like Skeksis pitted against the gentle Mystics. In a plot that borrows liberally from Tolkein, two elfin Gelflings are tasked with spiriting the powerful Dark Crystal away from the Skeksis before the alignment of three suns.

1983

Cabbage Patch craziness

Harrods is swamped with shoppers on 1st December, as they descend on the store to grab this festive season's must-have toy - a Cabbage Patch doll. Despite their strange, pudgy faces, which everyone, even the buyers, agree are rather ugly, the Cabbage Patch phenomenon has caused violent riots among shoppers in the US.

Just Seventeen

On 20th October, comes the launch of *Just Seventeen* magazine, a fresh new title aimed at teenage girls, heavy on fashion, heartthrobs and pithy advice, and light on the soppy romance photo-stories which magazines like *My Guy* peddle. *J-17* doesn't patronise its readers, has some great cover giveaways and feels like the ideal read for any sophisticated 1980s teen.

Tootsie

Tootsie steals the hearts of UK audiences when it opens on 28th April. Sydney Pollack's direction and Dustin Hoffman's entertaining turn as a difficult, out-of-work actor who lands a plum role in a primetime soap by becoming 'Dorothy Michaels', brings the screwball comedy of the 1930s bang up to date. There's an underlying message about gender and male privilege, but it's delivered without losing any of its sparkle. As she becomes an unlikely standard bearer for feminism, 'Dorothy' falls in love with his/her co-star played by Jessica Lange, who won an Oscar for Best Actress. A dragged-up delight.

I'll have a 'P' please, Bob

Blockbusters, a quiz game for sixth-formers hosted by Bob Holness, first airs on ITV on 29th August. More intellectually rigorous than the majority of teatime quiz shows, one solo player battles a team of two as they make their way across a board of interlocked hexagons by answering general knowledge questions linked to the letter on each hexagon. The winner goes on to try their luck at the Gold Run, with a chance to stay and defend their champion status each week.

Cheers to that

Channel 4 builds a reputation for sniffing out great American sitcoms, beginning with *Cheers* which it presents for the first time on 4th February. Set in a Boston bar where 'everybody knows your name', the wisecracks flow as freely as the beer.

Tweenyboppers

Minipops airs for the first time on Channel 4 on 8th February. Featuring pre-teen children impersonating current pop stars and singing along to chart hits, the appearance of these mini-me popstrels with crimped hair and eyeliner is controversial to say the least and after one season, the ill-judged *Minipops* is dropped.

1983

The A Team
On the run from the US government, 'for a crime they didn't commit', ex-commandos The A-Team become the action-adventure sensation of 1983. First screened on ITV on 22nd July, it's the de facto star, the muscular Mr T as B.A. Baracus, with his acres of gold chains, surly countenance and magical, mechanical know-how, who becomes a cult figure. Of course, nobody's perfect and B.A.'s Achilles heel is his fear of flying; 'I ain't getting on no plane' becomes one of the show's memorable catchphrases.

Tucker's Luck
The first episode of Tucker's Luck, a Grange Hill spin-off series, begins on BBC2 on 10th March. Featuring one of the most popular characters from Grange Hill's original cast, it follows the teenage Peter 'Tucker' Jenkins (Todd Carty) as he negotiates life, work (or lack of it) and girls after leaving school.

Blue Peter's sunken garden vandalised
The decline of civilisation can perhaps be pinpointed to the moment in November 1983 when Blue Peter's Italian sunken garden is vandalised. Viewers are horrified as Janet Ellis confirms that the upturned sundial, ripped-up plants and oil on the pond are due to senseless vandalism. Percy Thrower finds it hard to hold back the tears and in a moment of political incorrectness, suggests the perpetrators are 'mentally ill'.

Thrills and chills
The golden age of the music video has truly arrived when Michael Jackson's Thriller is screened at the ungodly hour of 1:05am on Channel 4, introduced by Jools Holland of The Tube. Zombies, teen movie schtick and gobsmacking dance routines combine to make this a major multimedia event, at a time Jackson is reaching the peak of his solo success.

Swatch out
Swatch watches are launched on 1st March, Switzerland's riposte to the growing dominance of digital watches from Asia. Swatches are analogue, quartz time pieces, but they're also affordable and their colourful, simple design make them a classic 1980s accessory.

Caped crusaders
Early October sees the advent of two animated superheroes. On 3rd October, the lantern-jawed, fruit-fuelled Bananaman, who originated in the comic Nutty, comes to life on BBC1, voiced by members of The Goodies. Superted airs a day later, also on BBC1, almost a year after he had first been shown on Welsh TV channel, S4C. Originally created by Mike Young as a series of books, written to help cure his young son's fear of the dark, Superted, a toy factory reject, is brought to life by a visiting alien from the Planet Spot and given superpowers.

1983

MUSIC

Blue Monday
19th March 1983 Breaking new ground musically, technically and commercially is *Blue Monday* by New Order. It uses a synth bassline, a sequencer and a drum machine. Sampling Kraftwerk's *Uranium* and echoing Donna Summer's *Our Love* and the soundtrack of *The Good, the Bad and the Ugly*, it's an extraordinary amalgam of sound and voice that is a hit twice during 1983, in twelve-inch and standard format versions.

Wizards of Oz
Men at Work lead a succession of Australasian bands to big success in the UK and US. With its ironic articulation of Antipodean clichés, their *Down Under* becomes almost a second Australian anthem, while 1983 sees Michael Hutchence's INXS (photo) debut in New York and Icehouse build their reputation by supporting David Bowie on tour. Nick Cave and the Bad Seeds emerge from the ashes of the much-admired Birthday Party, while Rick Springfield and the Little River Band each have a strong run of hits in more conventional soft rock mode in the US. Uncompromising and politically active, long-timers Midnight Oil are on the cusp of an international breakthrough as the year ends.

Pink Floyd on hiatus
21st March 1983 After releasing *The Final Cut*, which is largely the work of Roger Waters, Pink Floyd dissolve into acrimony. For the next four years the members will focus on solo work and dealing with legal action around the right to use the Pink Floyd name.

Duran Duran
26th March 1983 Hitting No. 1 for the first time - and doing so just one week after the single's release - are new romantic pin-up boys Duran Duran with *Is There Something I Should Know*. Thanks to their super-glamorous and very MTV-friendly videos, Simon Le Bon and friends are the hottest UK property in the US at the moment, where audience hysteria is likened to Beatlemania. They are named after a character in the 1964 sci-fi film *Barbarella* starring Jane Fonda.

Billy's innocent
The album of the year has to be Billy Joel's multi-platinum *An Innocent Man*, on which Long Island's finest pays homage to the singers and groups who influenced him. The songs brilliantly capture the styles, characteristics and qualities of the Drifters (the title track), Motown (*Tell Her About It*), doo wop (*The Longest Time*) and the Four Seasons (*Uptown Girl*). More than a tribute, it's a series of loving re-creations with nostalgically choreographed videos to match.

1983

Bowie and Nile
9th April 1983 It's a marriage made in heaven - David Bowie teaming up with ex-Chic guitarist and producer Nile Rodgers for a chart-topping album and single, both called *Let's Dance*, that do not pretend to be anything more than solid slices of ultra-funky contemporary dance music. *China Girl* and *Modern Love* are also hits from the same album, the warm reception to which encourages Bowie to tour for the first time in five years.

MY FIRST 18 YEARS
TOP 10 1983

1. **Billie Jean** *Michael Jackson*
2. **War Baby** *Tom Robinson*
3. **Lovecats** *The Cure*
4. **Karma Chameleon** *Culture Club*
5. **Every Breath You Take** *The Police*
6. **IOU** *Freeez*
7. **Islands in the Stream** *Dolly Parton, Kenny Rogers*
8. **Come Dancing** *The Kinks*
9. **Back on the Chain Gang** *The Pretenders*
10. **Heartache Avenue** *The Maisonettes*

Soul brothers
Young white soul boys are in their element in UK pop in the 1980s. Paul Weller launches the Style Council with Mick Talbot to create the

Otis Redding/Curtis Mayfield style soul he adored as a teenager. Spandau Ballet swap outrageous new romantic get-ups for a smart-suited new look and storm the chart with *True*. And Paul Young (photo), has the temerity to cover a hallowed Marvin Gaye classic, *Wherever I Lay My Hat (That's My Home)*, and take it No. 1.

Pointed politics
Politics is part of the pop mix in 1983. Written in the wake of the Falklands War, two of the most pointed songs of the year both originate on Elvis Costello's *Punch the Clock* album - *Shipbuilding* and *Pills and Soap*. Beautifully covered in deadpan style by Robert Wyatt, once of Soft Machine, *Shipbuilding* is a swipe at the prospect of a closed-down British industry being revived for making battleships, told from the conflicted perspective of an unemployed man.

Thrashing it out
25th July 1983 The thrash metal genre arrives with a vengeance with *Kill 'Em All* by Metallica, a four-piece formed in 1981 by Lars Ulrich and influenced by the UK bands who comprised the 'new wave of heavy metal' at the time. Metallica combine speed and energy with a Zeppelin-esque density of sound and soon find themselves one of the big four of the metal scene alongside Anthrax, Slayer and a band formed by ex-member Dave Mustaine, Megadeth.

PHOTO CREDITS Copyright 2024, TDM Rights BV.
Photos: **A** Getty Images - Hulton Archive - Getty Images / **B** Mirrorpix - Getty Images / **C** Tony Duffy - Getty Images / **D** PA Images - Getty Images / **E** PA Images - Getty Images / **F** Brownie Harris - Corbis Historical - Getty Images / **G** Mirrorpix - Getty Images / **H** Anwar Hussein - Getty Images Europe - Getty Images / **I** Heritage Images - Hulton Archive - Getty Images / **J** Ullstein Bild - Getty Images / **K** Denver Post - Getty Images / **L** Avalon - Hulton Archive - Getty Images / **M** Ronald Grant Archive - Mary Evans / **N** AF Archive - Universal Pictures - Mary Evans / **O** Art Zelin - Archive Photos - Getty Images / **P** Ronald Grant Archive - Mary Evans / **Q** Ronald Grant Archive - Mary Evans / **R** Avalon - Hulton Archive - Getty Images / **S** AF Archive - Mary Evans / **T** Jean-Louis URLI - Gamma-Rapho - Getty Images / **U** Fin Costello - Redferns - Getty Images / **V** Michael Putland - Hulton Archive - Getty Images / **W** Krasner Trebitz - Redferns - Getty Images.

1984

SPORT

Torvill and Dean's golden moment
One of the most iconic moments in sporting history takes place at the Winter Olympics in Sarajevo, appropriately on 14th February. The United Kingdom's Jane Torvill and Christopher Dean skate a risky routine of fluid grace and breath-taking romance to Ravel's Bolero in the free dance competition, earning them an unprecedented perfect score of 6.0 from every judge for artistic impression. The routine is watched by 23 million Britons at home.

Lewis leads the way at the Olympics
Carl Lewis equals Jesse Owens' Olympic tally of 1936 by winning four gold medals, in the 100m, 200m, 4x100m relay and long jump. Seb Coe overcomes a period of injury and equals his own medal tally, by once again winning gold in the 1500m and silver in the 800m. Tessa Sanderson gains gold for Great Britain in the javelin, as does Daley Thompson in the decathlon. Steve Redgrave gets the first of his five rowing gold medals in the men's coxless fours. The LA Olympics has been a ritzy, glitzy affair, and one that shows hosting the Games can be a commercial success.

West Indies overwhelm England's cricketers
A majestic West Indies side under Clive Lloyd thrashes David Gower's England 5-0 in the summer Test series; the only instance where England have suffered such a resounding whitewash at home.

The fall
South African athlete Zola Budd, who breaks American Mary Decker's 5000m world record in January, controversially gains a British passport on 6th April allowing her to compete at the Olympic Games in Los Angeles. When Budd (who runs barefoot) and Decker meet in the 3000m Olympic final more controversy follows. Budd makes her way to the front of the pack and Decker, pinned behind, trips over Budd's heel, and falls on her hip. Decker fails to finish the race and Budd comes seventh.

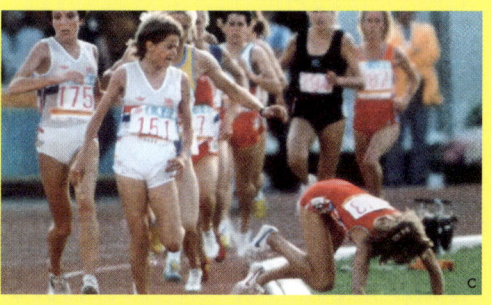

6 JAN 1984
The British turn their backs on cigarettes as anti-smoking group ASH say two million have given up in the last two years.

9 FEB 1984
As open civil war erupts in Beirut, 400 Britons are evacuated from the city.

28 MAR 1984
Nissan select the north-east town of Washington, near Sunderland, as the location for its new UK car plant.

1984

Turnaround for the Toffees
Everton end a fourteen-year trophy drought and emerge from the shadow of their Merseyside sibling, Liverpool, by winning the FA Cup Final, beating Watford 2-0 on 19th May. It's a pivotal moment for manager Howard Kendall and his team signalling the beginning of purple patch of success.

Olympic boycott
8th May 1984 In retaliation for the decision of the US to boycott the Olympic Games in Moscow in 1980, the Soviet National Olympic Committee boycotts the Los Angeles Olympic Games. All Eastern Bloc countries with the exception of Romania also confirm their non-participation.

Miners' strikes
12th March 1984 The National Union of Mineworkers go out on strike in protest at government plans that will see the closure of most of Britain's remaining coal pits. Clashes between police and miners in April and May continue into June, when the 'Battle of Orgreave' results in over 120 injuries and 95 arrests in one of the most violent incidents of the dispute. A mass lobby by miners at the Houses of Parliament ends in violence and 120 arrests, and in September the strike is ruled unlawful.

Chatham Dockyard closes
31st March 1984 The Medway in Kent witnesses an end to over 400 years of shipbuilding at the Chatham Dockyard, as it is closed for the final time. 84 acres of the Dockyard is preserved as a heritage attraction, telling the story of shipbuilding on the site since the reign of Elizabeth I.

DOMESTIC NEWS

Halfpenny withdrawn
1st February 1984 The government announces that the halfpenny is to be withdrawn from circulation at the end of the year. Whilst the new decimal version of the coin has only been in circulation since 1971, the country has had halfpennies since 1672.

WPC Yvonne Fletcher
17th April 1984 A gunman inside the Libyan Embassy shoots and kills WPC Yvonne Fletcher and wounds 11 others during peaceful protests outside. Following the shooting, armed police lay siege to the building, and Britain severs diplomatic ties with Libya.

21 APR 1984
Return of the groundbreaking US series *Cagney and Lacey* to BBC1.

19 MAY 1984
Poet and protector of Britain's building heritage, Sir John Betjaman dies at his Cornish home, aged 78.

22 JUN 1984
The first Virgin Atlantic flight to New York takes off from Gatwick, with fares costing £99.

1984

Thames Barrier opened
8th May 1984 The Queen formally opens the Thames Barrier, a new system designed to protect London from flooding. High tides and storm surges have threatened the capital since the Roman period, and this new barrier will allow authorities to close the 520m width of the river when the city is in danger.

Abbeystead disaster
23rd May 1984 An explosion at a waterworks' valve house in Abbeystead, Lancashire, kills sixteen people. The explosion is caused by a build-up of methane gas that investigators determine has seeped into the pipes from nearby coal deposits, igniting when the valves were opened.

Hong Kong agreement
19th December 1984 After months of negotiations, Britain and China sign the Sino-British Joint Declaration, which agrees the return of the British Overseas Territory of Hong Kong to Chinese control.

Brighton hotel bombing
12th October 1984 The entire cabinet are the intended targets of a Provisional IRA bomb planted in the Grand Hotel in Brighton. The hotel is hosting the Conservative Party conference, and the explosion is intended to strike after Prime Minister Margaret Thatcher and her fellow ministers have arrived. Five people, including MP Anthony Berry, are killed and several more are seriously injured and trapped in the rubble.

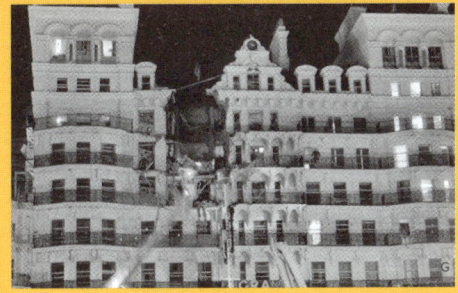

BT privatised
20th November 1984 Shares in British Telecom go on sale after plans for the privatisation of the company were unveiled in 1982. The government retain 50% of the shares, whilst over two million members of the public choose to invest, amounting to approximately 5% of the population.

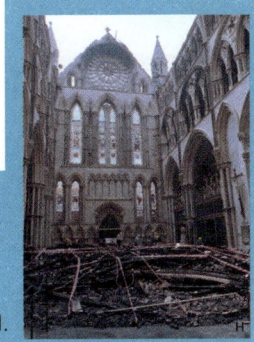

York Minster fire
9th July 1984 The country watches on in horror as a fire breaks out in the early hours of the morning at York Minster. Quick-thinking firefighters choose to collapse the roof of the South Transept, where the fire has started, in a successful attempt to prevent the fire from spreading, and the rest of the medieval building is saved.

12 JUL 1984
Robert Maxwell acquires Mirror Group newspapers and states his editors will be 'free to produce the news without interference'.

4 AUG 1984
The BBC continues its coverage of the Los Angeles Olympics until 4am each day, and supplements this with Ceefax Olympics AM.

29 SEP 1984
A huge IRA arms cache is discovered on board an Irish trawler sailing off the south-west coast of Britain.

1984

Gorbachev Visits UK
16th December 1984 The UK welcomes Soviet politburo member Mikhail Gorbachev on a week-long semi-official tour of the country. Gorbachev meets government ministers and politicians, and tours factories and cities, meeting with Prime Minister Margaret Thatcher at Chequers. Her verdict that 'we can do business together' proves prophetic as he shows himself to be a reformer seeking closer ties with the West.

FOREIGN NEWS

First compact computer
24th January 1984 Apple launches the first compact computer with the Apple Macintosh 128k. The Macintosh has 128 kilobytes of RAM and its own operating system, Mac OS. The computer has no hard drive, and to keep the device as quiet as possible, Steve Jobs insists that no fan be built in.

CIA chief kidnapped
16th March 1984 The ongoing war in Lebanon claims another high-profile victim. The CIA's station chief in Beirut, Willliam Buckley, is kidnapped by the Islamic Jihad and dies in captivity.

ROYALTY & POLITICS

Birth of Prince Harry
The Princess of Wales gives birth to a second son on 15th September. The following day it is announced the new baby prince will be given the names Henry Charles Albert David, although he quickly becomes known as Prince Harry.

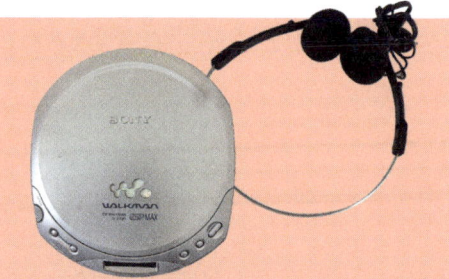

Sony markets the Discman
19th November 1984 Just as its original Walkman design boosted sales of cassettes to unprecedented levels, so Sony's Discman is set to do exactly the same for the new compact disc format. More robust and user friendly than the Walkman, the Discman is the ultimate aid to personalised music listening.

1 OCT 1984
Dr. David Jenkins, the outspoken Bishop of Durham, makes a public attack on Margaret Thatcher's social policies.

20 NOV 1984
McDonald's makes its 50 billionth hamburger.

19 DEC 1984
Mrs. Thatcher signs the Sino-British Declaration handing Hong Kong to China, ending 155 years of British rule in the colony.

1984

HIV positive
23rd April 1984 US Department of Health and Human Services Secretary Margaret Heckler announces that the cause of AIDS – the HIV virus – has been discovered by Dr Robert Gallo and colleagues at the National Cancer Institute. She reveals the development of a diagnostic blood test to identify infection and holds out the hope that a vaccine against AIDS will be produced within two years.

Reagan re-elected
6th November 1984 Ronald Reagan secures a second term as US President with a landslide win over his Democrat opponent Walter Mondale. Reagan achieves nearly 70 per cent of the popular vote and wins all the states except Washington DC and Mondale's home state of Minnesota.

Bhopal
3rd December 1984 Methyl isocyanate escapes from a Union Carbide factory in the Indian city of Bhopal. In a short time, this poisonous gas cloud kills more than 8,000 people outright and affects over half a million people. The final death toll is estimated at over 20,000. It is the worst industrial accident in history and results in criminal prosecutions against Union Carbide and individuals running the factory.

ENTERTAINMENT

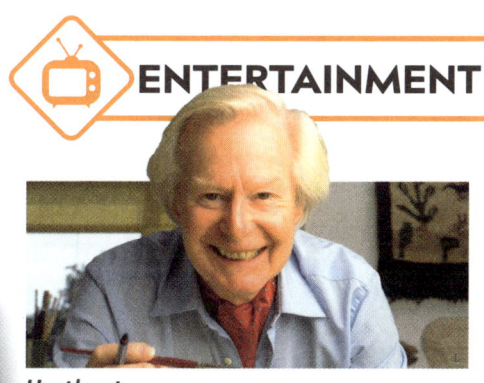

Hartbeat
Tony Hart has been the go-to man for art on children's TV for twenty years, first with *Vision On*, and then *Take Hart*. *Hartbeat* is the latest iteration, airing for the first time on 14th September. It retains all the familiar aspects of previous programmes, including his plasticine sidekick, Morph, and The Gallery segment where viewers send in their own artwork. But there are updates too. The set is jazzier, Tony has female co-presenters and occasionally he invites a graphic designer onto the programme to show how to create designs on a computer.

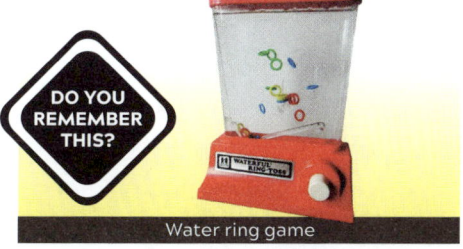

Water ring game

Consumer trends
While McDonald's proclaims the consumption of its 50 billionth hamburger, new global business launches in 1984 include Papa John's Pizza, Dell Computers and LA Fitness. Wrist watch calculators are the must-have gadgets of the year. In the fast rising world of video games, Commodore International founder Jack Tramiel founds Tramel Technology, buys the consumer assets of Atari Inc from Warner Communications and renames the company Atari. The biggest selling toys on the planet are Hasbro's Transformers, cleverly promoted via a cartoon TV series. The Cambridge Diet is launched in Europe and Blue Nun white wine with its distinctive dark bottle and blue labelling enjoys its best year for sales since launching in the 1920s. It's also a peak year for Filofax sales and power dressing as yuppie culture takes hold.

1984

The Box of Delights
The Box of Delights, BBC1's adaptation of the 1935 fantasy novel for children by John Masefield, broadcasts between 21st November and 24th December. At a cost of £1 million, it is the most expensive children's production the BBC has ever undertaken and wins several awards for its special effects. A landmark moment in children's television drama, *The Box of Delights* quite literally lives up to its name.

Mousse mania
First developed by L'Oréal in France, hair mousse becomes the favoured product to give your bonce the necessary 'bouff' as hair styles become progressively voluminous. L'Oréal's Studio Line range, with geometric, primary coloured packaging, is aimed at a younger customer; whereas its Freestyle product promises soft, sculpted waves for a sophisticated look.

Just like that
On 15th April, comedian and magician Tommy Cooper has a heart attack and collapses on stage at Her Majesty's Theatre during a live television broadcast to an audience of 12 million. He dies soon afterwards in Westminster Hospital. The following month, on 28th May, Eric Morecambe also dies after suffering a heart attack following a performance at a charity event at the Roses Theatre in Tewkesbury the day before.

Pranks a lot
Game for a Laugh first appeared on screens in 1981, dreamt up by ITV as a light entertainment rival to BBC1's *The Generation Game*. Hosted by a quartet of presenters perched on high stools, Henry Kelly, Matthew Kelly, Sarah Kennedy and Jeremy Beadle offer a mixed buffet of practical jokes, candid camera-style 'gotcha' moments and some of Britain's most bizarre eccentrics. The series continues until 1985 and on 25th August this year, a *GFAL* special 'Best of' programme is aired.

Tales of the River Bank
Following a successful film in 1983, a stop-animation TV series based on Kenneth Grahame's *Wind in the Willows* begins on ITV on 27th April. Produced by the Manchester-based Cosgrove Hall, already with well-established successes such as *Danger Mouse*, *Chorlton and the Wheelies* and *Jamie and the Magic Torch*, the *Wind in the Willows* characters are voiced by British acting's finest including Peter Sallis as Ratty, David Jason as Mr Toad and the recently knighted Sir Michael Hordern as Badger.

1984

'Listen very carefully, I shall zay this only once'

René Artois is a French café owner, who simply wants a quiet life, but what with his nagging wife, complicated affairs with his waitresses, his involvement with the French resistance, the permanently suspicious occupying Nazis, a policeman prone to malapropisms ('Good moaning'), some stranded British airmen and the whereabouts of a painting of 'The Fallen Madonna with the Big Boobies', there is never a dull moment in 'Allo 'Allo, which begins on BBC1 on 7th September. 'Allo 'Allo is farcical fun, awash with exaggerated accents, national stereotypes and catchphrases. It runs for nine series and eighty-five episodes until 1992.

A new old Bill

The uniformed officers and detectives of Sun Hill police station make their debut on ITV on 16th October following a successful one-off 1983 drama called Woodentop. The Bill remains on screens for the next 26 years, the UK's longest-running police drama.

Spitting Image

British satire is alive and well and finds a new outlet in the form of puppetry when Spitting Image first broadcasts on ITV on 26th February. Lampooning politicians, the royal family and various public figures and celebrities, Spitting Image puppets includes Margaret Thatcher as a cigar-smoking tyrant in a pin-striped suit, a gin-swilling Queen Mother and a bumbling Ronald Reagan, the nuclear button unnervingly close to his bedside.

Body conscious

The Body Shop, originally a single shop founded by Anita Roddick in Brighton in 1976, has rolled out across the country by the mid-1980s, tempting shoppers with a whole new experience in beauty retail. The environmentally friendly products and the company's ethical practices are part of the appeal, but the shops are an Aladdin's Cave of novel smells and magical potions, with glass pipettes inviting us to sniff the various perfume oils and bottles bearing the brand's distinctive green labels. Fruit glycerine soaps, bath pearls, Japanese washing grains, cucumber cleansing milk, White Musk and Dewberry are just some of the tempting products concocted by this revolutionary retailer.

Gremlins and Ghosties

Comedy, horror, action, and special effects combine in two of this year's biggest movie blockbusters when Gremlins and Ghostbusters are both released on 7th December. Gremlins is given a 15 rating after American parents who had taken small children to see the film in the summer discovered that cute furry Gizmo actually spawns a marauding bunch of reptilian imps who go on a gruesome murder spree. Ghostbusters (given a PG rating) has the odd terrifying moment too but it's all very tongue-in-cheek and carried along by Ray Parker Jr.'s bouncing soundtrack. Who you gonna call?

1984

This is Spinal Tap
Mocumentary rockumentary *This is Spinal Tap* follows the rise and rapid descent (mostly the latter) of the English metal band Spinal Tap, whose past members of whom have perished in the most ludicrous circumstances, as these rock losers try to tour their latest album, *Smell the Glove*, around the US to a rapidly diminishing fanbase. Treading a genius line between subtlety and stupidity, *This is Spinal Tap* sets the standard for all future on-screen spoofs, in time becomes nothing short of a cult sensation.

Mini-series addicts
British viewers can't get enough of American mini-series and this year sees a TV blockbuster based on a literary bonkbuster. Richard Chamberlain is sexy priest Father Ralph and Rachel Ward is Meggie in *The Thorn Birds*, based on Colleen McCullough's sprawling tale of forbidden love.

Nineteen-eighty-score
George Orwell's dystopian vision *1984* is ably transferred to the big screen by writer and director Michael Radford, with John Hurt as Winston Smith and Richard Burton playing O'Brien, his last screen role. The film is overshadowed by a row over the soundtrack. Radford wants a classical score. However, Virgin Films, who have provided finance for the movie, insist on a score of pop electronica by Eurythmics and release an album which includes the band's top 10 hit *Sex Crime* (1984).

***Crackerjack* the last broadcast**
Crackerjack has been a stalwart of the BBC's children's programming since 1955, during which time it has been hosted by Eamonn Andrews, Leslie Crowther, Michael Aspel, Ed 'Stewpot' Stewart and Stu 'Crush a Grape' Francis. It blends comedy sketches and music acts with the long-running 'Double or Drop', a quiz where kids have to keep a grip on a mounting pile of prizes, as well as cabbages given for wrong answers.

United Colours of Benetton
Oliviero Toscani, creative director of Benetton, photographs the first multi-racial advertisement for the clothing brand, which is at the height of its desirability. As the decade progresses, the provocative nature of the Italian brand's campaigns continues to be a talking point.

 # MUSIC

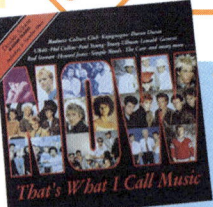

The time is Now
17th January 1984 At No. 1 in the album chart is the very first compilation album in the hugely popular *Now That's What I Call Music* series. It comprises a whopping total of 30 current hits and is heavily promoted by television advertising. The series runs to 116 individual releases and lasts for four decades.

1984

Elton marries
14th February 1984 Elton John bemuses friends, fans and the gay community by marrying recording engineer Renate Blauel. The couple divorce four years later.

Marvin shot dead
1st April 1984 Now living at his parents' home in Los Angeles because they fear he is suicidal, Marvin Gaye is shot dead by his father during a violent family row. Marvin Gaye Sr receives five years for voluntary manslaughter.

Frankie say…
13th January 1984 Dominating 1984 are Liverpool club band Frankie Goes to Hollywood. They're a phenomenon through the brilliance of record label ZTT's promotion campaign, not to mention those iconic 'Frankie say' T-shirts. They court controversy from the start: *Relax*, backed by a video that is famously banned by the BBC yet still stays at No. 1 for nine weeks and on the chart for almost the whole year. The nuclear war-themed *Two Tribes* has a spoken section advising what to do in the event of an attack. From here, however, it is all downhill, as the US largely ignores them and MTV won't touch their videos.

Starlight Express
Starlight Express, the train engine musical with music by Andrew Lloyd Webber and lyrics by Richard Stilgoe, opens at the Victoria Palace Theatre on 27th March. Arlene Phillips choreographs the cast who perform entirely on roller skates.

George in a whisper
Youth unemployment is rising and, for some, now is the time to form a band and turn being on the dole to productive use. That's the idea behind Wham! - best pals George Michael and Andrew Ridgley - and it's the philosophy behind *Wham Rap* that launches the boys in 1982. Two years on, they're ruling the pop roost with such hymns to hedonism as *Wake Me Up Before You Go-Go* and *Club Tropicana*. But the ambitious George surprises all and sundry with *Careless Whisper*, a cutting, mature break-up ballad that's full of self-recrimination and regret. Released under his own name rather than Wham!, it's one of the records of the decade.

All hail Madonna
27th January 1984 Is the UK ready for Madonna? A singer-dancer from Detroit with a brilliant grasp of look, fashion and choreography, she makes an arousing *Top of the Pops* debut with *Holiday*. Back in the US she films *Desperately Seeking Susan*, marries actor Sean Penn and closes the year with the image-defining *Like a Virgin*, produced by Nile Rodgers.

1984

Tina is back

No comeback is more deserved than Tina Turner's. She left husband Ike in 1978 after over a decade of abuse and has spent much of her time since playing nostalgia shows. Asked to guest on records by Sheffield electro band Heaven 17 and boosted by David Bowie's verbal support, she re-launches her career in astonishing style with the UK-made *Private Dancer* album and singles *Let's Stay Together* and *What's Love Got to Do with It*.

MY FIRST 18 YEARS — TOP 10 — 1984

1. **Careless Whisper** George Michael
2. **Radio Gaga** Queen
3. **Girls Just Wanna Have Fun** Cyndi Lauper
4. **White Lines** Grandmaster Flash & Mel Melle
5. **I Feel for You** Chaka Khan
6. **Smalltown Boy** Bronski Beat
7. **Nightshift** The Commodores
8. **Move Closer** Phyllis Nelson
9. **Last Christmas** Wham!
10. **Let's Stay Together** Tina Turner

Prince of sales

7th July 1984 Prince Rogers Nelson, known to all as Prince, is an icon in the US but has been awaiting a UK breakthrough for years. Now it comes via the rock-soul hybrid *When Doves Cry* from his semi-autobiographical movie *Purple Rain*, the soundtrack of which sells over 20 million albums and sits atop the US chart for 24 weeks. He writes, produces and plays every instrument on the track but - curiously for a dance record, and in typically perverse Prince fashion - he omits a bassline.

Band Aid

25th November 1984 Following a distressing BBC TV news report about the famine in Ethiopia, Bob Geldof of the Boomtown Rats has an idea. He calls Midge Ure of Ultravox and together they write a song, *Do They Know It's Christmas*, to raise money for relief charities. They call on all the music stars they know to join them for the recording at Trevor Horn's studio - and dutifully, early on a Sunday morning, most of the biggest names in UK pop music turn up including George Michael, Paul Young, Sting, Status Quo, Spandau Ballet, Duran Duran, Bananarama, Bono and - hotfooting it late from New York on Concorde - Boy George. The record is pressed and on sale within ten days and by mid-December it's at No. 1. By the time Christmas 1985 rolls around, Band Aid's single will have raised £8 million and inspired a US counterpart, *We Are the World*, and the most famous concert in music history - Live Aid.

1985

MY FIRST 18 YEARS

SPORT

Everton denied treble
18th May 1985 Manchester United beat Everton 1-0 at Wembley to win the FA Cup, denying Everton 'the Treble'. Having already secured victory in the Football League for the first time in fifteen years, Everton's hopes of a historic treble had been raised after their victory in the European Cup Winners' Cup just three days before the Wembley final.

Heysel Stadium disaster
29th May 1985 39 football fans are killed, and hundreds injured, as Juventus beat Liverpool in the European Cup. The victims are mostly Juventus fans who get crushed against a wall which then collapses, whilst fleeing a confrontation with Liverpool fans. An increasing culture of football hooliganism is blamed, and both the FA and UEFA impose bans on English teams playing in Europe. seventeen Liverpool fans are found guilty of manslaughter.

Becker wins Wimbledon
7th July 1985 Unseeded seventeen-year-old Boris Becker stuns the tennis world by beating Kevin Curren to become Wimbledon champion. It is the first time a player from Germany has won the championship, and Becker soon becomes an iconic figure in tennis, going on to win 64 titles. The women's event is won for the sixth time by Martina Navratilova in her fourth consecutive Wimbledon final.

Davis vs Taylor
27-28th April 1985 Steve Davis and Dennis Taylor meet in the World Snooker Championship Final, in what is considered by many to be the greatest snooker match of all time. With Davis having led for most of the sessions, the Championship comes down to the potting of the final black ball. Both players miss the shot several times before Taylor pulls off a surprise victory. The match is often credited with reviving the sport in the 80s and 90s.

JAN 1985
Vodafone launch the first UK mobile phone network.

9 FEB 1985
Madonna releases album *Like a Virgin*.

3 MAR 1985
UK Miner's Strike ends after a year of industrial action and violent clashes.

23

1985

England regain ashes
2nd September 1985 The Australian cricket team's six-Test tour of England is won by the hosts in the final Test. England are victorious after a more than 350-run batting partnership between Graham Gooch and David Gower, which sees them win the final Test by 94 runs and an innings.

Newry mortar attack
28 February 1985 A Royal Ulster Constabulary police station in Newry, County Down, is struck by mortar shells fired by the Provisional IRA; nine officers aged 19-41 are killed. Over 30 people are injured, including civilians, and the day is dubbed 'Bloody Thursday' by the British press.

DOMESTIC NEWS

Sinclair launches C5
10th January 1985 Sir Clive Sinclair launches his iconic but short-lived Sinclair C5, an electrified, one-person tricycle able to travel 20 miles before it needs a charge. Sinclair hopes the C5 will prove a popular mode of transport and replace petrol engines in the future, but sadly, despite proving a lot of fun, the product sells only 17,000 units and ceases production in August.

Bradford City Stadium fire
11th May 1985 Horror unfurls at a Third Division football match between Bradford City and Lincoln City when a fire starts in the main stand. Multiple fire hazards within the stadium, combined with windy weather, mean the whole stand is engulfed in less than four minutes, claiming the lives of 56 fans, and injuring over 260 more. Dramatic photos of the fire transfix a grieving nation, and calls are made for changes to safety regulations when it is revealed that exits were padlocked, barring escape routes.

Red telephone boxes
17th January 1985 The newly privatised British Telecom announce that they will phase out their iconic red telephone boxes. A huge campaign is launched to save them, but BT insist that they are rarely used and are expensive to clean and maintain. In response many local authorities give their phone boxes protected status, and over 2,000 are listed.

11 APR 1985
An eighteen-month-old baby becomes the youngest person in the UK to die in the AIDS epidemic.

22 MAY 1985
James Bond film, *A View to a Kill* permieres, it's the last to star Roger Moore.

23 JUN 1985
An Air India Boeing 747 disappears off the Irish coast after a bomb detonates killing all 325 people onboard.

1985

Hole in the ozone
16th May 1985 Three scientists associated with the British Antarctic Survey, Joe Farman, Brian Gardiner and Jonathan Shanklin, discover a hole in the planet's ozone layer over Antarctica. Their research suggests that a group of chemicals known as chlorofluorocarbons are to blame.

White House Farm murders
7th August 1985 Grandparents Nevill and June Bamber, their daughter Sheila, and her six-year-old twin children are found shot dead in their home in a killing that horrifies the country. The investigation soon focuses on the Bambers' other child, Jeremy, who had claimed to be away from home at the time. Jeremy is found guilty of murder and sentenced to life in prison.

Manchester air disaster
22nd August 1985 55 people are killed when a British Airtours flight from Manchester to Corfu suffers damage to an engine and abandons take off. The accident causes a fire in one of the plane's underwing fuel tanks, and issues with the plane's emergency exits mean that only 80 of the 135 people on board make it off safely.

Broadwater Farm riot
6th October 1985 The death of a 49-year-old black woman, Cynthia Jarrett, who dies of heart failure during a police search, leads to a riot on the Broadwater Farm council estate in Tottenham. With tensions already enflamed following the Brixton riots a few days before, the violence leads to the murder of PC Keith Blakelock, who trips and falls whilst attempting to protect the London Fire Brigade from attack. He is set upon by a crowd armed with knives and other weapons.

Comic Relief launched
25th December 1985 Comedians Richard Curtis and Sir Lenny Henry found charity Comic Relief in response to the Ethiopian famine. Whilst Live Aid and Band Aid are the talk of the summer, Comic Relief proves to have much more longevity as it begins a biennial fundraising event, the first of which takes place in 1986. Becoming enormously popular for showing famous people doing silly things, the event becomes 'Red Nose Day' in 1988.

Titanic located
1st September 1985 The wreck of famous ocean liner the RMS *Titanic* is discovered by a joint French and American expedition, 3,700 metres below the surface of the North Atlantic. A few days later, the explorers take the very first photographs and footage of the wreck, showing it in two pieces rather than intact as had previously been believed.

6 JUL 1985
At Wimbledon, Martina Navratilova beats Chris Evert in 3 sets in the women's singles final.

22 AUG 1985
A terrible month for air travel sees three disasters across the globe claim the lives of 711 people.

19 SEP 1985
A magnitude 8 earthquake strikes Mexico City, killing over 5000 people.

1985

ROYALTY & POLITICS

Queen tours Caribbean
9th October 1985 The Queen embarks on a royal tour of the Caribbean. Flying in to Belize, she will spend almost a month on board the Royal Yacht *Britannia* with Prince Philip, as they visit Belize, Bermuda, the Bahamas, St Kitts and Nevis, Dominica, St Lucia, St Vincent and the Grenadines, Grenada and Trinidad.

First black council leader
30th April 1985 The country gains its first black council leader, when Bernie Grant is elected leader of Haringey Council in London. Born in Guyana, he is a member of the Labour Party, and later becomes MP for Tottenham.

Anglo-Irish agreement signed
15th November 1985 Prime Minister Margaret Thatcher and Irish Taoiseach Garret FitzGerald sign the Anglo-Irish Agreement at Hillsborough Castle. The agreement gives the Irish government an advisory role in Northern Ireland in a move that it is hoped will lessen the violence of the Troubles.

FOREIGN NEWS

Angel of Death
June 6 1985 The skeleton of Josef Mengele turns up in a grave near São Paulo in Brazil, proof that the 'Angel of Death' is no longer alive. Mengele is responsible for the deaths of hundreds of thousands of Jews in the Auschwitz concentration camp during World War II.

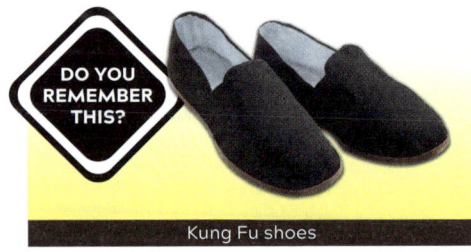

DO YOU REMEMBER THIS? Kung Fu shoes

---

9 OCT 1985
Strawberry Fields memorial to John Lennon is revealed in Central Park, NYC.

21 NOV 1985
Soviet Leader Mikhail Gorbachev and US President Ronald Reagan hold productive meetings in Geneva in what Reagan calls a 'fresh start'.

9 DEC 1985
Argentinian Junta leaders Jorge Videla and Emilio Massera are sentenced to life imprisonment.

1985

Apostle of peace
April 7 1985 The new leader of the Russian Communist Party, Mikhail Gorbachev, announces a unilateral moratorium on the deployment of the SS-20 medium-range missiles in Europe, valid until the end of November. Gorbachev indicates that he is looking for peace. With a five-year plan, he hopes to save the Soviet Union, which is in decline due to a very expensive war in Afghanistan and economic malaise. 'Uskorenie' (accelerated economic development), 'perestroika' (thorough reforms), and 'glasnost' (openness and transparency) are the main lines of his policy.

Schengen
June 14 1985 On a boat on the Moselle near the Luxembourg village of Schengen, the heads of government of the Benelux nations, West Germany and France agree that border controls between those countries will gradually disappear. This creates a 'Schengen area' without internal border controls on persons and goods.

Rainbow Warrior
The Greenpeace flagship, the Dutch *Rainbow Warrior*, sails to New Zealand for a demonstration against French nuclear tests. But things don't get that far, because in the port of Auckland, agents of the French intelligence service DGSE commit an attack on the ship with the blessing of French President Mitterrand. The *Rainbow Warrior* is sunk with mines secretly attached to the boat by divers. A Dutch photographer is killed in the attack. 'Opération Satanique' causes a major diplomatic row.

AIDS wave
October 2 1985 When American film star Rock Hudson dies of AIDS, his suffering and death make a deep impression. The masses now realize what AIDS is and the damage the disease causes. New statistics show that the number of AIDS patients in Europe has tripled in one year, to 1,126 registered cases.

ENTERTAINMENT

We are sailing
Howard's Way, a saga of yachts and yuppy types, begins on BBC1 on 1st September. It's a sort of British *Dynasty*, but set on the Hampshire coast instead of Colorado, and with deck shoes and jumpers casually tied round the shoulders instead of sequins and shoulder pads.

1985

Victoria Wood As Seen on TV
The Beeb lures multi-talented comedian Victoria Wood away from ITV, and the result is *Victoria Wood As Seen on TV*, which first airs on BBC2 on 11th January. Wood, who writes all sketches, is given a decent budget, creative freedom and comes up with comedy gold. The show is bursting with what quickly become some of television's finest moments, from spoof soap *Acorn Antiques* to Julie Walters as a doddery waitress in the 'Two Soups' sketch; Wood as Ena Sharples in a 1960s episode of *Coronation Street* grimly predicting the endings of numerous characters, to musical numbers like the uproarious *Ballad of Barry and Freda - Let's Do It* where the line 'Beat me on the bottom with a *Woman's Weekly*' encapsulates her down-to-earth genius.

No Limits
A programme that combines pop music clips with young presenters roaming the country to share the best bits of the UK's different regions, *No Limits* is the brainchild of Jonathan King, who has been doing much the same thing with his own show *Entertainment USA*. *No Limits* begins on BBC2 on 30th July, presented by Jeremy Legg and Lisa Maxwell, who are later replaced with jokey pair Tony Baker and Jenny Powell.

The Broom Cupboard
As part of an overhaul of Children's BBC, Phillip Schofield appears from a control desk called 'The Broom Cupboard' on 9th September, where he provides links between programmes with the help of a furry friend called Gordon the Gopher. When Schofield begins presenting Saturday morning show *Going Live!*, Gordon goes with him, and The Broom Cupboard is occupied by Andy Crane and Edd the Duck. Andi Peters and Zoe Ball are two more who cut their presenting teeth in the country's best-known confined space.

Looking for love
Cilla Black plays cupid as host of ITV's new Saturday night fixture, Blind Date, which begins 30th November. With three possible dates hidden behind a screen, a contestant must decide which one they'd like to go on a date with according to how promising their answers are to three questions. After a round-up from 'Our Graham' (the voice of Graham Skidmore) the pair see each other for the first time as the screen falls back, and then learn whether they're going to the Caribbean or Clacton for their date.

I'll be back
Ex-body builder Arnold Schwarzenegger's wooden acting and deadpan delivery is just what director James Cameron needs for the cyborg assassin - *The Terminator* - sent from the future to destroy the mother of the boy who will grow up to lead a human resistance against Skynet's machines. Arnie's monotone promise 'I'll be back' proves propitious as *The Terminator* franchise goes on for five sequels.

1985

Eastenders

13 million viewers tune in on 19th February to watch the first episode of BBC1's brand new soap, *Eastenders*. Set in the fictional borough of Walford in east London, the residents live in the characterful Albert Square, where, for some reason, London's soaring house prices are never discussed and local boozer the Queen Vic acts as a stage for feuds, punch-ups, scandals, revelations and even murder. The first episode sets the tone for a soap where trouble and strife are rarely far away. *Eastenders*, pitched to compete with ITV's *Coronation Street*, provides drama and characters to equal those of the Street, and soon its tropes and famous lines become part of soap opera lore, whether that's the inevitable black cab, hailed to spirit away departing characters, or Barbara Windsor's Peggy Mitchell screaming, 'Get outta my pub!'

Girls on Top

Dawn French, Jennifer Saunders, Tracy Ullmann and Ruby Wax are four mismatched flat mates in *Girls on Top*, a female riff on *The Young Ones* format, first shown on ITV on 23rd October. Wax plays to type as a loud, brash American, French is a militant feminist who works at *Spare Cheek* (a skit on *Spare Rib*), Saunders is her doltish school friend, Ullmann a manipulative nymphomaniac, while veteran actress Joan Greenwood plays their eccentric landlady. Ullman departs after the first series to find stardom in the US, and after a second series in 1986, the cast are killed off allowing French and Saunders to tread their own paths, right to the top.

Levi's 5 'Oh!' 1

A new advertising campaign for Levi's 501, the 'original shrink-to-fit' jeans, has TV viewers looking as stunned as the ladies in the 1950s laundromat who watch in awe as Nick Kamen strips down to his boxers to wash his favourite jeans, to the strains of Marvin Gaye's hit, *I Heard it Through the Grapevine*. The commercial is a sensation; it leads to rocketing sales of 501 jeans. Gaye's song takes to the charts and Kamen, with his demi-god looks, has his own moment of pop stardom.

Back to the Future

In *Back to the Future*, Michael J. Fox stars as Marty McFly, the high school kid who time travels back to 1955 in a bid to keep his parents together so that he can be born. Already a heartthrob thanks to his role in the US sitcom *Family Ties*, *Back to the Future* turns Fox into a movie megastar.

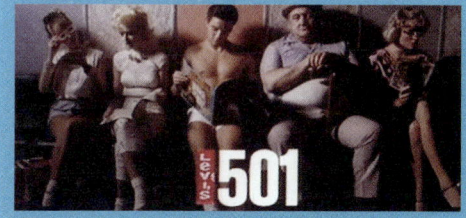

1985

Cute + cuddly = cash
The cuddly Care Bears are first created by artist Elena Kucharik for American Greetings in 1981. Each one's tummy bears the insignia of a special emotion, and they live in the clouds in the faraway realm of Care-a-lot (aah). *A Care Bears* cartoon series for television and *The Care Bears Movie* this year guarantee the plush toy Care Bears are a money-spinner.

To the barricades
The Royal Shakespeare Company English-language production of Schönberg and Boublil's musical adaptation of Victor Hugo's novel, *Les Misérables*, opens at the Barbican Centre on 8th October and transfers to the Palace Theatre on 4th December. At the time of writing it is estimated that 132 million around the world have seen *Les Mis*, and it is the second-longest West End show after *The Mousetrap*.

Brat Pack's *Breakfast Club*
Arguably the ultimate teen flick. *The Breakfast Club* director and producer John Hughes assembles a group of young actors who become part of a set the media dub 'The Brat Pack'. Forced to endure a weekend detention at school in each other's company, a group of teenagers begin the morning as strangers but as they reveal their hopes, fears and frailties, depart united by their shared experience. The film relies largely on sharp dialogue rather than action, and with the talented cast and an 80s soundtrack led by Simple Minds' *Don't You Forget About Me*, it's a surprisingly emotive piece of cinema.

Rock me Amadeus
Tom Hulce brings some rock-star swagger to the role of the eighteenth century's musical prodigy in the film version of Peter Shaffer's play about Mozart which has its UK theatrical release on 17th January. F. Murray Abraham is the embittered court composer Salieri, whose consuming jealousy of the clownish Mozart's genius sours his entire career. *Amadeus* wins eight Academy Awards including Best Picture.

 # MUSIC

USA for Africa
28th January 1985 Prompted by the UK Band Aid charity single, dozens of US music stars pool their talents to record an American equivalent - *We Are the World*, written by Michael Jackson and Lionel Richie and released under the name USA for Africa. Performers include Ray Charles, Billy Joel, Bob Dylan, Smokey Robinson, Kenny Rogers, Diana Ross, Tina Turner and Bruce Springsteen. The record raises $50 million for famine relief.

Red Wedge
21st March 1985 A spine-tingling moment on *Top of the Pops* as Billy Bragg performs his unequivocally pro-miners and anti-Thatcher song, *Between the Wars*. Billy goes on to form the Labour Party-supporting musicians' collective Red Wedge with Paul Weller and Jimmy Somerville. Gigs and tours follow but, with as many critics on the left as on the right, it is wound up in 1990.

1985

Going digital
13th May 1985 Led by guitarist brothers Mark and David Knopfler, Dire Straits are trailblazers for the new compact disc era with *Brothers in Arms*, one of the first to be recorded digitally rather than on analogue magnetic tape. It is the first album to sell more via the CD format than on vinyl and includes the self-deprecating *Money for Nothing*.

Springsteen fever
3rd July 1985 A month after his marriage to Julianne Phillips in Oregon and in the middle of an exhilarating 156-date world tour to promote his *Born in the USA* album, Bruce Springsteen plays three epic dates at Wembley Stadium. Such is the Springsteen fever overwhelming the UK this summer that his previous six albums all enter the chart on re-release.

Tipper's crusade
13th May 1985 Tipper Gore, wife of Senator Al Gore, forms the Parents Music Resource Center (PMRC) with three other 'Washington wives' to combat what they see as excessive reference to sex, violence, drugs and the occult in rock lyrics. Although much derided, they succeed in persuading the music industry to add 'parental advisory' stickers to products deemed likely to cause offence.

Live Aid
13th July 1985 With wall-to-wall live television coverage, the momentous Live Aid concert takes place in Wembley Stadium and JFK Stadium in Philadelphia. Thanks to Concorde, Phil Collins performs at both. Status Quo open the London show with *Rockin' All Over the World*, with Queen, the Who, U2, Elton John and David Bowie all following. In Philadelphia, performers include the Beach Boys, the Pretenders, Santana, Neil Young, Duran Duran and a specially re-formed Led Zeppelin, who hate their performance so much they remove it from the official video. The total amount raised by both concerts is estimated at $150 million.

In Dublin's fair city
29th June 1985 Currently the top band on the planet thanks to their *The Unforgettable Fire* album, U2 come home to Dublin to play to a 55,000-strong audience at Croke Park. It is their biggest concert in their homeland to date.

Beatles publishing sold
6th September 1985 An unamused Paul McCartney discovers that the Northern Songs publishing catalogue containing most of the songs he composed with John Lennon has been sold to Michael Jackson.

1985

Angels and sisters
27th July 1985 Eurythmics - the oldest, canniest and most musically interesting of all the UK's many UK electro duos - miss out on Live Aid because of Annie Lennox's throat problems but top the UK chart with *There Must Be An Angel*, featuring Stevie Wonder on harmonica. Three months later they collaborate once more with soul music royalty - Queen of Soul Aretha Franklin - on the anthemic *Sisters Are Doin' It for Themselves*.

MY FIRST 18 YEARS TOP 10 — 1985

1. **Material Girl** Madonna
2. **Dancing in the Street** Mick Jagger & David Bowie
3. **Saving All My Love for You** Whitney Houston
4. **Between the Wars** Billy Bragg
5. **Would I Lie to You** Eurythmics
6. **Nightshift** The Commodores
7. **Frankie** Sister Sledge
8. **Running Up That Hill** Kate Bush
9. **A New England** Kirsty MacColl
10. **Glory Days** Bruce Springsteen

Open | Search | Scan

Norway's year
19th October 1985 Dedication pays off in the end. That's the lesson of Norwegian trio A-Ha's *Take On Me*, which has just been released for the third time in two years. Promoted this time by an award winning pencil-drawn animated video, it helps A-ha become the first Norwegian act ever to top the US chart.

Lionel makes history
9th November 1985 Four years after leaving the Commodores (photo), Lionel Richie is now the leading solo act in the US. He moves on from steering the USA for Africa project to create history with *Say You Say Me* from the movie *White Nights*. He is the only composer ever to have written nine No. 1s in nine consecutive years. Now planning his next album and single, *Dancing on the Ceiling*.

1986

MY FIRST 18 YEARS

SPORT

Chelsea win Full Members Cup
23rd March 1986 Chelsea become the first winners of the new 'Full Members Cup', a competition designed to fill the scheduling gap left by UEFA's ban on English clubs playing in European competitions. The final at Wembley sees an incredible fight back from Manchester City, who at one point are 5-1 down, to set the final score at 5-4 to Chelsea.

Argentina win World Cup
29th June 1986 Argentina secure victory in the 1986 FIFA world cup final in Mexico City, with a 3-2 win against West Germany. Argentinian captain Diego Maradona celebrates the win just a week after breaking English hearts with his famous 'hand of God' goal in their 2-1 defeat of England in the quarter-final.

Birmingham Superprix
24th August 1986 The inaugural Birmingham Superprix kicks off in the city centre, becoming the first motorsport street race to be held in mainland Britain. Part of the Formula 3000 Championship, the race is red flagged when bad weather leads to a crash, with Spanish driver Luis Pérez-Sala taking the win.

Liverpool victorious
5th May 1986 Liverpool beat Chelsea 1-0 to win the First Division title for the 16th time, a new record. Five days later they defeat local rivals Everton 3-1 to win the FA Cup in the first all-Merseyside final.

More hooliganism
8th August 1986 The future of English participation in European football is placed in further doubt when violence breaks out between Manchester United and West Ham fans onboard a ferry to Amsterdam. The clubs are both due to play friendlies in the city, whilst UEFA maintain their ban on English clubs in European competitions for a second season.

16 JAN 1986
Police arrest 2 IRA-terrorists in Amsterdam who had escaped from the Maze prison in 1983.

17 FEB 1986
Single European Act signed to establish the goal of a single market by 1992.

31 MAR 1986
Greater London Council abolished along with several other metropolitan county councils.

1986

DOMESTIC NEWS

Channel Tunnel planned
12th February 1986 France and the United Kingdom sign the Franco-British Channel Fixed Link Treaty to initiate the creation of a Channel Tunnel. The idea of a permanent tunnel connecting the two countries has been around since the early 1800s, but now the idea becomes a reality as the Eurotunnel Group is formed in August to finance and build the project.

John McCarthy kidnapped
17th April 1986 The Lebanon hostage crisis continues as British journalist John McCarthy (left) is kidnapped by Islamic jihadists in Beirut. In retaliation for US airstrikes in Libya, McCarthy is captured by gunmen on his way to the airport and held for over five years.

Northern Ireland Assembly dissolved
24th June 1986 Attempts to restore the devolution of power to Northern Ireland fall apart as the dissolution of the Assembly is ordered by the Secretary of State. Ian Paisley and his Democratic Unionist Party members refuse to leave their seats, leading to ugly scenes as they are dragged out by the Royal Ulster Constabulary.

New exams launched
September 1986 14-year-olds across Britain begin their new 'GCSE' courses, which replace the old GCE 'O' Levels and CSEs. The first exams will be sat in 1988.

Babes in the Wood murders
9th October 1986 Nine-year-old Nicola Fellows and her friend, ten-year-old Karen Hadaway, are reported missing near Brighton. The following day, their bodies are found in Wild Park. Russell Bishop, a twenty-year-old roofer, is soon arrested and charged, but thanks to errors in the investigation is acquitted, and will not be brought to justice until 2018.

M25 opens
29th October 1986 The London Orbital Motorway is finally completed 11 years after the first section opened in 1975. At almost 120 miles long, it opens as the longest ring road in Europe.

14 APR 1986
Desmond Tutu elected Archbishop of Cape Town, South Africa.

17 MAY 1986
Chicken Song by Spitting Image becomes number one in the UK Singles Chart.

8 JUN 1986
Alleged Nazi Kurt Waldheim elected President of Austria.

1986

Childline opens
30th October 1986 A new telephone counselling service for children and young people launches in the UK. Childline is open 24 hours a day, 365 days a year, and is launched by Esther Rantzen at the BBC, who hopes it will help to intervene and save the lives of children in danger across the country.

Shetland Chinook crash
6th November 1986 A Chinook helicopter crashes into the ocean on the approach to Sumburgh Airport on the Shetland Islands. The helicopter is acting as a shuttle, carrying workers from the nearby Brent Oilfield back to the island, and comes down with 47 people on board, only two of whom survive.

AIDS crisis campaign
21st November 1986 Amid a rising death toll and estimates that as many as 30,000 people may be infected across the country, the government launches a £20 million campaign to raise awareness of the dangers of HIV, known as the 'Don't Die of Ignorance' campaign.

UNESCO designates UK sites
November 1986 The UK gains its first UNESCO World Heritage Sites, as places including Stonehenge, Durham Cathedral, Ironbridge Gorge and Giant's Causeway are officially recognised for their cultural significance.

British gas privatised
8th December 1986 Following the 'If you see Sid... tell him!' advertising campaign, 4 million people apply for shares of British Gas as it is floated on the stock exchange. The initial share offering gives the company a valuation of around £9 billion.

ROYALTY & POLITICS

The Westland affair
9th January 1986 Two cabinet ministers resign over the so-called 'Westland Affair' in a debacle that comes close to unseating the Prime Minister. In a cabinet disagreement over the future of Westland Helicopters, Secretary of State for Defence Michael Heseltine resigns after claiming Margaret Thatcher will not allow a full discussion of the issue at cabinet. Trade and Industry Secretary Leon Brittan follows when it is revealed he leaked confidential letters to the press.

Queen hit by eggs
February 1986 Queen Elizabeth is struck by an egg whilst touring in New Zealand. The Queen and Prince Philip are targeted by two assailants protesting an 1840 treaty made between the British Crown and New Zealand Maoris. The Queen is unharmed, and later jokes that she 'prefers her New Zealand eggs for breakfast'. She is clearly not deterred from public duty, as later in the year she becomes the first British monarch to tour China.

---

1 JUL 1986
Unemployment hits a post-war high of 3,280,106 meaning almost 15% of the workforce are affected.

19 AUG 1986
National Bus Company privatised as Devon General bought out by management.

8 SEP 1986
The Oprah Winfrey Show is first broadcast in the US.

1986

Prince Andrew marries
23th July 1986 The Queen's third child, Prince Andrew, marries Sarah Ferguson at Westminster Abbey. In honour of the event, the Queen makes the new couple the Duke and Duchess of York.

Archer resigns
26th October 1986 Deputy Chairman of the Conservative Party Jeffrey Archer resigns over a *News of the World* story that claims he paid a prostitute £2,000 to leave the country.

Pogo Ball

FOREIGN NEWS

Challenger disaster
28th January 1986 Immediately after the launch of the Challenger space shuttle, things go horribly wrong. A sealing ring on a thruster malfunctions and gas and fuel begin to leak. After 73 seconds, the Challenger turns into a huge fireball. One of the seven-person crew is 37-year-old teacher Christa McAuliffe, who Americans had already taken to their hearts. The launch is recorded and broadcast on television with a delay. The crew compartment, human remains and other fragments from the shuttle are recovered during a three-month recovery operation. The space shuttle programme is suspended for three years.

People power
25th February 1986 The twenty-year dictatorship of President Ferdinand Marcos of the Philippines ends when he is forced into exile by what is described as a 'people power' revolution and, crucially, the removal of US support. Corazon Aquino, widow of the murdered opposition leader, becomes President.

1 OCT 1986
'Big Bang' Day in London Stock Exchange as computerisation is introduced and foreign companies are welcomed.

22 NOV 1986
Mike Tyson becomes youngest heavyweight champion of the world at 20 years old.

9 DEC 1986
First case of bovine spongiform encephalopathy is diagnosed in British cattle as the BSE crisis unfolds.

1986

Iran-Contra affair
21st November 1986 On this day, as investigations into the Iran-Contra affair continue, Lieutenant Colonel Oliver North and his secretary begin shredding documents implicating them in selling weapons to Iran and using the proceeds to fund the Contra rebels in Nicaragua. Although Iran was and remains under an arms embargo, it emerges that a secret deal to sell arms was made to try to facilitate the release of US hostages then held in Lebanon. President Reagan denies all knowledge.

Olof Palme
28th February 1986 Swedish Prime Minister Olof Palme and his wife are shot dead in the street in central Stockholm after a visit to the cinema. The murder of a democratically elected head of government is a huge shock in normally peaceful Sweden and far beyond.

ENTERTAINMENT

The Color Purple
Stephen Spielberg takes a step away from fantasy and sci-fi to direct the film version of Alice Walker's book *The Color Purple*, with newcomer Whoopi Goldberg revelatory as a wonderfully expressive Celie, and Oprah Winfrey making her screen debut as Sofia. UK audiences get to see it on 11th July.

Chernobyl burns
26th April 1986 The worst nuclear disaster in history unfolds. Due to human error during a safety test, explosions occur in nuclear reactor 4 of the Chernobyl nuclear power plant in Ukraine, then part of the Soviet Union. The first explosion blows away the 2,000-ton lid of the reactor vessel. The graphite blocks catch fire and the power plant continues to burn for ten days. The fire releases enormous amounts of radioactive materials into the atmosphere. Communication about the catastrophe from the Soviet authorities is slow. More than 100,000 residents from the immediate area are evacuated. Chernobyl and the larger Pripyat turn into ghost towns. The radioactive cloud spreads rapidly across Europe and Asia. Thousands of kilometres away, radioactive particles flutter down. To prevent further spread of radioactive materials, a gigantic concrete sarcophagus is built around the nuclear reactor in Chernobyl. Although the first explosion kills just 31, thousands to tens of thousands of people die due to the effects of radioactive radiation, mainly from cancer.

1986

Neighbours
The inhabitants of Ramsay Street, Erinsborough are introduced to British viewers at 1:25pm on 27th October, as part of its new daytime scheduling. *Neighbours* tackles the same themes as other soaps but it has the exotic appeal of being Down Under in houses and with weather less familiar to British viewers. It's also populated by a clutch of teenage characters who soon gain thousands of British fans. The burgeoning romance of Scott and Charlene, played by Jason Donovan and Kylie Minogue, sees the show enjoy peak viewing figures when their wedding takes place in 1988, with both actors using their characters' relationship as a platform for their music career. Australia seems to be having a moment with the Poms, as film comedy *Crocodile Dundee*, starring Paul Hogan, is also released this year, on 12th December.

Top Gun
'I feel the need, the need for speed!' Thrilling fighter jet sequences, Harley Davidsons, jukebox crooning, beach volleyball and a locker room bristling with testosterone: Tony Scott's *Top Gun* delivers a glossy, action-packed adrenalin rush which catapults Tom Cruise as 'Maverick' into Hollywood's super-league. A thundering soundtrack which includes Kenny Loggins' *Danger Zone* keeps up the pace and Berlin's *Take My Breath Away* spends four weeks at No.1 after the film's UK release on 3rd October.

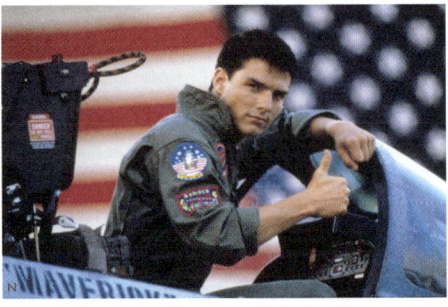

Bobby Ewing's soapy return
The makers of *Dallas* like nothing better than leaving its viewers teetering on the edge of a cliffhanger at the end of each season, and season 9 is no exception when Pam finds husband Bobby lathering himself in the shower. Barely cliffhanger material you might think, except Bobby was killed off at the end of season 8. The entirely logical explanation for Bobby's resurrection, revealed in season 10, is that Pam had dreamt the entire past 31 episodes.

Out of Africa
'I had a farm in Africa'. So begin Karen Blixen's memoirs, translated to the screen by Sydney Pollack in a sweeping romance in which the majestic Kenyan countryside shares top billing with Meryl Streep as Blixen, and Robert Redford as the dashing adventurer, Denys Finch-Hatton, into whose arms she falls. *Out of Africa* is one of those stately, heart-swelling, must-see movies. Not only does it scoop eight Academy Awards but it leaves many wishing they too could have their hair washed by Robert Redford!

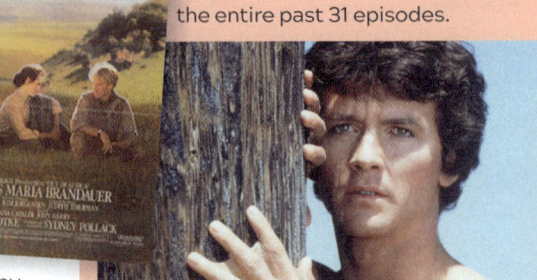

1986

Merchant Ivory - a very British film partnership
Released in the UK on 18th April, *A Room with a View* cements the reputation of producer-director team Ismail Merchant and James Ivory for gorgeous, literary period films. It also thrusts Helena Bonham-Carter into the spotlight as she plays Lucy Honeychurch, the young woman whose romantic awakening takes place against picturesque Tuscan scenery. A sterling British cast including Maggie Smith, Denholm Elliott, Julian Sands and Daniel Day-Lewis lend admirable support.

Racy *Riders*
Riders by Jilly Cooper, is published this year, the first book in the author's steamy Rutshire Chronicles; a racy page-turner about the rivalries and love affairs in the world of competitive showjumping.

Bread
The first episode of *Bread* airs on BBC1 on 1st May and introduces viewers to the Boswells, a close-knit, working-class family presided over by matriarch and staunch Catholic Nelly 'Ma' Boswell, whose disgust at her husband's mistress 'Lilo' Lill leads to her frequently spitting the line, 'She is a tart!'. Nelly's brood of four sons and a daughter, through back handers, dodgy deals and dole diddling keep the family finances afloat with the day's 'bread' (money) donated to a chicken-shaped pot every episode under the watchful eye of their indomitable mother.

Lovejoy
Ian McShane is lovable rogue *Lovejoy*, an antiques dealer and part-time detective with an eye for a bargain as he tootles around the pretty Essex and Suffolk countryside wheeling and dealing. The first series begins on 10th January.

I have a cunning plan
The first series of *Blackadder*, set in the fifteenth century, had enjoyed modest success but the arrival of his descendant, Edmund Blackadder, a suave and shrewd Elizabethan courtier, in *Blackadder II* on 9th January, makes this historical comedy, a nationwide favourite. Rowan Atkinson's wily Edmund is both supported and hampered by his loyal, turnip-eating servant Baldrick whose cunning plans to get his master out of his latest scrape are invariably rejected. The rest of the cast provide brilliant Tudor caricatures.

The Singing Detective
Dennis Potter's *The Singing Detective* starring Michael Gambon as the hospitalised detective Philip Marlow, reminiscing about his childhood and unravelling mysteries in his head, airs on BBC1 on 16th November. Potter suffered from the same painful skin disease as his character and was sometimes forced to write with his pen tied to his wrist, as Philip does in the final episode.

1986

Casualty rates
Casualty begins on BBC1 on 6th September, a hospital drama set in the accident and emergency department of Holby City Hospital, in a fictional area of Bristol. Written by Jeremy Brock and Paul Unwin, who based the storylines on observations they had personally made in NHS hospitals, the show is initially planned to run for fifteen episodes. Instead, its popularity leads to it becoming a more permanent fixture and *Casualty* goes on to become the longest-running medical drama in the world.

Fashion fix
Style mavens get a weekly fashion fix with the launch of BBC1's *The Clothes Show* on 13th October. Presented by designer Jeff Banks, who developed the idea out of the fashion slot he had on *Pebble Mill at One*, his co-host is Selina Scott, and they are later joined by fashion journalist and cool cat Caryn Franklin. Together they bring news from the catwalks, show viewers how to create budget looks at home, investigate great arbiters of style, and run a nationwide model competition.

Trouble and strife
Tensions are high in the Queen Vic on 16th October as two of *Eastenders*' most popular characters, Den and Angie Watts (Leslie Grantham and Anita Dobson) have an entire half hour devoted to their marriage breakdown and a surprising denouement. Den wants a divorce, and to leave Walford behind to make a new life with his mistress Jan. Angie tries to distract him and reveals to Den that she has only six months to live, obliging him to promise to stay with her.

The video age
The Chart Show begins on Channel 4 on 11th April, launching its first episode with the music video *What You Need* by INXS. Created to rival *Top of the Pops*, but without any cheesy DJ presenters, *The Chart Show* has in fact no presenters at all.

The Golden Girls
The Golden Girls comes to Britain this year, with the first episode broadcast on Channel 4 on 1st August. The chemistry between Bea Arthur as Dorothy, Betty White as Rose, Rue McClanahan's Southern belle Blanche and Estelle Getty as Dorothy's feisty, wise-cracking mother is irresistible as the four characters rub along together in the Florida house they share.

 MUSIC

West End boys
11th January 1986 Just as the electro pop era appear to be passing, another solemn-looking pair of Brits in long coats appears. The Pet Shop Boys offer a new slant, however. A former journalist with *Smash Hits*, Neil Tennant and synth-playing partner Chris Lowe write smartly rhymed lyrics to disco rhythms and deliver them in a passionless, almost bored style. With its echoes of Grandmaster Flash and T. S. Eliot's *The Waste Land*, *West End Girls* is the first No. 1 of 1986 and announces a duo who will still be having hits nearly 40 years later.

1986

Europe rocks
6th December 1986 With an apocalyptic lyric partly inspired by David Bowie's *Space Oddity*, *The Final Countdown* tops the UK chart for two weeks for Swedish hard rock band Europe.

Sister in control
4th February 1986 Working with producer-writers Jimmy Jam and Terry Lewis, Janet Jackson emerges from brother Michael's shadow with breakthrough album *Control* and single *What Have You Done for Me Lately*. In a year when Michael releases no new material, Janet fills the vacuum with her own pot-pourri of funk, soul and Paula Abdul-directed choreography.

Running the world
June 1986 Having had to turn down an invitation to play Live Aid, UK synth duo Tears for Fears back the next Ethiopian relief fund raiser, Sport Aid, by re-recording their BRIT Award-winning *Everybody Wants to Rule the World* as *Everybody Wants to Run the World*. The song was originally featured on the album *Songs from the Big Chair*, which achieved ten million sales in 1985 and established the band as a major force in the US.

Chain Reaction
8th March 1986 After Barbra Streisand and Dionne Warwick, newly married Diana Ross is the latest music diva to benefit from the hit writing skills of Barry, Robin and Maurice Gibb. A homage to her Motown past, *Chain Reaction* tops the UK and most overseas charts but flops completely in the US.

Arise, Sir Bob
10th June 1986 Dublin-born Bob Geldof receives an honorary British knighthood for his work raising money for famine relief in Ethiopia.

Last gigs
9th August 1986 At the end of a tour promoting the *A Kind of Magic* album and single, Queen play what will turn out to be their last concert with Freddie Mercury as lead singer, at Knebworth Park in Hertfordshire. A number of other leading bands play their last concerts this year - pending reunions, of course - including Madness, Boomtown Rats, Weather Report, Wham! and the Clash, while the Smiths drift inexorably towards disbandment.

Graceland controversy
25th August 1986 Paul Simon's *Graceland* album is released to a barrage of criticism over his decision to record in apartheid-gripped South Africa. Simon counters by pointing out his employment of and close collaboration with black musicians who wouldn't otherwise be heard anywhere in the West.

1986

Hip hop hybrid
New York hip hop kings Run-DMC didn't plan to smash genre boundaries with their take on a 1975 Aerosmith track, *Walk This Way*. With the latter's Steve Perry repeating the original's irresistible guitar riff, they create an eye-opening hybrid of rap and metal that defies US radio conventions and leads rock music into a whole new direction.

Bangles go manic
California's all-female Bangles become the UK's favourite American band of 1986 with the 1960s-styled guitar-and-harmonies hits *Manic Monday* (written by Prince), *Going Down to Liverpool* and *Walk Like an Egyptian*.

Blue collar rock
Maybe it's the Springsteen influence but 'blue collar rock' - rugged no-nonsense rock'n'roll aimed at a working-class audience - is in many ways the sound of 1986. Setting the standard is New Jersey boy Jon Bon Jovi and his band, whose *Slippery When Wet* album tops the US listings. The highlight is a blue collar anthem to cap them all - *Livin' on a Prayer*.

MY FIRST 18 YEARS
TOP 10 — 1986

1. **The Way it Is** Bruce Hornsby and the Range
2. **Sledgehammer** Peter Gabriel
3. **Caravan of Love** The Housemartins
4. **Addicted to Love** Robert Palmer
5. **Holding Back the Years** Simply Red
6. **Papa Don't Preach** Madonna
7. **Take My Breath Away** Berlin
8. **White Wedding** Billy Idol
9. **Kiss** Prince
10. **Word Up** Cameo

Hull of a band
20th December 1986 They look gawky, dance like dads at a disco and play up their roots in unfashionable Hull. But for all the Housemartins' comic veneer, *Happy Hour* delivers a strong pro-union and anti-Murdoch message. During the year-long miners' strike, Paul Heaton and friends played more gigs for miners' families than any other band in the country. A captivating album cheekily titled *London O Hull 4* is followed by an unexpected Christmas No. 1 - a lovely acapella version of the Isley Brothers' *Caravan of Love*.

PHOTO CREDITS Copyright 2024, TDM Rights BV.
Photos: A Hugh Hastings - Chelsea FC - Getty Images / B PA Images - Getty Images / C Mirrorpix - Getty Images / D Richard Baker - In Pictures - Getty Images / E PA Images - Getty Images / F Science Museum Group - / G Derek Hudson - Getty Images Europe / H PA Images - Getty Images / I MPI - Archive Photos - Getty Images / J Bettmann - Getty Images / K Ullstein Bild - Getty Images / L Wojtek Laski - Hulton Archive - Getty Images / M Comic Relief - Getty Images Europe - Getty Images / N Sunset Boulevard - Corbis Historical - Getty Images / O Bettmann - Getty Images / P BBC - Ronald Grant Archive - Mary Evans / Q Ronald Grant Archive - Mary Evans / R AF Archive - ITV - Mary Evans / S Ronald Grant Archive - Mary Evans / T BBC - Ronald Grant Archive - Mary Evans / U AF Archive - NBC - Mary Evans / V Kmazur - WireImage - Getty Images / W Michael Putland - Hulton Archive - Getty Images / X FG-Bauer-Griffin - Michael Ochs Archives - Getty Images / Y Paul Natkin - Archive Photos - Getty Images / Z BSR Entertainment - Getty Images.

1987

MY FIRST 18 YEARS

SPORT

Football firsts
1987 sees some footballing firsts, as Aldershot FC become the first team to win promotion through the new playoff system, Arsenal win the League Cup for the first time, and Coventry become first-time winners of the FA Cup.

First Rugby World Cup
22nd May 1987 The very first Rugby World Cup kicks off in New Zealand with a home side victory over Italy. 16 nations battle it out, with Wales proving the best performing home nation, securing third place over joint-hosts Australia. Favourites New Zealand go on to win the tournament with a 29-9 victory over France as the Webb Ellis Cup is lifted for the first time.

Great year for British golf
19th July 1987 Nick Faldo wins the Open Championship by just one stroke, becoming the first Englishman to claim the title since Tony Jacklin in 1969. One week later, Laura Davies, just 23 years old, wins the US Women's Open, having won the British Open the previous year.

Whitbread gold
6th September 1987 British athlete Fatima Whitbread puts in a wonderful performance at the World Athletics Championships to win the country's only gold medal with an incredible 76.64 metre throw in the javelin.

Cricket Cup and controversy
8th November 1987 England are defeated by Australia in the final of the Cricket World Cup in Calcutta, a disappointment that is followed in December by fractious scenes on the English tour of Pakistan. During the second test, Captain Mike Gatting and umpire Shakoor Rana engage in a foul-mouthed shouting match that is broadcast worldwide. Gatting issues Rana with a written apology.

DOMESTIC NEWS

Naji al-Ali shot in London
22nd July 1987 Shots ring out in London as Palestinian cartoonist Naji al-Ali is attacked outside the offices of Kuwaiti newspaper *al-Qabas*. Famed for his satirical cartoons lampooning politicians across the Middle East, his sharply critical commentaries earned him many enemies, including Yasser Arafat. His murder is still unsolved.

1 JAN 1987
British Airways is floated on the stock market ahead of its privatisation in February.

27 FEB 1987
The General Synod of the Church of England votes for legislation to allow the ordination of women priests.

24 MAR 1987
Soul Train Music Awards winners are Janet Jackson and Luther Vandross.

43

1987

MS *Herald of Free Enterprise*
6th March 1987 Tragedy strikes as car and passenger ferry the MS *Herald of Free Enterprise* gets into difficulty leaving the harbour of Zeebrugge in Belgium. The bow door of the ship is left open, allowing the ferry to flood with water and capsize, coming to rest on its side. Many stories of bravery emerge following the rescue attempts, but despite most of the 539 passengers and crew on board being rescued safely, 193 passengers lose their lives in the worst British maritime disaster in over 150 years.

Knightsbridge robbery
12th July 1987 Two men hold up the Knightsbridge Safe Deposit Centre and steal £60 million in what would prove to be one of the largest robberies in history. The mastermind, Valerio Viccei, is identified by a fingerprint at the scene and, despite having fled the country, is later arrested when he returns to pick up his Ferrari Testarossa.

Archer wins libel case
25th July 1987 Former Conservative deputy chairman Jeffrey Archer wins a libel case against the *Daily Star*, and the tabloid is forced to pay him £500,000 in damages. Despite this, he is found guilty of perjury in 2001 after providing a false alibi during the trial.

The Troubles
The Provisional IRA conduct a number of attacks in 1987, including a bomb at a British Army barracks in Rheindahlen, West Germany, which injures 31. In November, the Enniskillen bombing claims the lives of 12 people at a Remembrance Day service and injures over 60 who had gathered to commemorate the war dead. The IRA themselves suffer their biggest loss of the Troubles in May, when eight members are killed by the SAS in an ambush at Loughgall, County Antrim, in which a civilian is also killed.

Spycatcher causes trouble
31st July 1987 Trouble erupts over the publication of the book *Spycatcher*, an autobiography written by former MI5 officer Peter Wright. The book, which contains many embarrassing details about the activities of the secret services, is banned from publication in the UK. Gag orders are served to several newspapers who attempt to publish details of some of the allegations made, leading many to mock and ridicule the Law Lords. The book is eventually cleared for publication in 1988.

Hungerford massacre
19th August 1987 Gunman Michael Ryan goes on a rampage armed with handguns and a semi-automatic rifle in the town of Hungerford, Berkshire. He kills sixteen people, including his own mother, and injures sixteen more before turning the gun on himself.

---

3 APR 1987
Gorbachev offers to remove all Soviet short-range weapons from Eastern Europe.

11 MAY 1987
British Rail rebrands its second class as 'standard class' travel.

12 JUN 1987
Ronald Reagan challenges Mikhail Gorbachev to 'tear down' the Berlin wall.

1987

The Great Storm
15th - 16th October 1987 England is struck overnight by the 'Great Storm', hurricane force winds which cause extensive damage and claim the lives of 22 people in the UK and Normandy. An estimated 15 million trees are felled, several ships are wrecked and the whole of the National Grid South East power system is shut down. Initial weather predictions had assumed the storm would be limited to coastal areas, and BBC weatherman Michael Fish receives much criticism for appearing to downplay the severity of the approaching winds.

No sign of Nessie!
11th October 1987 A million-pound project to scan the entirety of Loch Ness in search of the Loch Ness Monster fails to get a glimpse of the legendary beast. Operation Deepscan deploys 24 boats with echo-sounding equipment to scan the waters, and despite encountering several unidentified objects, the results are written off as debris on the loch bottom and seals at play.

IKEA arrives in the UK
1st October 1987 The first IKEA store in the UK opens in Warrington, Cheshire. The Swedish store, founded in 1943, has been popular across the continent for decades and now for the first time Brits can get their hands on the reasonably priced flatpack furniture that makes the store famous.

King's Cross fire
18th November 1987 A terrible tragedy strikes the London Underground as a fire takes hold on an escalator at King's Cross Underground Station. The fire quickly burns out of control, filling the tunnels with noxious gases and claiming the lives of 31 people.

ROYALTY & POLITICS

1987 General Election
11th June 1987 Margaret Thatcher wins a third term in office as the Conservatives secure another landslide victory. Despite losing 21 seats Thatcher is still comfortable with 376, a majority of 102.

SDP merges with Liberals
6th August 1987 The Social Democratic Party votes to merge with the Liberal party in a move that sees leader Dr David Owen resign. He is replaced as leader by Robert Maclennan but founds a breakaway faction of the party to continue outside the proposed merger.

7 JUL 1987
Chessington Zoo reopens as a theme park, Chessington World of Adventures.

1 AUG 1987
MTV Europe launches; *Money For Nothing* by Dire Straits is the first video played.

1 SEP 1987
The Montreal Conference sees over 70 nations agree on measures to protect the ozone layer.

1987

Diana opens AIDS ward
9th April 1987 Princess Diana opens the Broderip Ward at the Middlesex Hospital, the first ward in the UK exclusively for the treatment of HIV and AIDS. The princess makes a stir when she shakes the hands of patients without wearing gloves, directly challenging the fear many people had of the disease.

Andy Warhol dies
22nd February 1987 Pop art godfather, film maker and entrepreneur Andy Warhol dies in New York, aged 58. In his time he has elevated such everyday things such as Campbell's soup cans to art. Out of his New York City studio The Factory came a revolution that swept the art world, while Warhol also made a huge contribution to the history of rock music through sponsoring and producing the Velvet Underground.

 FOREIGN NEWS

Political suicide
22nd January 1987 A bizarre scene on television in the US. R. Budd Dwyer, Pennsylvania's state treasurer, has been taking millions of dollars in kickbacks from a computer company and faces 55 years in prison. The day before the prison sentence starts, Dwyer holds a press conference. Everyone expects him to announce his resignation. But Dwyer takes a revolver from an envelope and shoots himself in the head.

Terry Waite kidnapped
20th January 1987 Terry Waite, the Archbishop of Canterbury's special envoy, is in Lebanon to attempt to negotiate the release of UK hostages held there when he himself becomes a victim of kidnapping. He will remain captive until 1991.

Waldheim banned
27th April 1987 The US Department of Justice declares Kurt Waldheim, former Secretary General of the UN and now the elected President of Austria, 'an undesirable alien' over his recently discovered role in Nazi persecution during the Second World War.

Black Monday
19th October 1987 The global stock exchanges are turning into battlefields. After five years in which stock prices rose by an average of 350 per cent, the bubble has suddenly burst. It's Black Monday: 600 billion dollars on the Dow Jones evaporates in one day. The exact cause of the sudden stock market crash is unclear.

30 OCT 1987
George Michael's debut album *Faith* is released.

18 NOV 1987
King's Cross fire kills 31 people on the London Underground.

1 DEC 1987
Construction begins on the Channel Tunnel.

1987

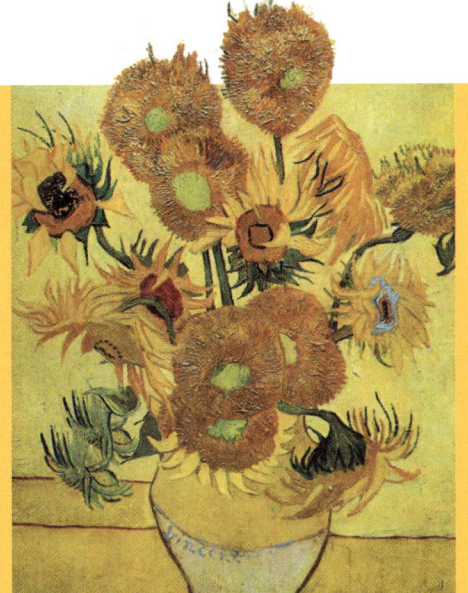

Very expensive Van Goghs
30th March 1987 Vincent van Gogh sets the record twice for the most expensive painting ever. A Japanese insurance company pays $39.7 million for *Vase of Fifteen Sunflowers* (1889) at an auction at Christie's in London. On 11th November, the controversial Australian businessman Alan Bond buys Van Gogh's *Irises* (1889) at Sotheby's for 49 million dollars.

Five billion
11th July 1987 UN figures reveal that the world's population now stands at five billion.

Rudolf Hess dies
17th August 1987 Rudolf Hess, Adolf Hitler's deputy, commits suicide at Spandau prison in West Berlin aged 93. He had been imprisoned since his conviction for crimes against peace in 1947.

INF Treaty
8th December 1987 In the White House, American President Ronald Reagan and Soviet leader Mikhail Gorbachev conclude a historic agreement. The superpowers agree that both sides will no longer possess, make or test ground-launched missiles with a range of 500 to 5,000 kilometres.

Flying stunt
28th May 1987 German teenager Mathias Rust performs a stunt that makes world news. The eighteen-year-old boy from Wedel rents a Cessna plane in Hamburg and flies to the Russian border via Iceland and Scandinavia. He flies on to Moscow and circles his plane a few times above the Kremlin, before landing the plane next to Red Square. He is arrested and sent to a labour camp. After fourteen months, Rust is pardoned.

ENTERTAINMENT

Through the Keyhole
Nosy types tune in to *Through the Keyhole* on 3rd April, as Lloyd Grossman snoops around celebrity homes while the panellists back in the studio, guided by David Frost, try to guess 'who might live in a house like this?' It's a perfect opportunity to see how the other half live and reminds us that money doesn't necessarily buy good taste.

47

1987

Going for Gold
Quiz show *Going for Gold*, presented by Henry Kelly, begins on BBC1 on 12th October. Seven contestants from different European countries battle it out through several rounds in a bid to make it to the grand final.

Prime Minister's questions
Prime Minister Margaret Thatcher appears on *Saturday Superstore* on 10th January, taking part in their Pop Panel, and burying the hatchet in the career of indie band Thrashing Doves by praising their latest hit. When teenager Alison Standfast rings in and persists in asking Thatcher where she will be in the event of nuclear war, asking bluntly, 'Haven't you got a bunker or something?', things suddenly feel rather awkward. *Saturday Superstore's* final episode is on 18th April and a new Saturday morning show, *Going Live!*, presented by Philip Schofield, begins in the autumn this year.

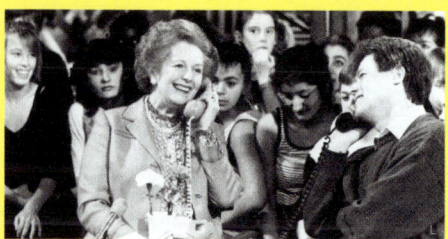

It's a Royal Knockout
The Royal Family appear on the small screen this year when they take part in *The Grand Knockout Tournament* on 15th June, with a medieval tournament theme. Organised by Prince Edward, there are four teams led by himself, the Princess Royal, and the Duke and Duchess of York, each aiming to raise funds for their individual charities. In support is an eclectic mix of celebrities from Meatloaf to John Mills participating in what some see as an undignified display of royal buffoonery (apparently the Queen disapproves). Nevertheless, *It's a Royal Knockout* raises £1.5 million and has an estimated global audience of 400 million.

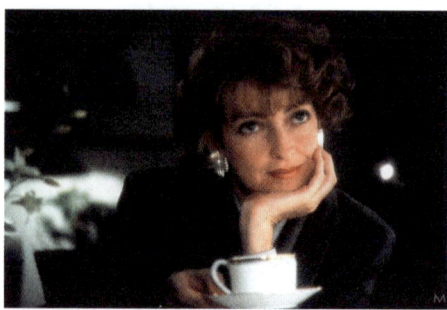

Coffee?
The first TV commercial for Nescafé Gold Blend airs this year, featuring yuppy neighbours Sharon Maughan and Anthony Head who begin a flirtation over coffee. Their on-screen chemistry leads to a series of adverts over the next six years in an ongoing will they/won't they soap opera. 30 million viewers tune in to see the finale where he finally professes his love. Meanwhile, Nescafé Gold Blend sales increase by 70%.

Bring me the finest wines
Richard E. Grant is the Withnail in *Withnail and I*, playing the hungover, loquacious libertine with boundless gusto. Withnail and Marwood (Paul McGann) are out-of-work actors who leave their squalid Camden flat for a holiday in the Lake District where they stay in a rundown cottage owned by Withnail's Uncle Monty. Full of memorable moments including the scene when Withnail strides into a Penrith tearoom and demands, 'We want the finest wines available to humanity. We want them *here*. And we want them *now*!', never has a miserable existence been quite so hilarious.

1987

The Untouchables
Released 18th September, the violent underworld of Prohibition-era Chicago is the backdrop to Brian de Palma's thrilling, *The Untouchables*, with Kevin Costner as Treasury agent Eliot Ness, who assembles a team of uncorruptible law men to dismantle the power base of mob boss Al Capone and bring him to justice. As Capone, Robert de Niro takes on another role requiring him to pile on the pounds, while Sean Connery wins Best Supporting Actor Oscar for playing heroic cop Jimmy Malone.

Thundercats - Innocence under siege
Lion-O, Cheetara, Panthro, Tygra et al thunder onto the small screen on 2nd January, a team of handsome cat-human heroes determined to save the Eye of Thundera from the Mutants of Plum-Darr and evil sorcerer, mummified Mumm-Raa. Along with other American imports like *Transformers* and *He-Man*, *Thundercats* is criticised not only for the level for violence, but also how commercially driven it is.

Chucklevision
Paul and Barry Chuckle bring a finely-tuned blend of slapstick, jokes and vivid characters to CBBC on 26th September in *Chucklevision*. They travel around on the Chuckmobile, mess up every job they take on and coin a series of catchphrases that infiltrate the subconscious of adults as well as children. Through a staggering 293 episodes over 22 years, 'From Me...To You' and 'No slacking' become part of the national lexicon.

Treets now M&M's

Blackadder the Third
Beginning on BBC1 on 17th September, *Blackadder the Third* transports Edmund Blackadder to the eighteenth century this time, where he is courtier and friend to Hugh Laurie's frightfully dim Prince of Wales, while Baldrick is still filthy, still stupid and still existing on a diet of turnips. Ben Elton and Richard Curtis have great fun with the Georgian references from Mrs. Miggins's Pie Shop to the episode where Baldrick accidentally burns Samuel Johnson's dictionary, obliging Edmund to re-write it in a weekend.

Logan's Eurovision Run
Following on from his 1980 success with *What's Another Year?* on 9th May, Irish crooner Johnny Logan returns to the Eurovision Song Contest, this time held in Brussels, for another stab at glory with *Hold Me Now*. He brings the title back home to the Emerald Isle and passes into Eurovision legend as one of only two double winners in the history of the competition. He also pens Ireland's 1992 winning entry, *Why Me?,* sung by Linda Martin.

1987

Morse code
A cerebral detective inspector who drives a Jaguar Mark 2 and has a fondness for real ale, opera and cryptic crosswords, *Inspector Morse*, first shown on ITV on 6th January, is a different animal to the traditional TV cop. In fact, Morse, who first appeared in a series of books by Colin Dexter, couldn't be more different than Jack Regan, the police character previously played by John Thaw in *The Sweeney*. The crimes are somehow more elevated too, being carried out among the dreaming spires of Oxford and surrounding countryside. Accompanied by the down-to-earth Geordie Sergeant Lewis (Kevin Whateley), Morse runs until 1993; at its peak drawing audiences of 18 million.

Top toys
Among this year's best-selling toys are Hasbro's My Little Pony, colourful equine figures with delicious names like Applejack and Peachy, with toy sales boosted by *My Little Pony - The Movie*. And firmly entrenched as a family favourite is Trivial Pursuit, the game of general knowledge based on the famous quotation from Pope's *Rape of the Lock* - 'What mighty contests rise from trivial things.'

Jailbirds
Prisoner Cell Block H, the Australian soap opera set in a women's prison, first airs on Central TV on 25th April (although Yorkshire TV has been showing it since 1984). It soon becomes a surprise, late-night ratings success.

 # MUSIC

House on fire
24th January 1987 Jack Your Body by Steve 'Silk' Hurley is the first record in the 'house' genre to top the UK chart. Originating in Chicago, house is a form of electronic dance music ruled by producer deejays such as Frankie Knuckles and Farley 'Jackmaster' Funk. In the UK, Beatmasters, Bomb the Bass and others are fuelling the Manchester-centred acid house boom to come.

Smiths to split
14th June 1987 The headline in *New Musical Express* reads 'Smiths to split'. It's premature, but it's correct: singer Morrissey and guitarist Johnny Marr are no longer talking. Marr is having much more fun working with Billy Bragg, Bryan Ferry and Talking Heads, while the opinionated, talented but difficult to like Morrissey is plotting a solo career.

1987

'Nobody puts Baby in the corner'
When Frances 'Baby' spends her summer at a holiday resort in upstate New York with her parents in 1963, she falls in love with Johnny, a dance instructor from the wrong side of the tracks whose moves and grooves are anything but polite. *Dirty Dancing*'s multi-million selling soundtrack includes the hit song, *I've Had The Time of My Life* - played during the film's climax when Baby and Johnny dance the routine they've practised and finally smash THAT lift. *Dirty Dancing* is a global sensation; UK audiences flock to see it when it opens on 16th October.

Def Jam
10th February 1987 Founded in 1985, producer Rick Rubin's New York-based Def Jam label is the epicentre of east coast hip hop with LL Cool J, the Beastie Boys and Public Enemy on its books. The latter's debut album *Yo! Bum Rush the Show*, released today, mixes in-your-face lyrics with radical political messaging.

Flower of Scotland
Just as the Pogues' *Fairytale of New York* is part of a venerable tradition of Irish diaspora songs, so the Proclaimers' *Letter from America* does the same for the Scottish emigration story. Twin brothers Craig and Charlie Reid are just the latest flowering of talent from Scotland.

Beasties in Britain
30th May 1987 Every couple of years, the UK press and publicity-seeking MPs create a media panic about some new band or style. This year their target is white hip hop trio the Beastie Boys, whose reputation follows them from the US. Tonight sees a particularly infamous gig in Liverpool including fights, missiles, a mini-riot and the arrest of Beastie Adam Horovitz, but did they really 'sneer at dying kids' as the *Daily Mirror* claims? Of course not.

D'Arby debut
13th July 1987 Attracting huge media attention is the debut album by Terence Trent D'Arby, R&B singer-songwriter whose rebel attitude saw him court martialled out of the Army in 1983. Entitled *Introducing the Hardline According to Terence Trent D'Arby*, it features four major hit singles including *Wishing Well*.

Blockbusters
Three blockbuster albums dominate the sales charts in 1987. Now the world's mightiest stadium band, U2 (photo) sell fourteen million with *The Joshua Tree*, which also wins the Grammy for best album and produces two US No. 1s. Michael Jackson's *Bad*, despite uneven reviews, produces five US No. 1s - a new record for any album. Then comes the biggest selling debut album ever: *Appetite for Destruction* from new hard rock icons Guns N' Roses.

1987

Family matters
Five Star seem to have it all: a solid disco-funk sound, cross-generation appeal, great choreography and TV-friendly looks. From Romford, Deniece Pearson and her four siblings are the missing link between the Jacksons and Sister Sledge.

MY FIRST 18 YEARS
TOP 10 — 1987

1. **I Knew You Were ...** Aretha Franklin & George M.
2. **So Strong** Labi Siffre
3. **Don't Dream It's Over** Crowded House
4. **La Bamba** Los Lobos
5. **Mary's Prayer** Danny Wilson
6. **With or Without You** U2
7. **I Think We're Alone Now** Tiffany
8. **Wonderful Life** Black
9. **Build** The Housemartins
10. **Wishing Well** Terence Trent D'Arby

Open Spotify | Search | Scan

Hit factory
The studio owned by production/writing team Mike Stock, Matt Aitken and Pete Waterman is called 'the hit factory' - and no wonder. Two No. 1s - *Respectable* by Mel and Kim (photo) and *Never Gonna Give You Up* by the boyish but big-voiced Rick Astley - follow hits for Dead or Alive and Bananarama, plus a dance track called *Roadblock* that they release anonymously to fool their critics. And all this is before a certain actress arrives from Australia to discuss making a record.

A Christmas fairytale
23rd November 1987 Irish punk folk band the Pogues record *Fairytale of New York* with Kirsty MacColl. Inspired by J. P. Donleavy's novel, it's a bruising but touching account of an Irish couple down on their luck in post-war Manhattan. Although a No. 2 hit, no one guesses how the song will keep coming back every Christmas and earn classic status - even if colourful language like 'scumbag', 'slut' and 'faggot' causes airplay issues in later years.

PHOTO CREDITS Copyright 2024, TDM Rights BV.
Photos: **A** Peter Robinson Empics - PA Images - Getty Images / **B** David Cannon Collection - Getty Images / **C** PA Images - Getty Images / **D** Roger Hutchings - Corbis Historical - Getty Images / **E** Keystone - Hulton Archive - Getty Images / **F** Georges De Keerle - Hulton Archive - Getty Images / **G** Anwar Hussein - Hulton Archive - Getty Images / **H** San Francisco Chronicals - Hearst Newspapers - Getty Images / **I** Universal Images Group - Getty Images / **J** Ullstein Bild - Getty Images / **K** Universal History Archive - Getty Images / **L** PA Images - Getty Images / **M** Ronald Grand - Mary Evans / **N** AF Archive - Alistar Picture Library - Mary Evans / **O** BBC Enterprices - Ronald Grant - Mary Evans / **P** Ullstein Bild - Getty Images / **Q** Carlton UK Productions - Ronald Grant Archive - Mary Evans / **R** Brian Rasic - Hulton Archive - Getty Images / **S** Archive Photos, Moviepix - Getty Images / **T** Dave Hogan - Hulton Archive - Getty Images / **U** Ron Galella Collection - Getty Images / **V** Ebet Roberts - Redferns - Getty Images / **W** Tim Roney - Hulton Archive - Getty Images / **X** Mike Prior - Redferns - Getty Images / **Y** Tim Roney - Iton Archive - Getty Images.

1988 — MY FIRST 18 YEARS

SPORT

Eddie the Eagle wins hearts
28th February 1988 The XV Winter Olympics in Alberta, Canada, draws to a close having made a star of one British athlete. Despite the representatives from Great Britain winning not a single medal across the games, the charm of Michael 'Eddie the Eagle' Edwards, Britain's first ever entry into the ski jumping event, captures the world's hearts. Edwards comes last in both the 70m and 90m events, despite setting a British record, but his enthusiasm is contagious, and wins him a legion of fans.

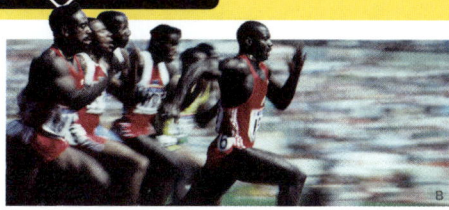

Seoul Summer Olympics
2nd October 1988 The British team return with five golds, ten silvers and nine bronzes from a games marred with controversy over drug taking. Canadian Ben Johnson (photo) is stripped of his 100m gold medal and world record when he tests positive for a banned substance, bumping Brit Linford Christie up to silver, and he is joined by nine other athletes across several disciplines who are all disqualified. Highlights of the games include US sprinter Florence 'Flo-Jo' Griffith-Joyner who secures gold in both 100 and 200m finals, and British gold for Steve Redgrave and Andy Holmes in the coxless Pairs.

Sandy Lyle wins US Masters
10th April 1988 The prestigious US Masters golf tournament falls to a Brit for the first time, as Scotsman Sandy Lyle takes the victory following an incredible fairway bunker shot and birdie putt that lives long in the memory.

European Championships
18th June 1988 England are knocked out of the Euros after losing all three group games and finishing bottom, a devastating result that is made even more sour by the arrest of over 100 fans for incidents of hooliganism. The tournament is eventually won by the Netherlands who beat the Soviet Union 2-0 in the final.

Exciting finishes in Cups
24th April 1988 A goal in the 92nd minute sees Luton Town FC secure a 3-2 victory over Arsenal in the final of the Littlewoods Football League Cup. The FA Cup also witnesses a fairytale result as Wimbledon FC beat league champions Liverpool 1-0 in the final after only two seasons in the first division, and Celtic do the double, coming from behind in the Scottish Cup Final to beat Dundee United with two late goals.

22 JAN 1988
Colin Pitchfork becomes first person convicted of murder based on DNA fingerprinting.

8 FEB 1988
Comic Relief's inaugural BBC 'Red Nose Day' raises over £15,000,000 for charity.

9 MAR 1988
Audrey Hepburn is appointed a UNICEF Special Ambassador.

1988

DOMESTIC NEWS

Railway killer sentenced
26th February 1988 One of the infamous 'Railway Killers', John Duffy, is sentenced to life imprisonment following a trial at the Old Bailey. He is convicted of two murders and four rapes, although he later admits to a further 17, conducted in dark places near railway stations. His accomplice in many of the attacks, David Mulcahy, is arrested in 1999.

Operation Flavius
6th March 1988 The deaths of three provisional IRA members at the hands of the SAS during 'Operation Flavius' in Gibraltar mark the beginning of a chain of violence, as the funerals of the three men are attacked by a loyalist paramilitary in the Milltown Cemetery attack. Three days later, during the funeral of a victim of the second attack, two British soldiers drive into the funeral procession, are dragged from their cars and shot, in what becomes known as the 'corporal killings'.

£1 note discontinued
11th March 1988 The £1 note, in circulation in one form or another since 1797, is no longer legal tender having been replaced with the £1 coin in 1983.

Piper Alpha disaster
6th July 1988 An explosion on board the Piper Alpha oil rig in the North Sea leads to its collapse and the deaths of 167 workers on board. Two would-be rescuers are also killed by the 200m-high flames. Only 61 of the 226 people on board are rescued and the disaster leaves behind enormous economic and ecological damage.

Pope heckled by Paisley
12th October 1988 During an address at the European Parliament, Pope John Paul II is heckled by Democratic Unionist Party leader and MEP Ian Paisley, who calls him the Antichrist. Paisley holds up a sign reading 'Pope John Paul II ANTICHRIST' and is forcibly removed from the chamber having been pelted with objects thrown by his fellow politicians.

IRA interviews banned
19th October 1988 The British government bans interviews with members of certain republican and loyalist organisations from being broadcast on radio or television, with the ban including the IRA and the Ulster Defence Association, among others. The move proves controversial as many in the media speak out against censorship, with multiple news outlets using professional actors to dub interviews instead.

---

5 APR 1988
A Kuwaiti airliner carrying members of the Kuwaiti royal family is hijacked in Iran.

1 MAY 1988
The first GCSE exams are sat by sixteen-year-olds across the country.

27 JUN 1988
Mike Tyson KOs Michael Spinks in 91 seconds.

1988

Clapham Junction crash
12th December 1988 A signal failure leads to a collision between two busy commuter trains just outside of Clapham Junction station. 35 people are killed, 69 seriously injured and over 400 people suffer minor injuries. The first people on the scene are students and staff from a nearby school, who are later commended by the Prime Minister for their assistance.

Lockerbie bombing
21st December 1988 A bomb on board Pan Am Flight 103 to New York detonates at 7pm over the town of Lockerbie, killing all 259 people on board and 11 people on the ground. The nation grieves as news channels capture shocking images of the wreckage-strewn town. In 2001 a Libyan intelligence officer, Abdelbaset al-Megrahi, is convicted of the bombing, and Libyan leader Muammar Gaddafi pays compensation to the victims.

Ashdown new leader
28th July 1988 Following the merger of the Social Democratic and Liberal parties, a new leader, Paddy Ashdown, MP for Yeovil, is elected to take the new Social and Liberal Democratic Party forward. He will remain their leader for 11 years.

Birth of Princess Beatrice
8th August 1988 The country is delighted with the news of the birth of Princess Beatrice, the first child of the new Duke and Duchess of York.

Currie causes outrage
3rd December 1988 Under-Secretary for Health Edwina Currie is forced to resign after she inspires widespread outrage by stating that most British eggs are infected with salmonella. The resulting 60% plummet in egg sales angers farmers, leads to the slaughter of four million hens, and earns her the nickname 'Eggwina'.

ROYALTY & POLITICS

Prince Charles avoids avalanche
10th March 1988 Prince Charles comes face to face with death on a skiing holiday in Klosters, Switzerland, when an avalanche claims the life of his companion Major Hugh Lindsey, a former equerry to the Queen.

1 JUL 1988
The Young British Artists display their work at Surrey Docks, London, in Damien Hirst's 'Freeze' exhibition.

21 AUG 1988
New licensing laws allow pubs to open between 11am and 11pm outside of Sundays.

11 SEP 1988
Steffi Graf completes a record four Grand Slams and an Olympic gold in one year with victory in the US Open.

1988

FOREIGN NEWS

Hole in the ozone layer
15th March 1988 A disturbing report from NASA shows that the ozone layer, which protects the Earth against UV radiation, is breaking down faster than thought.

Bush is President
8th November 1988 George Bush, who was Vice President during the Reagan administration and before that was one-time chief of the CIA, wins the US Presidential election. He defeats his Democrat challenger Michael Dukakis with over 53 per cent of the popular vote, despite having a somewhat gaffe-prone running mate in Dan Quayle.

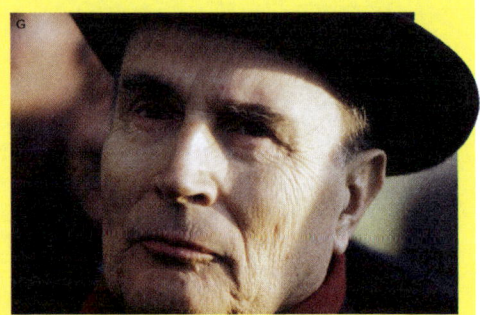

Soviets pull out
15th May 1988 As promised by Mikhail Gorbachev, the Soviet Union begins pulling out its forces from Afghanistan after more than eight years. Often referred to as 'Russia's Vietnam', the Afghan conflict revealed the ineffectiveness of Russian military tactics against a committed guerrilla army.

Airliner shot down
3rd July 1988 During rising Iranian-US tension in the Gulf a civilian Iranian airliner is mistakenly shot down by USS *Vincennes*, killing all 290 passengers and crew.

Mitterand re-elected
8th May 1988 Francois Mitterand is re-elected President of France, defeating former Mayor of Paris Jacques Chirac.

Zia is killed
17th August 1988 President Muhammad Zia-ul-Haq of Pakistan is killed alongside several of his military commanders and US ambassador Arnold Raphel when their plane crashes near Bahawalpur.

CDs outsell LPs
29th December 1988 Year-end figures show that compact discs are outselling vinyl records for the first time in the US, fuelled by major releases such as George Michael's *Faith* and Van Halen's *OU812*. Total CD sales for 1988 are 150 million compared to vinyl album sales of 72 million.

Air show deaths
28th August 1988 An air show disaster in Germany claims the lives of 70 people, the majority of them spectators, when three jets of an Italian demonstration team collide.

30 OCT 1988
Prince Charles speaks out against works of architecture, such as the National Theatre, that he feels are destroying the country's cities.

13 NOV 1988
Legandary McLaren driver Ayrton Senna wins his first Formula 1 World Drivers, Championship.

15 DEC 1988
Unemployment reaches an eight-year low at just over 2,100,000.

1988

ENTERTAINMENT

Bunny boiler
A one-night stand with a work colleague has serious repercussions for happily married Michael Douglas in *Fatal Attraction*, a thriller that turns out to be one of this year's biggest movie successes. Glenn Close plays the increasingly unhinged Alex, who takes rejection rather badly. *Fatal Attraction* opens at UK cinemas on 15th January.

Film love
It's an excellent year for arthouse cinema. *Distant Voices, Still Lives*, Terence Davies' elegiac film about his Liverpool childhood is released; Spanish auteur Pedro Almodovar wows with his *Women on the Verge of a Nervous Breakdown* (released in Spain this year), and then there is Guiseppe Tornatore's *Cinema Paradiso*, a film about the love of film. Its climactic ending, consisting of a cascade of censored film clips showing couples kissing, must surely be one of the greatest film finales ever.

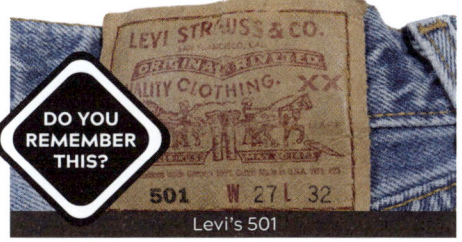
DO YOU REMEMBER THIS?
Levi's 501

Good Morning, Vietnam
Robin Williams' rapid-fire stand-up style finds a perfect outlet as he takes on the role of real-life U.S. Armed Forces DJ Adrian Cronauer in *Good Morning, Vietnam* released in the UK on 30th September. Director Barry Levinson decided to let Williams's natural knack for ad-libbing take centre stage and simply let the cameras roll during the broadcast scenes, with many of the manic monologues done off the cuff.

What a Relief
The first *Night of Comic Relief* takes place on 5th February - Red Nose Day - an eight-hour telethon featuring the best of British comic talent performing specially written sketches and skits to raise money for the Comic Relief charity. There's a special *Spitting Image* version of *Question of Sport*, a one-off *Blackadder* special called *The Cavalier Years*, a classic episode of *Dad's Army*, and much more, all presented by Lenny Henry and Griff Rhys Jones. *The Night of Comic Relief* raises £15 million.

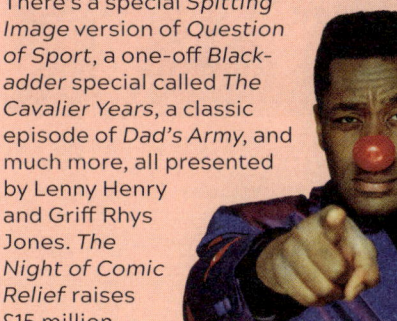

Fire! Fire!
London's Burning follows the lives and loves of the members of Blue Watch, a London Fire Brigade unit based in Blackwall, east London. Based on Jack Rosenthal's 1986 TV movie, the series begins on 20th February and continues until 2002, one of ITV's longest-running programmes after *Coronation Street* and *Emmerdale Farm*.

1988

Morning from Merseyside
Liverpool's recently restored Albert Dock is the setting for ITV's new show *This Morning* with husband-and-wife team Richard Madeley and Judy Finnegan. The two-hour show, beginning on 3rd October, brings together health and family topics, cooking, fashion, hair and beauty and celebrity interviews.

Cartoon capers
Seamlessly blending live action and animation, *Who Framed Roger Rabbit* is released on 2nd December, starring Bob Hoskins as private eye Eddie Valiant, with Kathleen Turner providing the husky voice of the iconic cartoon screen siren and sex symbol, Jessica Rabbit.

A Fish Called Wanda
Farcical comedy *A Fish Called Wanda*, starring Kevin Kline, Jamie Lee Curtis, Michael Palin and John Cleese (who is also co-writer), is released on 14th October. The ensemble cast gel brilliantly but it is Kline who wins an Academy Award for best supporting actor.

Red Dwarf
Red Dwarf, a sci-fi comedy, touches down on BBC2 on 15th February. Craig Charles is Dave Lister, an astronaut who has been in stasis for three million years and wakes to find he is drifting around space alone except for a hologram of former crew member, Rimmer (Chris Barrie), and The Cat (Danny John-Jules), a feline humanoid who has evolved from the cat he originally smuggled onto the ship. By series III, this raggle-taggle trio is joined by Kryten, a robot with self-confidence issues. They are steered around the universe under the deadpan guidance of the ship's computer, 'Holly'.

Through the wardrobe
BBC1's adaptation of *The Lion, the Witch and the Wardrobe* by C. S. Lewis begins in its early Sunday evening slot on 13th November. It has taken the BBC several years to acquire the rights to the book, during which time technology has advanced enough to make a convincing production using animation and special effects to successfully recreate the magic of Narnia. This includes a huge Aslan, operated with two people inside the lion's body and a series of complex electronics.

1988

Armchair shopping
Classy high street store Next launches the Next Directory this year, a mail order catalogue that is a cut above the rest. With a glossy magazine layout, fashion 'stories', exclusive designs and even fabric swatches, the Next Directory provides a luxe retail experience from the comfort of home.

Blood Brothers
Willy Russell's musical, *Blood Brothers*, about twin brothers separated at birth, originally makes its debut with a short run in Liverpool and the West End in 1983. But it is this year's revival at the Albery Theatre (later renamed the Noel Coward Theatre), beginning on 28th July, which goes on to become one of theatre's most successful musicals, running for 24 years and 10,000 performances.

Bough's off
Frank Bough has been a lynchpin of the BBC since 1963, a reliable presenter of breakfast news and sport with a smooth manner and penchant for sensible knitwear. Given Bough's squeaky-clean image, when the *News of the World* breaks a story alleging his involvement with cocaine and prostitutes, it's a scandal of epic proportions. Bough leaves the BBC in June.

Masquerade charade
When Kit Williams's exquisitely illustrated book *Masquerade* was published in 1979, it triggered a nationwide treasure hunt, as many tried to solve the book's fiendish, cryptic riddles to find a golden hare jewel buried somewhere in Britain. But on 11th December this year, the *Sunday Times* publishes a story about *Masquerade's* winner who had managed to find the location of the jewel through insider links.

Die Hard
Bruce Willis and Alan Rickman fully commit to their respective roles of tough, vest-wearing hero cop John McClane and saturnine bad guy Hans Gruber in *Die Hard*, a tightly plotted, compelling action flick, which goes on to become a winning formula followed by four more sequels.

Whose Line Is It Anyway?
Channel 4 launches *Whose Line Is It Anyway?* on 23rd September, presented by Clive Anderson where four quick-witted performers are given a series of improvisational challenges. Based on the original radio programme also aired this year, *Whose Line Is It Anyway?* is huge fun and makes stars of a number of rising British and American stand-ups and comic actors including John Sessions, Tony Slattery, Josie Lawrence, Mike McShane, Greg Proops, Paul Merton and Rory Bremner.

1988

That's Life – A moving moment
In February 1988, Nicholas Winton appears on *That's Life*, as presenter Esther Rantzen goes through his scrapbook from the time he had helped organise the rescue, transport and care of 669 mainly Jewish children from Nazi-occupied Czechoslovakia in 1939. During the programme, Rantzen tells Winton that the woman sitting next to him is Vera Gissen, who, as a little girl, was among those in his 'Kindertransport'. Three more of Winton's rescued children are also seated nearby. Winton is invited back on the show on 3rd July when Rantzen asks, 'Is there anyone who owes their life to Nicholas Winton?' When several rows of the audience stand up around him, it's one of the most moving and powerful moments in television history. Winton is knighted in 2003 and dies in 2015 at the age of 106.

Kylie's so lucky
20th February 1988 With one Australian No. 1 behind her – *The Locomotion* – Kylie Minogue starts recording *I Should Be So Lucky* with the hottest UK producers around, the team of Stock, Aitken and Waterman. Spending five weeks at No. 1, it begins one of the most enduring recording careers of the post-Beatle era. Kylie's success attracts a host of other soap opera stars to take a stab at the charts.

Tracy's triumph
11th June 1988 Stevie Wonder was to be the unannounced superstar of the Mandela concert at Wembley until a technical malfunction made it impossible for him to perform. In his place, with 45 minutes to fill, the little-known Tracy Chapman plays an impromptu acoustic set that turns her into an overnight star.

Girl power 80s style
Never has there been a year when the charts have been so dominated by female voices. Formerly of US all-girl band the Runaways, Belinda Carlisle kicks off 1988 at No. 1 with *Heaven is a Place on Earth*, to be followed by sixteen-year-old Tiffany with *I Think We're Alone Now* and Kylie's *I Should Be So Lucky*. Another teen star is the emerging Debbie Gibson, who writes her own material, while Robin Beck, Enya and Whitney Houston all have UK chart-toppers. And the most perfect pop record of the year? A tie between Yazz's (photo) *The Only Way is Up* and Fairground Attraction's *Perfect*, featuring the glorious voice of Glasgow folk and blues singer Eddi Reader.

MUSIC

Holly victory
19th February 1988 In an important test case, Holly Johnson of Frankie Goes to Hollywood wins the court action brought against him by record label ZTT, which sought to prevent him from signing with MCA as a solo artist.

1988

Celine's a winner
30th April 1988 Ne parlez pas sans moi wins the Eurovision Song Contest for Switzerland, performed by a little-known French-Canadian singer with a voice as big as her future - Celine Dion.

The Big 'O' departs
6th December 1988 The sudden death of Roy Orbison throws the future of the Traveling Wilburys into doubt. The Wilburys are the ultimate rock super-group - a part-time fun project for Roy and fellow veterans Bob Dylan, George Harrison, Tom Petty and Jeff Lynne, who elect to continue as a foursome.

Concert for Mandela
11th June 1988 Concert of the year is at Wembley Stadium - a multi-act 70th birthday tribute to anti-apartheid leader Nelson Mandela, who has been incarcerated on Robben Island for 25 years. Musically, the line-up is even more impressive than Live Aid, bringing together Sting, George Michael, Eurythmics, Al Green, Natalie Cole, the Bee Gees, Simple Minds, Whitney Houston, UB40, Dire Straits and South African music stars Miriam Makeba and Hugh Masekela.

Gangsta rap
8th May 1988 As rap's reputation for confrontation continues to close off many UK venues to visiting hip hop artists, Wembley Arena bars Run DMC. Rap's image is further dented - or enhanced, depending on your point of view - by the release of *Straight Outta Compton* by NWA in August, its advocacy of violence denying it airplay and incurring a warning from the FBI. As if NWA care: the album is certified platinum within a year and 'gangsta rap' is the new buzzword.

Elton wins his case
11th December 1988 The day before his libel case against The *Sun* is due to be heard, Elton John receives a million pounds in damages. He was suing the paper over drug and rent boy allegations that were wholly untrue.

1988

Motown is sold
6th July 1988 MCA Records buys Motown for $61 million, ending the latter's 30 years as an independent company.

Brosmania
For proof that the old-fashioned pop attributes of pretty faces, catchy tunes and ephemeral fame are re-asserting themselves, look no further than Bros, two twin brothers (Matt and Luke Goss) and their best mate Craig Logan, who debut with an anthem for the age of celebrity - *When Will I Be Famous*. The trio's eighteen months in the spotlight eventually dissolve into courtroom acrimony.

1. **Fast Car** *Tracy Chapman*
2. **Orinoco Flow** *Enya*
3. **When I Fall I Love** *Rick Astley*
4. **Rush Hour** *Jane Wiedlin*
5. **Don't Worry Be Happy** *Bobby McFerrin*
6. **Don't Be Cruel** *Cheap Trick*
7. **I Don't Want to Talk ...** *Everything but the Girl*
8. **A Little Respect** *Erasure*
9. **Girlfriend** *Pebbles*
10. **Sweet Jane** *The Cowboy Junkies*

Jackson v. Prince
14th July 1988 There's a clear hint of rivalry behind the respective touring plans of Michael Jackson and Prince. Jackson begins a UK visit with seven dates at Wembley Stadium. By the time of his last concert in September at Aintree Racecourse, he will have played in front of three quarters of a million Brits. Just two days after Jackson's last stadium date, Prince opens his European *Lovesexy* tour with seven nights at Wembley Arena and arrives onstage in a pink Cadillac.

In memoriam
Among the music greats leaving us this year are jazz trumpeter Chet Baker, aged 58, and singer and bandleader Brook Benton, 56. In March, Barry, Robin and Maurice Gibb mourn younger brother Andy who had three US No. 1s in 1977-78. David Prater, one half of soul duo Sam and Dave, dies in a car accident in April aged 50, and German singer Nico of Velvet Underground fame dies aged 49 in Ibiza from an untreated head injury.

PHOTO CREDITS Copyright 2024, TDM Rights BV.
Photos: **A** David Cannon Collection - Getty Images / **B** Ronald C. Modra - Getty Images North America - Getty Images / **C** PA Images - Getty Images / **D** PA Images - Getty Images / **E** Georges De Keerle - Hulton Archive - Getty Images / **F** Georges De Keerle - Hulton Archive - Getty Images / **G** Bernard Bisson - Sygma - Getty Images / **H** Sunset Boulevard - Corbis Historical - Getty Images / **I** Comic Relief - GettyImages Europe - Getty Images / **J** Ronald Grant Archive - Mary Evans / **K** BBC - Ronald Grant - Mary Evans / **L** BBC - Ronald Grant - Mary Evans / **M** Channel 4 Hat Trick Productions - Ronald Grant Archive - Mary Evans / **N** AF Archive - 0th Century Fox - Mary Evans / **O** PA Image - Getty images / **P** Michael Putland - Hulton Archive - Getty Images / **Q** Ullstein Bild - Getty Images / **R** Lynn Goldsmith - Corbis Historical - Getty Images / **S** Mirrorpix - Getty Images / **T** PA Images - Getty Images.

1989

MY FIRST 18 YEARS

SPORT

Faldo wins Masters
10th April 1989 Nick Faldo wins the Masters Tournament, becoming the first English player to take the trophy. Despite going into the fourth round five shots off the lead, Faldo makes it into a playoff with Scott Hoch and takes victory with a 25-foot putt on the second hole.

Hillsborough disaster
15th April 1989 Tragedy strikes the FA Cup semi-final between Nottingham Forest and Liverpool at Hillsborough, Sheffield, when a crush kills 97 fans and seriously injures 300 more. *Sun* prompts outrage by falsely claiming that survivors robbed the dying and attacked emergency services. Stadiums around the country move to remove perimeter fences and standing sections. A month later, Liverpool win the FA Cup final 3-2 over Everton, but Liverpool fans have to wait years for justice, with a second inquest finally finding that the victims were unlawfully killed in 1996.

Desert Orchid
16th March 1989 Fan favourite Desert Orchid wins the Cheltenham Gold Cup in an exciting finish. Despite setting off an 11-4 favourite, 'Dessie', as he became known, hated the mud and the left-handed track and was being tried over a far longer distance than he had run before. After the race his jockey, Simon Sherwood, stated that he had 'never known a horse so brave'.

Mansell wins Grand Prix
26th March 1989 British racing driver Nigel Mansell shocks fans in his first season with Ferrari by winning an unlikely Grand Prix in Brazil. The race is at the home track of his rival, Nelson Piquet, who many expect to dominate, but despite prior issues with the car's new semi-automatic gearbox, Mansell powers to victory.

First UK WWF event
10th October 1989 The London Arena plays host to the very first World Wrestling Federation event held in the UK. Known as the 'UK Rampage', it is broadcast live on the new Sky One channel and features top performers such as Hulk Hogan and Randy Savage, who battle it out for the Heavyweight Championship.

20 JAN 1989
George Bush Senior is sworn in as the 41st President of the United States.

2 FEB 1989
F. W. de Klerk replaces P. W. Botha as South Africa's National Party leader.

20 MAR 1989
Two superintendents of the Royal Ulster Constabulary are shot dead by the IRA.

1989

DOMESTIC NEWS

Kegworth air disaster
8th January 1989 Just weeks after the Lockerbie bombing, the country is brought to a standstill again as 44 people are killed when British Midland Airways Flight 092 crashes into an embankment on the M1.

Satanic Verses protests
14th January 1989 Protests in Bradford erupt over the publication in September 1988 of Salman Rushdie's *The Satanic Verses*, which some Muslims find offensive. Books are burned in the streets, and the following month the Iranian Ayatollah Ruhollah Khomeini issues a fatwa calling for Rushdie's death. In March diplomatic relations between Iran and the UK are broken over the book, and Rushdie is forced to go into hiding.

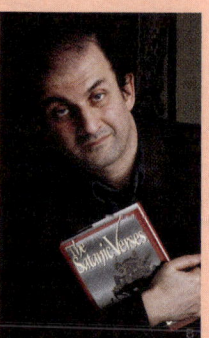

Sky Television launches
5th February 1989 Sky Television, the world's first commercial direct broadcast satellite system, launches. The system carries three new channels, Sky News, Sky Movies and Eurosport, alongside the already existing Sky Channel.

Lawyer murdered
12th February 1989 The murder of lawyer Pat Finucane by the Ulster Defence Association sends shockwaves across Northern Ireland when he is shot fourteen times whilst eating a meal at home with his wife and children. The British security services later admit collusion in the killing and issue an apology in 2011.

Serious Crime Squad disbanded
14th August 1989 Following repeated allegations of wrongdoing, the Serious Crime Squad of the West Midlands Police is broken up. Many detectives are suspended when stories of abuse and incompetence hit the news, most famously involving the wrongful convictions of the 'Birmingham Six' who alleged that they were beaten and deprived of food and sleep.

Marchioness disaster
20th August 1989 In the early hours of the morning the *Marchioness*, a pleasure boat, is struck twice by a dredger, the *Bowbelle*. The *Marchioness*, which had been hired for a birthday party, is forced onto her side, and sinks quickly, trapping many of the young partygoers inside. 51 of the 130 on board are killed.

5 APR 1989
Channel Tunnel workers strike for two weeks, over pay and working conditions.

2 MAY 1989
Prisoners at Risley Detention Centre riot, protesting on the roof for three days.

3 JUN 1989
Ayatollah Khomeini, who founded the Islamic Revolution in Iran, dies.

1989

Deal bombing
22nd September 1989 The Royal Marines School of Music at the Royal Marine Depot in Deal is bombed by the Provisional IRA. Eleven Royal Marine bandsmen are killed when the building collapses after the bomb explodes in the changing room.

Ashdown throws gauntlet
15th September 1989 Paddy Ashdown makes a rousing speech at the annual conference of the Social and Liberal Democratic Party, in which he calls for an 'end to Thatcherism'. A month later, the party is rebranded as the 'Liberal Democrats'.

ROYALTY & POLITICS

FOREIGN NEWS

Exxon Valdez oil spill
24th March 1989 The supertanker *Exxon Valdez* spills over 10 million gallons of crude oil into Prince William Sound after striking Bligh Reef off Alaska. It creates one of the worst environmental disasters in memory and affects 1,300 miles of coastline, killing wildlife, savaging the local economy and blighting Prince William Sound for years to come.

Diana visits New York
February 1989 Princess Diana makes her first solo trip to New York, with a brief to promote British industries abroad. She surprises many by visiting social projects in the more deprived areas of New York. This famously includes a visit to an AIDS ward in Harlem Hospital, where she hugs a young patient.

Communism falls
It is the year of the greatest upheaval in Europe since the French Revolution. Revolutions are overthrowing communism in almost all Eastern Bloc countries. People are also turning against communism in the Baltic states. On 23rd August two million people from the three different countries form a 600-kilometre-long chain between the capitals of Tallinn, Riga and Vilnius. In Czechoslovakia, hundreds of thousands of people jingle their keys in Prague in November, as a sign that they want to be freed from communism.

Princess Diana opens AIDS centre
25th July 1989 Diana, Princess of Wales, officially opens a new day centre for people with AIDS in Tulse Hill, London.

European elections
19th June 1989 The Labour Party secure big wins in the European Elections, earning 45 of the 78 constituencies up for grabs. This shows a big shift in fortunes for Labour, who have been out of power in the UK for over a decade.

9 JUL 1989
Boris Becker beats Stefan Edberg and wins his 3rd and last Wimbledon title.

1 AUG 1989
The last colliery in Kent closes, ending almost 100 years of mining in the Kent Coalfield.

7 SEP 1989
Heidi Hazell, wife of a British soldier, is killed by the IRA in West Germany.

1989

Perestroika too slow
26th March 1989 That major changes are afoot in the Soviet Union becomes crystal clear during the elections for the Congress of People's Deputies. For the first time, Russians are allowed to vote anonymously and candidates from outside the Communist Party are allowed to stand as candidates. The popular Boris Yeltsin (photo left), who has just been expelled from the party due to his criticism of Mikhail Gorbachev's too-slow *perestroika* (restructuring), wins in Moscow with an overwhelming score of 92 percent of the votes.

Tank Man
5th June 1989 A protest begins in Beijing's Tiananmen Square. Encouraged by developments in the Soviet Union and the Eastern Bloc, students and workers demand far-reaching reforms. The crowd in Tiananmen Square grows to more than a million demonstrators. Deng Xiaoping decides to put a rigorous end to the protest and sends tanks to the square. Between 3,000 and 10,000 people die during the action to clear the square. The most famous image is that of a man stepping in front of a column of tanks to block their way. Film and photo images of the unknown 'Tank Man' are going around the world.

The Wall falls
9th November 1989 Developments in the Eastern Bloc have a huge impact in East Germany, which is still trying to resist *glasnost* and *perestroika*. Tens of thousands of East Germans flee to the West. The socialist utopia is practically bankrupt and demonstrations against the regime are swelling in all major cities. On 7th November, the government collapses and the Politburo resigns a day later. Completely

unexpectedly, East Berlin party secretary Günter Schabowski gives a press conference on 9th November and announces that East German citizens will now be allowed to travel freely. To a question from an Italian journalist when exactly these rules will come into effect, Schabowski answers: '*Sofort, unverzüglich*'. (Immediately, immediately.) Immediately, tens of thousands of East Berliners gather at various border crossings in Berlin. The border guards, the Stasi and the army are completely overwhelmed. The Berlin Wall has fallen after 28 years. Before the end of the year, US President Bush and Russian leader Gorbachev will shake hands in Malta to mark the end of the Cold War.

17 OCT 1989
A large earthquake in San Francisco kills 63.

21 NOV 1989
Cameras are permitted in the House of Commons.

2 DEC 1989
Margaret Thatcher joins Mikhail Gorbachev and George Bush to declare the Cold War over.

1989

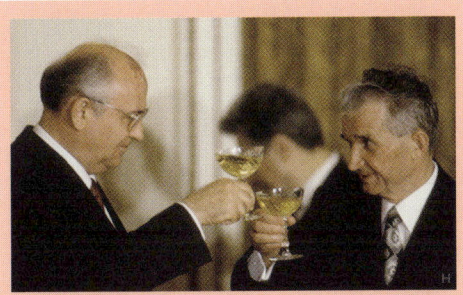

The next domino
16th December 1989 Following relatively bloodless revolutions in East Germany, Hungary and Czechoslovakia and the installation of new governments, Romania is the next domino to fall. It begins with demonstrations and ends on 22nd December when the army deserts President Nicolae Ceausescu and he is forced to flee. He and his wife are captured and executed on Christmas Day.

US invades Panama
20th December 1989 The US launches an invasion of Panama to oust President Manuel Noriega. He is captured on 3rd January and taken to the US for trial.

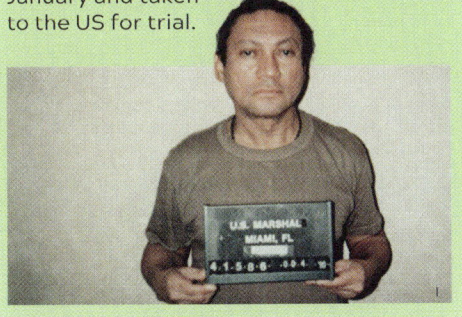

Gaming on the go
Nintendo brings out the Gameboy console this year, offering complete portability and games on the go. The Nintendo Gameboy costs £59.99 and comes with a variety of games such as *Super Mario Land* and *Tetris*. Adverts target cool, older gamers as well as kids, showing the Nintendo in use anytime, anywhere with the slogan, 'There's nowhere you can't play it'.

Dramatic beginnings
Three popular children's television dramas begin this year. First up is *Press Gang*, ITV's comedy drama about a junior newspaper run by kids from the local comprehensive school which first airs on 16th January. *Children's Ward* begins on ITV on 15th March, and on 8th November, *Byker Grove*, the gritty drama about the Geordie scamps at a Newcastle youth club, is first broadcast on BBC1. All three are seedbeds for some of television's best talent.

Kiss the boys
In 1987, *Eastenders* causes controversy when its gay character Colin Russell gives his boyfriend Barry a peck on the forehead. But that's nothing compared to the scene in this year's 24th January episode when Colin has a full-on snog with Guido Smith. It is the first mouth-to-mouth gay kiss on British television and sparks a torrent of complaints and abuse.

ENTERTAINMENT

Desmond's
Channel 4's comedy about a barber shop run by the Guyanese Ambrose family, *Desmond's* is less about haircuts (which are generally bad) and more about friendship and community. Episode one, the first of s71, airs on 5th January. Thirty years on from that date, writer Trix Morrell tells the *Guardian*, 'I didn't write *Desmond's* for black people. I wrote it for white people so they could see how black people really are.'

1989

Action Anneka

Anneka Rice has made a name for herself on Channel 4's *Treasure Hunt* where viewers are used to seeing her zipped into a boilersuit, hopping in and out of helicopters as contestants direct her next move by solving a series of puzzles. *Challenge Anneka*, which begins on BBC1 on 8th September, makes use of Rice's can-do attitude and action girl reputation as she takes on a series of tasks each episode, usually with a charitable focus.

When Harry Met Sally

A timely confluence of great writing from Nora Ephron, director Rob Reiner's comic touch, and Billy Crystal and Meg Ryan at the top of their game, *When Harry Met Sally* explores the truth in Harry's belief that, 'men and women can't be friends because the sex part always gets in the way'. The film goes on general release in the UK on 1st December and is remembered above all for the scene in a busy deli when Ryan demonstrates how easy it is to fake an orgasm. The follow-up line from a fellow diner, 'I'll have what she's having', is actually delivered by Reiner's mother, Estelle.

Blackadder Goes Forth

In Blackadder's fourth and final outing, first broadcast on 28th September, Edmund finds himself an officer in the trenches on the Western Front, more world weary and cynical than ever, which is no surprise when he's surrounded by imbeciles; a subaltern twit, George (Hugh Laurie), batman Baldrick and, safely in his chateau HQ, General Melchett (Stephen Fry) who is intent on sending his men to certain death. The last episode, *Goodbyee*, is disarmingly poignant as Blackadder assembles, ready to go 'over the top' in the 'big push', with the characters we've grown to know and love over the years. But this time, it really is goodbyee.

Maid Marian and her Merry Men

Tony Robinson (*Blackadder's* Baldrick) writes and stars in *Maid Marian and Her Merry Men*, starting on BBC1 on 16th November. It's a partly a broad comedy with physical jokes but also a sophisticated, cleverly scripted parody of the traditional Robin Hood story. The programme flips gender roles, with Maid Marian the idealistic and passionate leader of the forest-dwelling gang, and Robin an ex-tailor and all-round wet drip who insists everyone wears green 'to coordinate with the trees'. For those too young to watch *Blackadder*, *Maid Marian and her Merry Men* is a more than worthy substitute.

Acid house smiley

1989

Birds of Feather
Birds of a feather, flock together. That's what Sharon (Linda Robson) and Tracey (Pauline Quirke) do in this hit comedy, which first airs on BBC1 on 16th October. After their husbands are jointly sent down for armed robbery, Tracey moves from her grotty Edmonton flat to her sister Sharon's deluxe Essex home in Chigwell, where their neighbour, middle-aged man-eater Dorien Green (Lesley Joseph, upstaging everyone and wearing the hell out of leopard print) is a regular uninvited guest. Together they are the older, wiser and funnier flag bearers for the 'Essex Girl' of the 1990s.

The Cook, The Thief, His Wife and Her Lover
Peter Greenaway's stylish, opulent, unsettling film, released 13th October, is his damning indictment of Thatcher's government, metaphorically at least. Michael Gambon perfectly expresses the greed and excess of Tory Britain as the sadistic, violent Albert Spica, surrounded by henchmen and sycophants as they devour an ostentatious banquet each evening at his restaurant. Helen Mirren, exquisitely dressed in Jean Paul Gaultier, is his wife who begins an affair with a bookish diner under her husband's nose, while the cook provides cover for their passionate liaisons.

Bodacious!
Time-travelling twerps Bill (Alex Winter) and Ted (Keanu Reeves) enlist the help of Napoleon, Joan of Arc and 'So-crayts' to write their history paper (and avoid Ted being banished to military school) in *Bill and Ted's Excellent Adventure* released 10th August. Bill and Ted introduce audiences to phrases like, 'Bodacious' and 'Party on, dudes!' but above all, remind everyone to 'Be excellent to each other.'

A new era for *Batman*
Batman, released 11th August, goes from the kitsch, comic character of the past to a brooding, conflicted superhero of the present in a Tim Burton makeover which lays the foundation stone for comic-based blockbusters of the future. Michael Keaton is a darker Batman altogether, saving Gotham City while wrestling with the memories of his murdered parents. Jack Nicholson in daubed makeup as the Joker is a captivating baddie, his purple suit echoing various tracks throughout the film, provided by His Royal Purpleness, Prince.

My Left Foot
Daniel Day-Lewis deservedly wins Best Actor Oscar at the 1990 Academy Awards for his performance as Christy Brown in *My Left Foot*, while Brenda Fricker, playing his careworn mother, takes home the award for Best Actress in a supporting role, dedicating it to Bridget by saying, 'anyone who gives birth 22 times deserves one of these'. The story of Brown's remarkable life, where he overcame crippling cerebral palsy and prejudice to become a respected writer and artist, is unflinching but also uplifting.

1989

Nielsen gets naked
It's easy to forget Leslie Nielsen has spent decades as a serious actor, so easily does he slip into characters such as the incompetent detective Lieutenant Frank Drebin in *The Naked Gun: From the Files of Police Squad!*, which has its UK release on 10th February. Based on the comedy television series *Police Squad!* the film, and its two sequels, cement Neilsen's reputation as 'the Olivier of spoofs', a title suggested by American film critic Roger Ebert.

Rain Man
Rain Man, which UK audiences can see from 3rd March, wins four Oscars at the 61st Academy Awards. Tom Cruise and Dustin Hoffman are perfectly cast; Cruise as arrogant and shallow car salesman Charlie who learns his late father has left everything to a brother he never knew he had: autistic savant, Raymond (Hoffman). Their road trip across the country is a journey of understanding and self-discovery, as Charlie emerges from the experience a better and more decent man.

MUSIC

BRIT Awards chaos
13th February 1989 The annual showpiece BRIT Awards are televised live from the Royal Albert Hall. Everything that could go wrong does. The hosts, Samantha Fox and Mick Fleetwood, are completely mismatched and can't manage the autocue. Government minister Kenneth Baker is roundly booed, causing Cliff Richard to castigate the audience for their lack of respect. Boy George appears when the Four Tops are announced. Transatlantic links fail, some live performances are out of tune and some awards are not presented at all. From now on, the BRITs will be recorded the night before to ensure that the bad bits are edited out before broadcast.

Madonna v. the Vatican
2nd March 1989 Madonna is no stranger to controversy; she pushes the boundaries further with *Like a Prayer*, the video for which plays provocatively with Catholic iconography. The Vatican expresses outrage and a planned world tour is cancelled. Is she bothered? Not at all. The *Like a Prayer* album is the top selling record of 1989 at 15 million, beating Janet Jackson's *Rhythm Nation*, Phil Collins' *But Seriously* and a resurgent Cher's *Heart of Stone*.

1989

Mike and the Mechanics
25th March 1989 Phil Collins plays Great Train Robber Buster Edwards in *Buster* but his solo work has put his band, Genesis, on hiatus for a while. Fellow members Tony Banks and Mike Rutherford start other projects, the latter topping the US chart with *The Living Years* as leader of Mike and the Mechanics.

Boy band on the block
26th April 1989 Now undertaking their first UK tour, New Kids on the Block were formed in 1985 as a white answer to black teenage quintet New Edition. New Kids have tightly choreographed stage moves, carefully developed individual personas, sweet harmonies, all-round good looks and just a touch of bad-boy menace. With six US Top Ten records during 1989 including three No. 1s, they create the template for the Backstreet Boys, Take That, Boyzone and all the boy bands who follow in their wake.

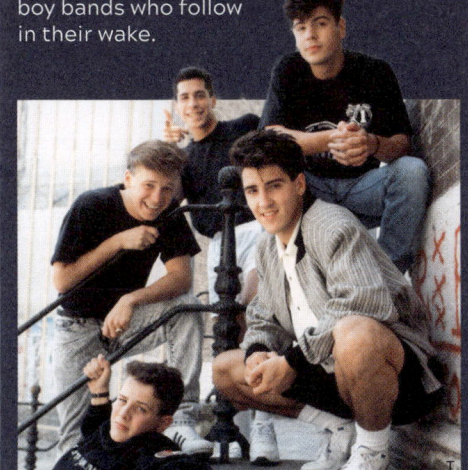

Soul II Soul
24th June 1989 That British-made black music is now a real force is clear from the rise of Soul II Soul, a collective founded by north Londoner Jazzie B (photo) and Bristol-based Nellee Hooper of Massive Attack. Caron Wheeler joins for *Back to Life*, now at No. 1 for four weeks.

Monkees reunite
9th July 1989 Following a successful tour featuring three of the original Monkees, Mike Nesmith joins Mickey Dolenz, Peter Tork and Davy Jones to receive their own stars on the Hollywood Walk of Fame.

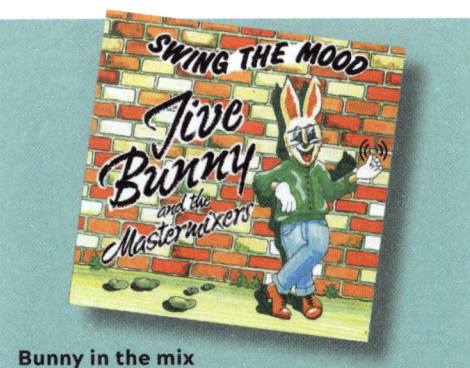

Bunny in the mix
5th August 1989 Every mobile DJ in the country envies John and Andy Pickles, who have hit on the simple idea of putting their megamix medleys on record. Taking the name Jive Bunny, they are now at No. 1 with *Swing the Mood* which combines nine 1950s rock'n'roll tracks with Glenn Miller's *In the Mood* and Chubby Checker's *Let's Twist Again*. The Jive Bunny formula will be good for two more No. 1s.

1989

Bangles break
21st September 1988 The Bangles split up just months after *Eternal Flame* - inspired by the flame burning on Elvis Presley's grave - is a transatlantic No. 1.

Death of Ewan MacColl
22nd October 1989 Ewan MacColl, father of Kirsty and the prime mover behind the UK's post-war folk music revival, dies aged 74. His songs include *Dirty Old Town* and *The First Time Ever I Saw Your Face*.

MY FIRST 18 YEARS TOP 10 — 1989

1. **Ride on Time** Black Box
2. **Wind Beneath My Wings** Bette Midler
3. **All Around the World** Lisa Stansfield
4. **When Love Comes to Town** U2 with B. B. King
5. **Love and Regret** Deacon Blue
6. **The Second Summer of Love** Danny Wilson
7. **Sowing the Seeds of Love** Tears for Fears
8. **If I Could Turn Back Time** Cher
9. **You Keep it All In** The Beautiful South
10. **Sweet Child of Mine** Guns N' Roses

Open | Search | Scan

Hello, Madchester
2nd December 1989 The appearance of Happy Mondays and the Stone Roses (photo) on the same edition of *Top of the Pops* awakens the world to the fast blossoming Manchester scene and rave culture in general. The peculiarly Mancunian mix of loopy electronic dance rhythms, chiming guitars, acid-laced bonhomie and baggy trousers, fused in clubs like the Hacienda, is going national. 'Madchester' has arrived.

Ice Cube goes solo
23rd December 1989 Ice Cube departs the most controversial rap band of all, NWA from Compton in Los Angeles. He is already recording his first solo album.

Housemartins go south
Following the end of the Housemartins, Paul Heaton and Dave Hemmingway retain their base in Hull and form a new five-piece, the ironically named Beautiful South. Beginning with a song about the cynical side of songwriting, *Song for Whoever*, they specialise in barbed wire lyrics couched in the sweetest of soul-influenced melodies.

PHOTO CREDITS Copyright 2024, TDM Rights BV.
Photos: **A** Phil O'Brien EMPICS - PA Images - Getty Images / **B** David Leveson - Hulton Archive - Getty Images / **C** Mirrorpix - Getty Images / **D** Allan Tannenbaum - Archive Photos - Getty Images / **E** TASS - Getty Images / **F** Archive Photos - Getty Images / **G** Ullstein Bild - Getty Images / **H** Georges Merillon - Gamma-Rapho - Getty Images / **I** Bettmann - Getty Images / **J** Robtek - Asset Assurance - Shutterstock / **K** AF Archive - Mary Evans / **L** AF Archive - BBC - Mary Evans / **M** Acstle Rock Entertainment - Ronald Grant Archive - Mary Evans / **N** AF Archive - Allstar Picture Library - Mary Evans / **O** Allarts Cook Elsevira Erato Films - Ronald Grant Archive - Mary Evans / **P** Sunset Boulevard - Corbis Historical - Getty Images / **Q** Universal History Archive - Universal Images Group Editorial - Getty Images / **R** Dave Hogan - Hulton Archive - Getty Images / **S** Paul Natkin - WireImage - Getty Images / **T** Michel Linssen - Redferns - Getty Images / **U** Mike Prior - Redferns - Getty Images / **V** Paul Natkin - WireImage - Getty Images / **W** Brian Rasic - Hulton Archive - Getty Images.

1990

MY FIRST 18 YEARS

SPORT

1990 Commonwealth Games
3rd February 1990 At the 14th Commonwealth Games, hosted by New Zealand, the medal table is topped by Australia, with England coming in second with an impressive tally of 128 medals, 46 of which are gold.

World Cup heartbreak
4th July 1990 England make it through to the semi-finals of the FIFA World Cup before losing in heartbreaking fashion to West Germany following a penalty shootout. West Germany go on to take the tournament in a 1-0 victory over Argentina, with England losing to tournament hosts Italy in the third place playoffs.

Shock Tyson defeat
11th February 1990 One of the biggest upsets in boxing history occurs when undefeated, undisputed heavyweight Champion of the World, Mike Tyson, is knocked out in the tenth round by the 42 to 1 opponent, Buster Douglas.

UEFA lifts ban
10th July 1990 Five years after it was implemented following the Heysel Stadium disaster, UEFA finally lifts its ban on English football clubs participating in European competitions. Incidents of football hooliganism have reduced over the previous year, and Manchester United celebrate a return to European football by winning the Cup Winners' Cup in the 1990-1991 season.

Hendry youngest champ
29th April 1990 Twenty-one-year-old Stephen Hendry secures victory over Jimmy White at the Crucible to become the youngest ever World Snooker Champion. Leading from the start, he wins the match 18-12 in a tournament that sees 18 century breaks.

21 JAN 1990
The first MTV Unplugged is aired, featuring the band Squeeze.

13 FEB 1990
Britain and France give Germany the OK to reunify.

2 MAR 1990
Gorbachev is elected President of the USSR.

1990

DOMESTIC NEWS

Stormy weather
1990 proves a year of extremes in weather as a series of storms, including the Burns Day Storm which kills 39 people, batter the country in January and February. August sees a formidable heatwave reach a high of 37.1°C, before heavy snow blankets the country in December leading to power cuts lasting several days.

Strangeways Prison riot
1st April 1990 Rioting breaks out at Strangeways Prison in Manchester, leading to 25 days of violence. Following several smaller protests, and growing frustrations at conditions in the compound, hundreds of prisoners riot following a service in the prison's chapel. One prisoner is killed, and 194 people, both prisoners and guards, are injured.

Poll tax riots
9th March 1990 The new Community Charge introduced by the government prompts rioting across the capital. Protesters object to the fixed rate tax, which would see all residents contribute the same amount to their local authority, regardless of income. The tax is introduced despite protests but is replaced just three years later with a new 'Council Tax' system.

MP killed by IRA
30th July 1990 Ian Gow, Member of Parliament for Eastbourne, is killed by the IRA after a bomb is planted under his car at home. His death comes just days after a bomb had targeted the Stock Exchange Tower in London, and weeks after a bombing at the Carlton Club which killed one and injured twenty. Later in the year, Air Chief Marshal Sir Peter Terry narrowly survives after being shot nine times by the IRA at home.

The Year of budget brands
1990 proves the year of discount shopping as three low-cost supermarket chains launch in Britain for the first time. German supermarket Aldi, Danish chain Netto, and British store Poundland all open their first UK branches in 1990, catering to customers looking for better value deals.

Brian Keenan released
24th August 1990 Northern Irish writer Brian Keenan is released from captivity in Beirut, Lebanon, having spent over four years as a hostage. His release leads to hope that his fellow hostages, including John McCarthy and Terry Waite, will soon be released as well.

---

27 APR 1990
Axl Rose of *Guns N' Roses* marries Erin Everly, daughter of Don Everly of the Everly Brothers.

1 MAY 1990
Imports of British beef banned by several European countries over BSE.

21 JUN 1990
Large earthquake in Iran kills 35-50,000.

1990

Channel Tunnel connected
1st December 1990 A major milestone is celebrated by workers on the Channel Tunnel as labourers on the French and British sides meet in the middle 40 metres below the seabed. The two countries are now connected by land for the first time in 8,000 years. Sadly, a more sombre milestone had been reached in May, when Billy Cartman became the sixth Briton to die during the tunnel's construction.

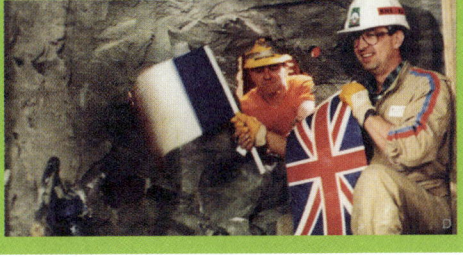

Contaminated blood scandal
11th December 1990 The British government announces that it will make available £42 million to be used as compensation for those affected by the 'contaminated blood' scandal in an out of court settlement. Over 1,200 haemophiliacs are known to have been infected with the HIV virus through transfusions which had been collected from unsafe sources, predominantly prisoners in the US. The true scale of the scandal does not become apparent for many years, as deaths from Hepatitis C are added to the equation and it emerges that over 30,000 people were affected. As of 2023 at least 3,000 people have died as a result.

ROYALTY & POLITICS

New princess born
23rd March 1990 Prince Andrew and his wife Sarah, the Duchess of York, welcome their second child, a baby girl. In December she is christened Princess Eugenie Victoria Helena of York at St Mary Magdalene Church, Sandringham. She is the first royal baby to have a public christening.

Deputy PM resigns
1st November 1990 Divisions in the Conservative Party widen as Deputy Prime Minister Geoffrey Howe resigns over European policy and the Community Charge. Twelve days later he delivers a blistering attack on Thatcher in his resignation speech during Prime Minister's Questions, accusing her of risking the country's future and undermining her cabinet colleagues.

BBC Radio 5 launched
27th August 1990 The BBC launch their first new radio station in over 20 years as Radio 5 hits the airwaves for the first time. Providing a mix of sport and educational programming, it also features children's shows, and will run until 1994 before being replaced by BBC Radio 5 Live.

3 JUL 1990
Members of 2 Live Crew formally charged with obscenity in Florida for performing the song *Me So Horny*.

27 AUG 1990
The BBC launch their first new radio station in over 20 years as Radio 5.

13 SEP 1990
The first episode of *'Law and Order'* created by Dick Wolf premieres.

1990

Thatcher falls
14th November 1990 Michael Heseltine announces a challenge to the leadership of Prime Minister Margaret Thatcher in what would prove to be the beginning of the end for her tenure as leader. Six days later, she falls short of an outright victory in the leadership contest and on the 22nd announces her resignation as leader. After eleven years as Prime Minister, she is replaced by her Chancellor, John Major.

Goodbye Charlie
1st January 1990 More than 200,000 West and East Germans celebrate New Year at the Brandenburg Gate in Berlin. Soon thousands of former East Germans storm the Stasi headquarters to view their files. On 29th January former leader Erich Honecker is arrested on suspicion of high treason. On 19th February at midnight, border guards begin demolishing the Berlin Wall in the heart of Berlin, near the Reichstag. The well-known guard post, Checkpoint Charlie, disappears and the original guardhouse is moved to a museum.

FOREIGN NEWS

Big Mac Soviet style
31st January 1990 The symbol of Western consumer society lands in the former epicentre of communism. The Berlin Wall is barely down before the very first McDonald's in the Soviet Union opens on Pushkin Square in Moscow. Thousands of Muscovites queue for a Big Mac. On the first day, 34,000 units are sold.

Not a mental illness
17th May 1990 At the start of the year, homosexuality is still on the list of mental diseases of the World Health Organisation (WHO) alongside schizophrenia, dementia and depression. Today it disappears from that list and the date is declared International Day against Homophobia, Biphobia, Transphobia and Intersexphobia.

We will rock you
3rd January 1990 Panamanian President Manuel Noriega is finally captured by US invasion forces. The dictator, controller of a large drug and money laundering network, has been hiding in the Vatican embassy. He surrenders after the Americans play loud hard rock music for days to break him mentally.

---

18 OCT 1988
Britain joins the European Exchange Rate Mechanism.

14 NOV 1988
Britain performs nuclear test at Nevada Test Site.

2 DEC 1988
Helmut Kohl becomes Chancellor of a united Germany.

1990

A wider web
13th November 1990 The Internet already has more than 300,000 hosts but Tim Berners-Lee wants to connect computers in an even smoother way. The UK software developer envisions a huge digital library that stores all information and human knowledge and is available to every computer user. Together with Robert Cailliau, he designs the system that forms the basis of the World Wide Web.

Hubble Space Telescope
24th April 1990 NASA and ESA launch the Hubble Space Telescope. The Hubble reveals spectacular secrets of the universe with its infrared camera and spectroscope, including the fact that the universe is expanding faster than thought. Its sensational and razor-sharp images stun the world.

Digital camera
15th November 1990 The new Dycam Model 1 - also known as Logitech Fotoman - is a revolutionary step in photography but is not a commercial success. As the first fully digital camera for consumers, it is easy to operate with just one shutter button. The days of taking a film roll to the chemist and waiting a week for your prints are over.

Mandela released
11th February 1990 After 27 years of incarceration, Nelson Mandela is released. South African President Frederik Willem de Klerk realizes that apartheid can no longer be maintained due to enormous internal and international pressure. The whole world watches as Mandela leaves prison near Cape Town, hand in hand with his wife Winnie. After his release, Mandela speaks to 100,000 people in the Johannesburg football stadium. Mandela becomes political leader of the ANC, and in May he begins negotiations with de Klerk. The end of apartheid is in sight.

Saddam invades Kuwait
2nd August 1990 Treated with kid gloves for years by western powers anxious to have a bulwark against Iran, Iraqi President Saddam Hussein becomes the world's bogeyman as he launches an invasion of neighbouring Kuwait. The UN condemns the invasion and an international community united since the end of the Cold War imposes a boycott and an ultimatum on Iraq: withdraw from Kuwait by 15th January or the UN will end the occupation by force.

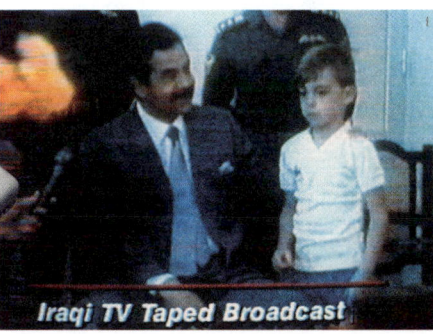

Herman the bull
16th December 1990 Herman is the first transgenic bull in the world. The outcome of genetic modification, he is the first bull to carry the human gene. The theory is that his female offspring will produce milk that contains anti-inflammatory protein but the milk of his 55 descendants proves unsuitable as medicine because there is too little of the protein in it.

1990

ENTERTAINMENT

Mr Bean
Airing on the first day of a new decade, rubber-faced Rowan Atkinson is the gawky, gauche, tweed-jacketed *Mr. Bean*, whose daily life is littered with misadventure and mishaps as he attempts to achieve apparently simple tasks in increasingly convoluted ways. Bean is largely non-verbal, communicating purely through physicality and unintelligible mumbling. Mr. Bean becomes one of Britain's best-loved and most exportable characters.

Baywatch
The show that launches a million posters, and inhabits the dreams of countless teenage boys, *Baywatch* comes to British TV screens on 6th January. Baywatch follows a lifesaving team in Los Angeles County, California, populated by various demi-gods and goddesses, including ex-Playboy model Pamela Anderson as P. J. Parker, and David 'The Hoff' Hasselhoff as Mitch Buchannon. In between rescuing weak swimmers or fending off shark attacks, the *Baywatch* lifeguards mainly run up and down the beach in slow-motion and conduct most of their business wearing the iconic *Baywatch* red swimsuit.

Pretty Woman
The basic premise of *Pretty Woman* may be questionable but it's hard not to fall in love with the romcom that revives Richard Gere's career and makes a star of Julia Roberts and her megawatt smile. Roberts plays Vivian, a streetwalker who by chance walks into millionaire businessman Edward's life. Their relationship, at first a business transaction, blossoms into romance. A feel-good fairy tale for modern times.

Teenage Mutant Hero must-haves
Leonardo, Raphael, Michaelangelo and Donatello, the pizza-loving, crime-fighting, sewer-dwelling *Teenage Mutant Hero (Ninja) Turtles* make their UK debut on 3rd January and by Christmas, their play figures are the UK's number one Christmas toy as Britain goes turtle crazy.

Keeping Up Appearances
The fact that Hyacinth Bucket insists her surname is pronounced 'Bouquet' tells you all you need to know about her. Patricia Routledge excels in the role as the overbearing and occasionally monstrous Hyacinth whose curtain twitching, candlelit dinner parties and 'RP' phone manner are all part of her drive to mix with the right crowd. If only her social aspirations weren't continually thwarted by her common as muck sisters, Daisy and Rose.

1990

Tip Top Tippety Top
Harry Enfield's Television Programme begins on 8th November where Enfield, along with pals Kathy Burke and Paul Whitehouse, introduces us to characters like Tim Nice-But-Dim, Mr. Cholmondeley-Warner (who presents everything in the style of a flickering 1940s newsreel), Wayne and Waynetta Slob (and baby Spudlika), The Scousers, and not forgetting over-the-hill radio DJs Smashie and Nicey. The show is rebirthed in 1994 as *Harry Enfield and Chums*.

The Little Mermaid
12th October 1990 After an extended fallow period, Disney adapts a well-loved fairy tale and finds its mojo again, casting its spell over Hans Christian Anderson's story, *The Little Mermaid*. Flame-haired Ariel makes a deal with the Ursula the sea-witch in order to become human and find true love with Prince Eric.

Twin Peaks
23rd October 1990 Co-created by Mark Frost and David Lynch, *Twin Peaks* subverts the traditional detective series with elements of the surreal and supernatural, and emerges as something much more original. Kyle McLachlan is FBI Special Agent Dale Cooper who arrives in the Pacific North West town of Twin Peaks to investigate the murder of prom queen Laura Palmer. So far, so typical, but *Twin Peaks*' dream-like weirdness and cast of eccentric characters wins it a cult-like following.

Supermodels
The supermodel phenomenon goes mainstream this year when George Michael features some of the world's most famous faces (and bodies) in his *Freedom: '90* music video. Soon, everyone knows the names of Cindy Crawford, Naomi Campbell, Linda Evangelista, Christy Turlington, Claudia Schiffer and the other Amazonian beauties who dominate catwalks and glossy magazine covers through the decade.

Masterchef
Masterchef, a competition for amateur cooks, begins on BBC1 on Sunday afternoon on 2nd July. Carried out in a hushed studio, it's presented by Loyd Grossman who goes off to 'cogitate' with a different chef and celebrity each week as they decide who goes through to the next round.

Beverley Hills 90210
90210 is the postcode of the exclusive Los Angeles enclave for the wealthy and well-heeled and when the Midwest-raised Walsh twins, Brandon and Brenda, touch down in the area after their father gets a job as accountant to the filthy rich, they take a while to fit in with their new, sophisticated school mates. Created by Aaron Spelling (whose daughter Tori is one of the stars), the series begins on 30th December. UK teenagers go mad for *Beverley Hills 90210* and especially its two dreamboat male leads, Jason Priestley and Luke Perry. Grange Hill was never like this.

1990

Married to the Mob
Martin Scorsese's *Goodfellas*, his operatic tale of an uneasy brotherhood of New York mobsters, hits cinemas on 26th October. Ray Liotta plays the central character and narrator, Henry Hill, whose entanglement with Jimmy (Robert de Niro), Tommy (Joe Pesci) and other neighbourhood crooks, brings a lavish lifestyle but at a cost. As Henry becomes increasingly mired in a life of crime and adultery, trust between the gang begins to crumble. With virtuoso performances from all cast members, it's Pesci, as the foul-mouthed psychopathic Tommy, who personifies the violent, bloody world of what the *Telegraph* review calls, 'Scorsese's explosive Mafia cocktail'.

Big Night Out
Surreal comedy reaches new heights as Vic Reeves and Bob Mortimer invite everyone along to *Vic Reeves Big Night Out* on 25th May, the most bizarre variety show ever created. Germinated as a comedy club night at the Goldsmith's Tavern in south-east London and with characters like bickering brothers Donald and Davy Stott, Wavey Davey and the Man with the Stick ('What's on the end of the stick, Vic?'), *Big Night Out* is bemusing, bonkers and utterly brilliant.

Home Alone
7th December 1990 John Hughes is the writer behind *Home Alone*, the box-office monster that makes a huge star of ten-year-old Macaulay Culkin. The film centres on Kevin McAllister, a kid accidentally left 'home alone' when his family travel to Paris for Christmas. Kevin defends the family home from two bungling burglars (Joe Pesci and Daniel Stern) by setting up a series of booby traps.

I don't BELIEVE it!
Everyone's favourite misanthrope, Victor Meldrew, is introduced to viewers on 4th January, with the first episode of new sitcom *One Foot in the Grave*. Richard Wilson plays Victor, whose enforced early retirement as a security guard has left him bitter, frustrated and at war with the world, causing him to voice his contempt with a variety of phrases, most famously uttering, 'I don't believe it!!' at the latest humiliating development. With Annette Crosbie as his long-suffering wife and Angus Deayton the neighbour who is convinced Victor is mad, *One Foot in the Grave* is darker than your average sitcom and is all the better for it.

Ghostly encounters
Ghost has its UK release on 5th October, and becomes 1990's highest-grossing film. Patrick Swayze is Sam, a ghost trapped in limbo after being mugged and murdered, who must find a way to protect his girlfriend Molly (Demi Moore) from those who killed him. Help comes in the unlikely form of Oda Mae Brown, a charlatan psychic played by Whoopi Goldberg. The film's iconic potter's wheel scene goes on to be much-parodied, even featuring in *Naked Gun 2 ½*.

1990

MUSIC

Hip hop lite
Representing a lighter, far less controversial stream of hip hop than society-defying NWA and Public Enemy are MC Hammer and Vanilla Ice. Hammer announces himself with *U Can't Touch This* and eye-poppingly baggy trousers. The much ridiculed Vanilla Ice (real name Robert Van Winkle) is the first solo white performer to embrace rap with UK No. 1 *Ice Ice Baby*, on which he makes liberal use of the bassline from the Queen-David Bowie track *Under Pressure*.

Nothing compares
3rd February 1990 Well known in new wave circles since the mid-80s, Irish singer Sinead O'Connor catapults to No. 1 in the US and UK with a stark, emotional version of a little-heard Prince song, *Nothing Compares 2 U*. The stripped back arrangement is the work of Nellee Hooper of Soul II Soul.

Solo Sting
12th February 1990 Seven years on from the break-up of the Police, Sting's support for environmental causes is unwavering. Tonight he joins Paul Simon, Bruce Springsteen, Jackson Browne and Herbie Hancock at a fundraiser in Beverly Hills for the Rainforest Foundation. His big solo hit this year is a remix of an earlier release, *An Englishman in New York*, a tribute to expatriate writer Quentin Crisp.

Concert for Mandela
16th April 1990 A packed Wembley Stadium hosts a televised tribute concert in honour of the recently freed Nelson Mandela. Artists performing include Peter Gabriel, Tracy Chapman, Simple Minds, Lou Reed and Neil Young.

Spike Island
27th May 1990 Manchester band the Stone Roses headline a concert at Spike Island in Widnes that becomes the stuff of legend. More than 30,000 attend 'the baggy Woodstock', but the Roses' seemingly inexorable rise is disrupted by disputes with their record label Silvertone, which delays the release of what should have been their breakout album - *Second Coming* - by four years.

Elton at No. 1 - at last
23rd June 1990 Nineteen years on from his first UK chart entry, Elton John finally achieves a solo No. 1 with *Sacrifice*. He divides all his royalties from the record between four nominated AIDS charities.

1990

World Cup fever
7th July 1990 Luciano Pavarotti, Placido Domingo and Jose Carreras join forces as 'the Three Tenors' at a televised concert in Rome to celebrate Italy's hosting of the FIFA World Cup. Back in England, a rare run to the semi-finals lifts *World in Motion* by the England World Cup Squad and New Order to No. 1 for two weeks.

Judas Priest verdict
24th August 1990 A six-million-dollar law suit against UK heavy metal band Judas Priest ends, brought by the parents of a teenage boy who shot himself after listening to one of their albums. The case rests on subliminal messages supposedly hidden on the record. A judge in Reno, Nevada, rules that the band was not responsible for the boy's actions.

The great deception
14th November 1990 The truth is out. After a malfunction on a live MTV show revealed that German duo Milli Vanilli were miming, producer Frank Farian admits that session singers had sung their parts on their records. The pair - Fab Morvan and Rob Pilatus - hit back by calling Farian 'a maniac'. The name of Milli Vanilli, who have sold over eight million records to unsuspecting fans, is now a byword for deception and fakery in the music business.

MY FIRST 18 YEARS — TOP 10 — 1990

1. **Tom's Diner** *Suzanne Vega*
2. **I'll Never Fall in Love Again** *Deacon Blue*
3. **There She Goes** *The La's*
4. **Groovy Train** *The Farm*
5. **Nothing Compares 2 U** *Sinead O'Connor*
6. **Dub Be God to Me** *Beats International*
7. **The Obvious Child** *Paul Simon*
8. **Birdhouse in your Soul** *They Might be Giants*
9. **Falling** *Julee Cruise*
10. **It Must Have Been Love** *Roxette*

Open | Search | Scan

Marital matters
21st November 1990 The day before Bill Wyman confirms his split from wife Mandy Smith (photo), Mick Jagger and model Jerry Hall tie the knot in Bali. Ronnie Wood can't attend as he is in hospital with two broken legs after a motorway accident.

PHOTO CREDITS Copyright 2024, TDM Rights BV.
Photos: **A** Jeffrey Asher - Archive Photos - Getty Images / **B** Simon Bruty - Getty Images / **C** Tom Stoddart - Hulton Archive - Getty Images / **D** PA Images - Getty Images / **E** David Levenson - Hulton Archive - Getty Images / **F** Anton Novooderezhkin TASS - Food Outlets Russia - Getty Images / **G** Dieter Palm - Moment Editorial - Getty Images / **H** Space Frontiers - Archive Photos - Getty Images / **I** Hulton Archive - Getty Images / **J** Peter Turnley - Corbis Historical - Getty Images / **K** Comic Relief - GettyImages Entertainment - Getty Images / **L** Fotos International - Archive Photos - Getty Images / **M** AF Archive - BBC - Mary Evans / **N** AF Archive - BBC - Mary Evans / **O** Frank Micelotta Archive - Hulton Archive - Getty Images / **P** Mikel Roberts - Sygma - Getty Images / **Q** Warner Bros - Ronald Grant Archive - Mary Evans / **R** Archive Photos - Moviepix - Getty Images / **S** ANP / **T** Ronald Grant Archive - Mary Evans / **U** Mick Hudson - Redferns - Getty Images / **V** Martyn Goodacre - Hulton Archive - Getty Images / **W** Glyn Howells - Hulton Archive - Getty Images / **X** David Hume Kennerly - Archive Photos - Getty Images / **Y** Bernd Mueller - Redferns - Getty Images / **Z** Julian Parker - UK Press - Getty Images.

1991

MY FIRST 18 YEARS

SPORT

Season's best
15th May 1991 Manchester United win the European Cup Winners' Cup, beating Barcelona 2-1 in Rotterdam. It is the first European success enjoyed by an English club since the lifting of the five-year ban on participation that followed the Heysel disaster in 1985. In domestic competition, Arsenal are league champions while North London rivals Tottenham win the FA Cup for a record eighth time, beating Nottingham Forest 2-1 in a game that sees a career-impacting injury to England midfielder Paul Gascoigne.

A new elite league
8th April 1991 The Football Association announces controversial plans to create a new 'super league' creaming off the top eighteen clubs in the current First Division. Agreement is reached during the autumn between the FA, the Football League and the clubs involved for the Premier League.

Sumo
9th October 1991 An official sumo wrestling tournament is mounted over five days at the Royal Albert Hall in London (photo) - the first outside Japan. Forty of Japan's leading wrestlers compete for the Hitachi Cup and the honour of winning the first foreign *basho*.

UK first in Tokyo
30th August 1991 Scottish 10,000 metre runner Liz McColgan wins the UK's first ever gold medal at the World Athletics Championships in Tokyo. In November she wins the New York City marathon, her first competitive attempt at the marathon distance.

Magic retires
7th November 1991 US basketball legend Magic Johnson of the Los Angeles Lakers announces his immediate retirement after revealing that he is HIV positive.

Australian victory
2nd November 1991 Australia wins the Rugby Union World Cup at Twickenham, beating England 12-6. It is the first World Cup to be held in the northern hemisphere, with matches spread across England, Wales, Scotland, Ireland and France.

3 JAN 1991
Iraqi embassy officials are expelled from the UK.

21 FEB 1991
British ballerina Dame Margot Fonteyn dies in Panama aged 71.

15 MAR 1991
Stansted Airport's new terminal building is opened by the Queen.

1991

DOMESTIC NEWS

Introducing TESSA
1st January 1991 A new acronym enters the financial lexicon - TESSA. The initials stand for 'tax exempt special savings account' and it is the brainchild of former Chancellor of the Exchequer John Major, now Prime Minister. Anyone over 18 can apply and save up to £9,000 free of UK income tax over a five-year period.

Mortar attack on No. 10
7th February 1991 With war in the Gulf in its third week and London on high alert, the Provisional IRA chooses this moment to launch what could have been a deadly mortar attack against 10 Downing Street. No one is hurt in the attack but all the windows of the Cabinet room are blown out. Eleven days later one person is killed by a bomb left at Victoria Station in London. In November, two IRA members are killed when the bomb they are planting explodes prematurely in St Albans, Hertfordshire.

Hillsborough inquest
28th March 1991 The inquest closes into the deaths of 96 fans in severe overcrowding at the FA Cup semi-final match at Hillsborough, Sheffield, in 1989. The coroner returns verdicts of 'accidental death' instead of the 'unlawful killing' verdicts which many of the fans' families had hoped for. The full truth about the police handling of the disaster emerges much later and the verdicts are finally overturned in April 2016 after many years of campaigning by supporters' groups.

M40 completed
16th January 1991 The M40 motorway between London and Birmingham is completed as the final section through Oxfordshire is opened to traffic.

Birmingham Six go free
14th March 1991 Following revelations that police fabricated evidence, the six men found guilty of the Birmingham pub bombings in 1974 that killed 21 people are freed by the Court of Appeal. Their convictions are declared unsafe and unsatisfactory, and they subsequently receive compensation of between £840,000 and £1.2 million.

Two million unemployed
15th March 1991 Unemployment figures reach two million in the UK - the highest in over two years.

20 APR 1991
Small Faces and Humble Pie singer-guitarist Steve Marriott is killed in a house fire.

4 MAY 1991
Death of comedian Bernie Winters of Mike and Bernie Winters fame.

23 JUN 1991
Sega launches a new video game - *Sonic the Hedgehog*.

1991

First Brit in space
18th May 1991 Sheffield-born scientist Helen Sharman makes history as the first UK citizen to go into space, as a member of the Soyuz TM-12 mission. She spends eight days in space, much of it on the Mir space station.

McCarthy and Waite freed
8th August 1991 In Lebanon, British hostage John McCarthy is freed by his captors after five years. The Archbishop of Canterbury's special envoy Terry Waite is finally freed on 18th November.

Hitting the heights
26th August 1991 One Canada Square is officially opened for business in the Docklands area of East London. It is the tallest building to date in the UK at 770 feet.

Riots across UK
August - September 1991 Rioting breaks out in Cardiff, Leeds, Birmingham, Dudley, Oxford and Tyneside.

TV-am to close
16th October 1991 Several of the best known ITV companies lose their franchises in the biggest shake-up of broadcasting since the 1960s. Among them are London's weekday service provider Thames Television and TV-am, the breakfast television service that has only been operating since 1983.

PC World arrives
18th November 1991 Indicating the huge growth in personal computing, computer retailer PC World opens its first store in Purley Way, Croydon.

Maxwell drowns
5th November 1991 Media magnate, *Daily Mirror* owner and former MP Robert Maxwell disappears from his yacht off the coast of Tenerife and is later found drowned. Suggestions of suicide are given credence when it emerges that he had removed £350 million from the *Daily Mirror* pension fund before his death. The Maxwell empire goes into receivership one month later with debts exceeding £1 billion.

Head of MI5
16th December 1991 The appointment of Stella Rimington is announced as the first female Director General of MI5, the UK's internal security service.

ROYALTY & POLITICS

Poll tax poleaxed
23rd March 1991 Prime Minister John Major tells the House of Commons that the contentious and unpopular Community Charge - disparagingly known as the 'poll tax' - is to be scrapped. It will be replaced by a more equitable Council Tax in 1993.

---

31 JUL 1991
125,000 pack into rain-soaked Hyde Park for a Luciano Pavarotti concert.

16 AUG 1991
Terminator 2: Judgement Day opens in UK cinemas.

19 SEP 1991
German tourists discover a mummy. Ötzi, as he is nicknamed, who lived more than 5,000 years ago.

1991

Major's charter
22nd July 1991 John Major unveils his government's White Paper detailing proposals for a 'Citizen's Charter'. Aimed at raising standards in public services, its measures guarantee redress when the service fails to reach established benchmarks. The announcement comes on the same day that the Bank of England closes down the Bank of Credit and Commerce International due to allegations of fraud. Numerous local authorities across the UK stand to lose millions from their investments in the bank.

Heading for separation
17th August 1991 Prince Charles and Princess Diana take a yachting holiday in Italy that is described in the press as a 'second honeymoon'. Royal watchers note an increasing distance between the couple. Diana is making her feelings known about the marriage in a series of secret tapes that author Andrew Morton is using as the basis for his forthcoming book, *Diana: Her True Story*.

By-election blues
7th November 1991 Two by-election results point to the likelihood of defeat for the Conservatives in the General Election due next year. Labour wins the safe Tory seat of Langbaurgh in north east England while the Liberal Democrats take Kincardine and Deeside in Scotland from the Conservatives.

Operation Desert Storm
15th January 1991 The international coalition's ultimatum to Iraq to leave Kuwait expires. A military offensive to liberate Kuwait is inevitable. The international coalition led by the US and backed politically by the Soviet Union launches the largest air offensive in history: Operation Desert Storm. Iraqi radar stations are disabled and military positions destroyed. Saddam, who has raised a huge and relatively modern army, presents himself as the great leader of the Arab world and tries to get other Arab countries on his side with Scud attacks on Israel. The coalition is superior in the air and defeats almost the entire Iraqi air force and navy to prepare for the ground offensive that starts on 24th February. After seven weeks of bombing, the Iraqi army offers little resistance. On 27th February, French troops reach Kuwait City. That evening, Iraq surrenders and accepts all UN resolutions regarding the withdrawal from Kuwait. As they retreat, Iraqi troops set fire to Kuwait's oil fields.

FOREIGN NEWS

WWW launched
6th August 1991 Tim Berners-Lee introduces the World Wide Web project and software on the alt.hypertext newsgroup. What is effectively the world's first website, 'info.cern.ch', is now publicly available.

---

6 OCT 1991 — The final episode of *Dallas* is transmitted in the UK.

3 NOV 1991 — Ayrton Senna wins his third and last World Drivers' Championship.

1 DEC 1991 — Ukrainian people vote for independence.

1991

Mobile phone revolution
1st July 1991 The Global System for Mobile Communications (GSM) is the new standard for mobile telephony. The second generation of mobile phones (2G) use a digital system for the first time, have much better sound, are ready for the introduction of SMS and come equipped with a SIM card, which allows you to make calls abroad and exchange phones without any problems. By the end of the millennium, more than 500 million people worldwide have a mobile phone.

Yugoslavia breaks up
May - June 1991 After the fall of East Germany, almost all communist regimes in the Eastern Bloc have collapsed. The federation of states that is Yugoslavia also falters, with Slovenia the first to declare its independence in June. The conflict explodes when Croatia holds a referendum in May and breaks away. It is the start of a bloody civil war which will also spread to Bosnia-Herzegovina.

A coup in Moscow
19th August 1991 Communist hardliners stage a coup in Moscow. Soviet Union President Gorbachev is placed under house arrest at his dacha in the Crimea. But the President of the Russian republic, Boris Yeltsin, elected only in July, sides with Gorbachev. He climbs on a tank in front of the parliament building and addresses the crowd, after which the army rallies behind him. One by one, the Soviet republics secede, beginning with Estonia. After 72 hours the coup leaders are captured and Gorbachev returns, but the days of the Soviet Union - and Gorbachev's presidency - are numbered. The white-blue-red flag of Russia is hoisted, with Yeltsin an unassailable leader with the backing of the Russian parliament. On Christmas morning, Gorbachev resigns. There is no Soviet Union left to govern.

ENTERTAINMENT

Dances with Wolves
8th February 1991 Kevin Costner turns to directing with *Dances With Wolves*, an epic three-hour Western in which he also takes the leading role as the Civil War veteran who becomes fascinated with the Native American Lakota Sioux. Costner's ambitious film is spectacular to look at; romantic, heartbreaking, often humorous, and portrays the Lakota tribe with respect and admiration. Costner proves himself as a director when *Dances With Wolves* gallops away with seven Oscars this year, including Best Picture.

Band tragedy
16th March 1991 The country music community is no stranger to tragic events but today's news is off the scale. Seven members of Reba McEntire's backing band are killed together with her road manager when their plane crashes in California. Reba dedicates her next album to them, *For My Broken Heart*.

1991

You've Been Framed
With video camera ownership on the rise, TV prankster Jeremy Beadle presents *You've Been Framed* from 16th April on ITV, a show with a simple formula. Members of the public send in their funny home videos and receive a payment of £100 (later rising to £250) if their film features. Each week we laugh out loud at babies falling asleep face first in their porridge, kids being tipped out of swings or crashing a sledge, and deckchairs collapsing under stout aunties.

The Darling Buds of May
David Jason and Pam Ferris star as Pa and Ma Larkin which begins on 7th April on ITV. The Larkins and their sunny Kentish idyll enchant the nation. We fall for Pa's charm and his cheeky wheeling and dealing ways; and swoon at Ma's gargantuan plates of food and her infectious laughter. *The Darling Buds of May* celebrates the sheer joy of living. It also makes a star of Catherine Zeta Jones, in her breakout role as eldest of the Larkin brood, the ravishing Mariette.

The Commitments
The Commitments is released on 4th October. Jimmy Rabbitte wants to bring the sound of soul to the world and Dublin is the place to start because, as Jimmy says, 'we're the blacks of Europe'. Audition flyers bring forth a dubious set of hopefuls before he discovers some musical diamonds in rough including the obnoxious Deco whose Joe Cocker-esque voice and swagger make him a shoo-in as lead singer. The band enjoys local success until personal grievances and rivalries cause its short-lived harmony to fracture. But while it lasts, *The Commitments* is foot-tappingly good for the 'soul'.

Cue *Big Break*
BBC's *Big Break* begins on 30th April, hosted by Jim Davidson, with ex-player John Virgo as referee. Contestants team up with well-known snooker stars including Stephen Hendry, Jimmy White and Ray Reardon, combining their general knowledge and potting skills to win prizes. Each week, Virgo sets up a trick shot for the losers to attempt in order to win a consolation prize.

1991

Robin Hood: Prince of Thieves
Robin has an American accent, Alan Rickman hams it up as the dastardly Sherriff of Nottingham and Bryan Adams (photo) spends a gazillion weeks at No. 1 with an earworm theme song; *Robin Hood: Prince of Thieves*, released 19th July, is a monster hit. It's a hugely entertaining, rip-roaring adventure, blending the swashbuckling of Errol Flynn-era Robin Hood with a historic authenticity (except, perhaps, Kevin Costner's mullet).

Rock *Bottom*
Bottom features Rik Mayall and Ade Edmondson as Richie and Eddie, two revolting losers who share a flat in Hammersmith where they are on a perpetually unsuccessful quest to sleep with women. Building on the relationship between Rick and Vyvyan in *The Young Ones* and their own friendship, *Bottom* is puerile, nihilistic, but undeniably funny. It comes to an end in 1995 after Mayall explains, 'We'd already hit each other with everything in the flat.'

Misery
Kathy Bates wins a Best Actress Academy Award for her portrayal of Annie, the obsessive fiction fan who rescues but then holds best-selling author Paul (James Caan) captive in her remote Colorado cabin when she discovers he plans to write off her favourite character, Misery Chastain. Paul's injuries and the film's violence increase in tandem with Annie's escalating mania and one scene involving a sledgehammer and Paul's feet makes audiences let out a shocked groan in unison. Stephen King offers *Misery* as one of his favourites among the many film adaptations of his books.

Creature Comforts
The *Creature Comforts* advertisements for the electricity board win Best Commercial of the Year. *Creature Comforts* features a variety of plasticine animals voiced by ordinary people with different regional accents. The endearing combination of the Aardman creatures with everyday human dialogue (complete with ums and aahs) is completed by a concluding voiceover from the king of funny animal voices, Johnny Morris.

Sega Game Gear
The Game Gear, Sega's riposte to Nintendo's Game boy is launched this year. It lacks the neat dimensions of the Gameboy and guzzles batteries but is redeemed by a strong selection of software to choose from with popular games including *Sonic the Hedgehog 2*, *Gunstar Heroes* and *Prince of Persia*.

1991

Thelma and Louise
Ridley Scott's cinematic eye gives *Thelma and Louise* a majestic backdrop, but it's the relationship of the two women whose road trip goes badly wrong that is the lynchpin of this groundbreaking film. Louise (Geena Davis) is a pretty but downtrodden housewife, Thelma (Susan Sarandon), her older, wiser waitress friend. As they hit the road in a bid to get away from it all, the men they meet along the way are the catalysts for a spiralling chain of disastrous events that turn Thelma and Louise into criminals on the run.

House of Eliot
31 August 1991 Fans of vintage fashion and the 1920s are in for a treat with *House of Eliot*, BBC1's new period drama. Beatrice and Evangeline Eliot are enterprising sisters with a talent for sewing and a passion for fashion. When their domineering father dies leaving them penniless, they turn their hobby into a dressmaking business that eventually, over three series, grows and flourishes into a successful couture house.

 # MUSIC

Billion dollar deal
11th March 1991 The deals keep getting bigger and bigger. Michael Jackson signs for Sony for one billion dollars just days after sister Janet signs for Virgin for $30 million, making her the highest paid female recording star ever. No doubt taking note is Mariah Carey, Columbia's top signing of 1990, who reaches No. 1 with her self-titled debut album. Meanwhile, old stagers the Rolling Stones conclude a comparatively modest $20 million deal with Virgin.

Silence of the Lambs
Anthony Hopkins creates one of cinema's most complex and memorable monsters when he pulls on a boilersuit and transforms into Hannibal 'the Cannibal' Lecter in this year's massive screen event, *Silence of the Lambs*. Trainee FBI agent Clarice Starling (Jodie Foster) must enlist the help of Lector, an incarcerated intellectual with a taste for human flesh, in her bid to track down a killer. Their uneasy relationship is compelling, while the more gruesome scenes have cinema audiences jumping in their seats before they go home vowing to avoid fava beans and a nice glass of chianti in future.

1991

Nat and Natalie
27th July 1991 As part of an album tribute to her late father Nat King Cole, Natalie Cole records his signature song, *Unforgettable*, interwoven with his original 1951 recording. It is the first 'virtual duet' in recording history.

Seattle spirit
24th September 1991 'Grunge' goes international with the release of Nirvana's album *Nevermind*. Grunge is a blend of punk rock and heavy metal created by a handful of alternative bands from the Seattle area. Though interpreted as a teen anthem for the 90s, the single *Smells Like Teen Spirit* is more a song about not being ready to leave your teens behind.

Freddie's gone
24th November 1991 Freddie Mercury of Queen dies from bronchial pneumonia resulting from AIDS. Though there has been plenty of conjecture, his condition has been kept secret from fans and the media. His death explains why there was such a retrospective character to the last Queen album, *Innuendo*, released in February. Songs such as *The Show Must Go On* and *These are the Days of Our Lives* now sound like epitaphs. *Bohemian Rhapsody* is re-released and spends five weeks at No. 1.

Trip hop
While Happy Mondays, the Stone Roses and the Charlatans keep eyes fixed on Manchester, the Bristol club scene offers a different psychedelic/electronic hip hop fusion – 'trip hop'. The scene's leaders are Massive Attack, a collective built around Adrian 'Tricky' Thaws. Signature single *Unfinished Sympathy* has an almost Gothic grandeur enhanced by a full orchestra recorded at Abbey Road.

REM go mainstream
REM, for so long the Georgia-based kings of small-scale, stripped-down US alternative rock, move into the big time with the album *Out of Time* and two breakthrough singles, *Losing My Religion* and the sunshine-fuelled *Shiny Happy People* featuring Kate Pierson from the B-52s. Their jangled, angular sound and Michael Stipe's intense vocals won't change but the scale of their success will.

KLF calling
Nobody knows what KLF – the Kopyright Liberation Front – will do next. Bill Drummond and Jimmy Cauty's idea is to embarrass the music industry at every opportunity, whether by sampling all and sundry without permission or creating havoc at the BRIT Awards. This year's stunt – their last under the KLF banner – is to make a nonsense record, *Justified and Ancient*, with country music queen Tammy Wynette. Only *Bohemian Rhapsody* prevents it from reaching No. 1.

1991

Take That formed
23rd November 1991 Wanting to create a UK New Kids on the Block, music entrepreneur Nigel Martin-Smith launches a five-piece boy band. Initially called Kick It but renamed Take That, they make their chart debut with *Promises*.

MY FIRST 18 YEARS
TOP 10 — 1991

1. **Smells Like Teen Spirit** *Nirvana*
2. **Sit Down** *James*
3. **Promise Me** *Beverley Craven*
4. **Gypsy Woman** *Crystal Waters*
5. **Whole of the Moon** *The Waterboys*
6. **This is Your Life** *Banderas*
7. **Fall at Your Feet** *Crowded House*
8. **Get Here** *Oleta Adams*
9. **Losing My Religion** *REM*
10. **The One and Only** *Chesney Hawkes*

Open Spotify | Search | Scan

Miles Davis
28th September 1991 Miles Davis, the most admired and influential figure in post-war jazz, dies of a stroke at 65.

They're too sexy
Pure raunchy fun is the best way to describe the fashion world send-up *I'm Too Sexy*, which sticks at No. 2 in the UK for weeks on end without ever dislodging the incumbent No. 1 by Bryan Adams. It's the inspired work of brothers Fred and Richard Fairbrass and guitarist Rob Manzoli in the guise of Right Said Fred.

Mood of the moment
With profound changes underway to the geo-politics of Europe, two records capture the times. *Right Here, Right Now* by Jesus Jones was written while the band were in Romania shortly after the fall of Ceausescu. *Wind of Change* from veteran German rockers the Scorpions (photo) hits the European charts during a summer in which the Soviet Union disintegrates and Cold War fears seem to be banished forever.

PHOTO CREDITS Copyright 2024, TDM Rights BV.
Photos: **A** Getty Images - Hulton Archive - Getty Images / **B** Chris Cole - Getty Images / **C** Sean Dempsey - PA Images - Getty Images / **D** PA Images - Getty Images / **E** Mattbuck - / **F** Rick Maiman - Sygma - Getty Images / **G** Universal Images Group - Getty Images / **H** TASS - Getty Images / **I** Archive Photos - Moviepix - Getty Images / **J** Ronald Grant Archive - Mary Evans / **K** Ronald Grant Archive - Mary Evans / **L** Ronald Grant Archive - Mary Evans / **M** Barry Batchelor - PA Images - Getty Images / **N** Mick Hutson - Redferns - Getty Images / **O** Daily Mirror - Mirrorpix - Getty Images / **P** MGM - AF Archive - Mary Evans / **Q** Michael Archives - Moviepix - Getty Images / **R** Paul Natkin - Archive Photos - Getty Images / **S** Paul Bergen - Redferns - Getty Images / **T** Paul Natkin - WireImage - Getty Images / **U** FG Baue - Griffin - Michael Ochs Archives - Getty Images / **V** Dave Hogan - Hulton Archive - Getty Images / **W** Tim Roney - Hulton Archive - Getty Images / **X** Richard E Aaron - Redferns - Getty Images.

1992 — MY FIRST 18 YEARS

SPORT

Shots down
25th March 1992 Aldershot Town - nicknamed 'the Shots' - face bankruptcy and resign from the Football League. They are followed five months later by Maidstone United whose debts mean that they cannot fulfil their fixtures. Both clubs are relaunched by groups of fans but have to start again in the lower leagues of the English football pyramid.

Botham joins Durham
25th April 1992 England's legendary all-rounder Ian Botham makes his first County Championship appearance for Durham versus Leicestershire, in his new club's debut season in the competition. Although Durham finish bottom of the Championship table, glory days await - notably in the late 2000s, when they win the Championship twice in consecutive seasons.

Premier League kicks off
15th August 1992 Just three weeks before the inaugural season of the Premier League begins, Alan Shearer becomes the most expensive footballer in UK history when he signs for Blackburn Rovers from Southampton for £3.6 million.

Euro 1992
10th - 26th June 1992 England and Scotland both qualify for the 1992 European Championships, hosted by Sweden, but fail to progress beyond the group stage. The tournament is won by outsiders Denmark who defeat Germany 2-0. Denmark were a late addition to the competition following the exclusion of Yugoslavia due to the conflict there.

Barcelona Olympics
25th July - 9th August 1992 British athletes perform well at the Olympic Games in Barcelona, taking a total of five golds, three silvers and twelve bronze medals. The high points from a UK point of view are on the track and on the water: Linford Christie's gold in the 100 metres and Sally Gunnell's in the 400 metres hurdles, with Mathew Pinsent and Steve Redgrave winning the coxless pairs and Garry Herbert and Greg and Jonny Searle victorious in the men's coxed pair. The most moving moment in the whole two weeks comes when UK runner Derek Redmond tears his hamstring in the 400 metres semi-final yet insists on hobbling to the end. He completes the final lap with the help of his father. The crowd responds with a standing ovation.

---

16 JAN 1992
Eric Clapton performs on MTV's *Unplugged*, the recording of which becomes the best selling live album of all time.

15 FEB 1992
Jeffrey Dahmer found guilty of killing 15 men.

26 MAR 1992
Mike Tyson sentenced to ten years for rape of Desiree Washington.

1992

Mansell retires at the top
13th September 1992 Having won the Formula One season with five races to spare just a month before - so becoming the first Brit to take the title since James Hunt in 1976 - British driver Nigel Mansell ends an outstanding career by announcing his retirement from Formula One.

Death of Leonard Cheshire
31st July 1992 Leonard Cheshire dies in Suffolk at the age of 74. One of the most decorated of all the RAF's wartime pilots, he founded the disability charity that bore his name and was married to fellow disabled champion Sue Ryder.

DOMESTIC NEWS

More bloodshed in Ulster
17th January 1992 At the start of another turbulent year in Northern Ireland, a Provisional IRA bomb kills eight Protestants working on a British Army construction project at Teebane. In a reprisal attack on 5th February, loyalist gunmen kill five Catholics in a Belfast betting shop. The Belfast shootings come during a first-ever visit to the six counties by a serving President of Ireland, Mary Robinson.

Baltic Exchange bombed
10th April 1992 One day after the General Election, the IRA bombing campaign against London continues. Three people are killed and 91 injured when the Baltic Exchange building in the City is targeted at 9.20am. It is the single most powerful bomb to strike London since the wartime Blitz. During the following night a bomb badly damages a major traffic intersection at Staples Corner in North London.

Welcome, Super Mario
11th April 1992 The Super Nintendo home video game console is launched in the UK along with the best selling Super Mario World game.

New banknotes issued
29th April 1992 A new ten-pound banknote is issued by the Bank of England depicting the author Charles Dickens, one of a new series of notes honouring great Victorians. It remains in circulation for eleven years.

---

12 APR 1992
Euro Disney Paris opens.

9 MAY 1992
37th Eurovision Song Contest; Linda Martin representing Ireland wins singing 'Why Me' in Malmo.

30 JUN 1992
Margaret Thatcher enters House of Lords as Baroness Thatcher of Kesteven.

1992

Fairtrade UK
26th June 1992 The Fairtrade Foundation is launched in the UK as an arm of the global Fairtrade movement. The Co-Op becomes the first supermarket to market a Fairtrade product - Cafedirect coffee.

Classic FM on the air
7th September 1992 With a policy of playing only classical music, Classic FM becomes the very first national commercial radio station to open in the UK. It is the brainchild of the Great Western Radio (GWR) group and Andrew Lloyd Webber's Really Useful Group.

Coal mine closures
13th October 1992 Trade Secretary Michael Heseltine announces the closures of 31 of the 50 remaining UK coal mines. With memories of the recent miners' strike still sharp, the decision is seen even by sections of the Conservative press as a betrayal. One hundred thousand march in London against the closures a week later.

Women can be priests
11th November 1992 In a momentous and far-reaching decision taken after many hours of intense debate, the General Synod of the Church of England votes to allow women to be ordained into the priesthood.

ROYALTY & POLITICS

'Annus horribilis'
6th February 1992 As the Queen celebrates four decades since her accession to the throne, 1992 becomes what she will later call an 'annus horribilis' (miserable year). In June, Andrew Morton's book *Diana: Her True Story* is published with revelations of adulterous behaviour by Prince Charles and Diana's five suicide attempts. In March, the Duke and Duchess of York separate after five years of marriage. In April, Princess Anne announces her divorce from Captain Mark Phillips after nineteen years. In November, a major fire destroys part of Windsor Castle and controversy follows over whether taxpayers should pay for the repairs. In December, it is confirmed that Charles and Diana have separated but have no plans for divorce. To cap it all, the Queen is now obliged to pay tax for the first time.

10 JUL 1992
Albert Pierrepoint, the UK's long-time official hangman, dies aged 87.

1 AUG 1992
Sexual Offences (Amendment) Act 1992 becomes law, giving lifelong anonymity to victims of sex crimes.

30 SEP 1992
A new, smaller 10p coin enters circulation.

1992

Election '92
9th April 1992 John Major's Conservatives win the General Election with a majority of 21 seats. The party secures the highest vote - over fourteen million - ever attained by any party in British electoral history. The final figures are 336 Conservative seats, 220 for Labour and 22 for the Liberal Democrats.

FOREIGN NEWS

Blue helmets
Under its new Secretary General, the Egyptian Boutros Boutros-Ghali, the United Nations blue helmeted peacekeepers are active in more regions and countries than ever. The blue helmets operate in the conflict zones of the Middle East, India, Angola, Somalia, Mozambique and Cambodia. On 21st February, the UN Security Council approves Resolution 743 to send a peacekeeping force to Yugoslavia.

Kinnock resigns
13th April 1992 Following Labour's election defeat, party leader Neil Kinnock resigns. The process of electing a new leader begins, ending with the victory of Shadow Chancellor of the Exchequer John Smith in the final ballot on 17th July. He defeats fellow candidate Bryan Gould with over 90 per cent of the vote.

Maastricht Treaty
7th February 1992 With the signing of the new Maastricht Treaty, the EEC becomes the European Community (EC), a partnership with common foreign and security policies and justice and home affairs policies. The European Parliament will have more legislative and supervisory power.

Black Wednesday
16th September 1992 On a day destined to be remembered as 'Black Wednesday', the government faces a humiliating climbdown when it is forced to withdraw sterling from the European Exchange Rate Mechanism (ERM) after insisting it would not do so. The withdrawal causes real damage to the Conservatives' reputation for safe handling of the UK economy, leading to a decline in the opinion polls and eventual electoral defeat in 1997.

---

26 OCT 1992
The last Russian troops leave Poland.

25 NOV 1992
Czechoslovakia votes to split the country into two separate nations, the Czech Republic and Slovakia.

31 DEC 1992
Breakfast television company TV-am makes its final broadcast.

1992

Civil war in Bosnia
5th April 1992 After Slovenia and Croatia, Bosnia-Herzegovina declares its independence from Yugoslavia. Just as in Croatia, this leads to civil war. The Serbian minority declares its own Serbian Republic which, under the control of Radovan Karadžić and Radkol Mladić and with the support of the Yugoslav army, besieges Sarajevo and commits mass murders in villages and towns in eastern Bosnia to 'cleanse' the region. Bosnian Muslims and Croats are mistreated, starved, abused and murdered.

Rodney King riots
29th April 1992 The acquittal of four Los Angeles police officers, on trial for beating up an unarmed black man, Rodney King, in March 1991, sparks six days of rioting, causing 63 deaths.

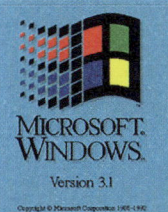

Opening Windows
6th April 1992 The newly released Windows 3.1 becomes the most widely used operating system for personal computers. Windows 3.1 bundles together the popular word processor Microsoft Word with Microsoft Excel, Microsoft PowerPoint and Microsoft Mail.

Clinton and Bush
3rd November 1992 In the US Presidential election, the incumbent George H. W. Bush (photo right) is defeated by Democratic Party candidate and Arkansas Governor Bill Clinton (photo left). The charismatic Clinton wins the elections by a huge margin and becomes the 42nd President.

First text message
3rd December 1992 Vodafone employee Richard Jarvis is sipping a drink when he receives the first ever text message on his mobile phone. The message says 'Merry Christmas' and comes from software programmer Neil Papworth of tech company Sema Group, which has been hired by Vodafone to develop a messaging service for pagers and mobile phones. What we now know as SMS - the Short Message Service - is born.

ENTERTAINMENT

You've been Tango'd
'Orange Man' the advertising campaign for Tango fizzy orange drink airs this year. The citrussy taste sensation is personified by an impudent bald, orange man who appears out of nowhere to give Tango drinkers a sloppy kiss or a slap around the chops. 'You know when you've been Tango'd' becomes part of common parlance used especially to describe anyone who has overdone the fake tan!

1992

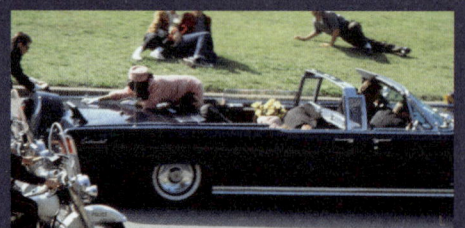

Who shot JFK?
24th January 1992 Writer and director Oliver Stone isn't afraid to tackle America's big questions. He explored the ordinary man's experience of the Vietnam War in *Platoon* and *Born on the Fourth of July* and this year, in *JFK*, he asks perhaps the biggest question of all – who killed John F. Kennedy? He asks it already knowing there will be no answer. Nevertheless, with Kevin Costner as dogged New Orleans district attorney Jim Garrison, and Gary Oldman as Lee Harvey Oswald, *JFK* sums up the frustrations, paranoia and mystery surrounding one of the twentieth century's defining events. A gripping and brilliantly crafted piece of filmmaking.

Where's my Willy?
Eastenders says goodbye to one of its most loyal cast members on 14th May when Willy, the pet pug belonging to Ethel Skinner, is diagnosed with cancer and Ethel makes the heartbreaking decision to have him put down. Having served on *Eastenders* since its first episode, Willy dies in real life just two weeks after his final scene.

Eldoradon't
After much fanfare, what will turn out to be one of the BBC's most expensive and embarrassing misfires begins on 6th July. *Eldorado* is a new soap, hoping to capture the sun-soaked success of *Neighbours* with a dash of *Dynasty* glamour. With a largely inexperienced cast, much of the acting is wooden, the storylines cringeworthy and the setting of an ex-pat community in Spain fails to engage audiences who prefer the homely familiarity of East End cockneys, or Manchester landladies. *Eldorado* limps on for just 156 episodes.

Gladiators...Ready!
10th October 1992 Can you feel the power of the *Gladiators*? UK audiences certainly can as ITV's *Gladiators* pits have-a-go contestants against twentieth-century Gladiators – a toned and honed assembly of musclemen and Amazons – ready to scupper the mere mortals as they scamper through a series of obstacle courses and challenges in the gladiatorial arena. Footballer John Fashanu and ex-TV-am weather girl Ulrika Johnson keep the energy high octane as hosts and stoke up the screaming audience.

Men Behaving Badly
If 'laddish' behaviour is becoming a defining feature of the 1990s, then *Men Behaving Badly*, written by Simon Nye, is the flagship for the movement. The first series, beginning on 18th February, pairs Gary (Martin Clunes) with flatmate Dermot (Harry Enfield) but Dermot is replaced in series 2 by Tony (Neil Morrissey), and the sitcom transfers to BBC1 where a later, post-watershed slot allows some colourful language and mild sexual content alongside the boozing and carousing. The result is one of the most popular comedies of the decade. As teenage boys in grown men's bodies, Gary and Tony, whose long-suffering love interests are Dorothy (Caroline Quentin) and Deborah (Leslie Ash), are the Likely Lads for a bolder, brasher era.

1992

Nude is *The Word*
Channel 4's live, late-night show *The Word* has courted controversy from its launch in 1990 but its dubious reputation reaches new highs (or lows?) this year when all-female grunge band L7 perform their single *Pretend You're Dead* and singer and guitarist Donita Sparks pulls down her jeans and knickers and carries on the performance naked from the waist down. Presenter Terry Christian remarks afterwards, 'It's gonna be one of those shows innit?'. Often tasteless but never dull, *The Word* is essential post-pub viewing and provides many a watercooler moment with its rich tapestry of outrageous moments. In 1995, *The Word* has the last word and comes to an end.

Later... with Jools Holland
Originally the music strand of *The Late Show*, *Later... with Jools Holland* begins on 8th October. Holland has a relaxed but efficient presenting style as he introduces around five musical acts, of different genres, who take turns to play live, sometimes accompanied by Holland on the piano. *Later...* continues to bring both established and undiscovered music acts to TV screens for the next 30 years, while the show's annual *Hootenany* is a New Year's Eve tradition.

In a *Heartbeat*
10th April 1992 Nick Berry had set hearts a-flutter as Simon Wicks in *Eastenders* and sealed his star status with a no. 1 single, *Every Loser Wins* in 1986. His next move is to fill the lead role in ITV's new period drama *Heartbeat* as PC Nick Rowan, alongside Niamh Cusack as Rowan's doctor wife. Set in the North Riding of Yorkshire around the fictional village of Aidensfield, it stays for eighteen series, attracting audiences of over 13 million at the peak of its popularity.

DO YOU REMEMBER THIS?

Raider

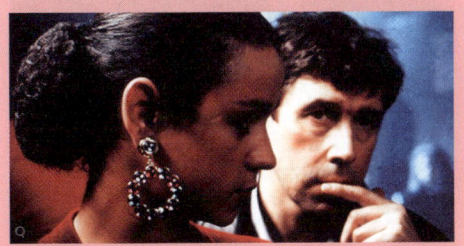

The Crying Game
30th October 1992 Neil Jordan wins the Oscar for Best Screenplay for his low-budget indie sleeper hit, *The Crying Game*. Set in Northern Ireland, Stephen Rea is an IRA operative whose capture and role in the death of a British soldier (Forest Whitaker) leads to him seeking out the man's lover. Complex, multi-layered and sexually subversive, *The Crying Game* surprises with a story that meanders unexpectedly off course and an ending that nobody sees coming.

1992

Blobby blunders in
Mr Blobby makes his debut on BBC1's *Noel's House Party* on 24th October as Noel Edmonds' sidekick and chief troublemaker. An over-sized, goggle-eyed, yellow spotted avacado-shaped figure the colour of pink blancmange, Blobby's unintelligible language (he can only say 'Blobby') makes him sound like he's drowning, and his main talents appear to be bumping into everything and falling on top of everyone. Inexplicably, Mr. Blobby becomes a huge star and even has a No. 1 Christmas single in 1993 with, *Mr. Blobby*. A nadir in the cultural history of Western civilisation.

Party on!
22nd May 1992 Wayne's World developed from a short sketch on the American show *Saturday Night Live*. The film's two leads, Wayne and Garth, coining a whole new collection of universally copied catch-phrases from 'Schwing!' to 'Party on!' and 'We're not worth, we're not worthy!' The film's most famous scene, when Wayne and Garth head bang along to Queen's '*Bohemian Rhapsody*' while driving an AMC Pacer, propels the song to No. 2 in America and reignites interest in the band despite the death of Freddie Mercury.

The Big Breakfast
Channel 4 launch weekday morning show *The Big Breakfast* on 28th September, aiming to pull in a younger audience with its light-hearted and fast-paced format. Broadcast from a real house in Bow, east London, presenters Chris Evans and Gaby Roslin are joined by puppets Zig and Zag, and Paula Yates who conducts flirtatious celebrity interviews on a double bed, including a notorious 1994 chat with INXS sexpot Michael Hutchence that has the nation yelling, 'Get a room!'

Ab Fab
PR guru, neurotic hypochondriac and Christian Lacroix devotee Edina 'Eddie' Monsoon (Jennifer Saunders) is introduced to audiences for the first time on 12th November with the start of *Absolutely Fabulous* on BBC2. Together with her best friend Patsy Stone (Joanna Lumley), Eddie attempts to keep up with the cool kids, spends lavishly at 'Harvey Nicks', tries every New Age fad going, and mostly leaves the running of her company to her spaced-out PA, Bubble (Jane Horrocks) all under the disapproving gaze of sensible daughter Saffie (Julia Sawalha). Quickly established as a comedy classic, *Ab Fab* is a mischievous and outrageous send-up of the fickle world of fashion and celebrity.

1992

Reimagining the Western
Some might say Clint Eastwood has made the Western his speciality but as director and star, he brings an unprecedented depth and darkness to *Unforgiven*, a brooding reinvention of the genre, released in cinemas on 18th September. As William Munny, he's a grizzled ex-mercenary riding out to claim one last bounty with his sidekick Ned (Morgan Freeman) as he takes up the cause of women in a brothel who seek vengeance for a knifed and disfigured young prostitute. Critically acclaimed, *Unforgiven* wins Eastwood two Oscars for Best Picture and Best Director while Gene Hackman gains one as Best Supporting Actor for his turn as the callous sheriff, Little Bill.

Remembering Freddie
20th April 1992 The stars gather at Wembley Stadium to pay tribute to the late Freddie Mercury, with all profits going to a new Mercury Phoenix Trust in aid of AIDS research. Performers include Elton John, David Bowie, George Michael, Annie Lennox and Guns N' Roses.

MUSIC

Bodyguard bonanza
The biggest song of 1992 is actually twenty years old. Dolly Parton's *I Will Always Love You* is the centrepiece of the Whitney Houston-Kevin Costner movie *The Bodyguard*. A hugely powerful vocal performance, Whitney's single tops the US chart for fourteen weeks and the UK chart for ten, while the soundtrack becomes the top selling movie album ever at 45 million plus.

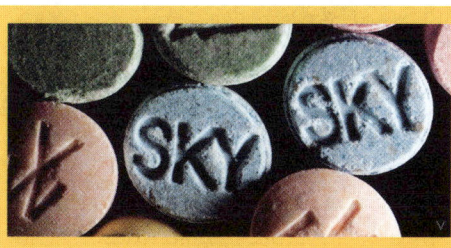

Clampdown on raves
22nd – 29th May 1992 As unauthorised rave events mushroom in warehouses and on farmland, the chaos at a week-long free festival at Castlemorton Common in the Malvern Hills prompts government action. A bill is introduced in Parliament to make illegal outdoor festivals which play 'sounds wholly or predominantly characterised by the emission of a succession of repetitive beats'. The Criminal Justice and Public Order Act becomes law in 1994.

Sex by Madonna
20th April 1992 Madonna signs a seven year multimedia deal worth $60 million with Time Warner, making her the most powerful woman in global entertainment. Her activities this year include a new album, *Erotica*, and a coffee table book of erotic self-portraits simply titled *Sex*.

Madness at Madstock
8th August 1992 Madness re-form and headline a 'Madstock' concert in Finsbury Park, close to their Camden Town stamping ground. Supporting act Morrissey, now solo after leaving the Smiths, is bombarded with coins and cans when he sings *National Front Disco* wrapped in a Union Jack.

1992

Nirvana at Reading
30th August 1992 Nirvana play a muddy Reading Festival in front of 40,000 fans. It will be their last live performance in the UK. Despite the media storm surrounding the Cobain-Love marriage and drug use, drummer Dave Grohl describes it as 'a wonderful show - and it healed us for a little while'.

MY FIRST 18 YEARS
TOP 10 — 1992

1. **Under the Bridge** Red Hot Chili Peppers
2. **I Can't Dance** Genesis
3. **Winter** Tori Amos
4. **Friday I'm in Love** The Cure
5. **Would I Lie to You** Charles and Eddie
6. **Sleeping Satellite** Tamsin Archer
7. **Walking on Broken Glass** Annie Lennox
8. **Damn I Wish I was You Lover** Sophie B. Hawkins
9. **The Days of Pearly Spencer** Marc Almond
10. **It Must Be Love** Madness

First Mercury Prize
9th September 1992 The prestigious Mercury Prize is awarded for the first time. Conceived to honour the most innovative UK or Irish album of the year, it goes to Scottish rock band Primal Scream for *Screamadelica*. They proceed to lose their £20,000 prize cheque in the celebrations.

Country matters
23rd November 1992 Billy Ray Cyrus's dippy line-dancing tune *Achy Breaky Heart* is one of the biggest global hits of the year. Elsewhere, veteran Willie Nelson is selling better than ever despite owing enormous sums in unpaid tax, while names like Joe Ely, Iris Dement, Vince Gill and especially Garth Brooks - fifth best selling act of 1992 at ten million albums - are leading country's new wave.

Sinead controversy
3rd October 1992 Sinead O'Connor incurs the wrath of American Catholics by tearing up a picture of Pope John Paul II on the *Saturday Night Live* show. She explains that it was a statement against child abuse in the Catholic church.

Mariah and the MiniDisc
7th December 1992 Challenging the compact disc is a new music format - the MiniDisc, developed by Sony. Released today is the format's first commercial release, Mariah Carey's *Unplugged*, comprising live recordings from her recent MTV show. The MiniDisc never takes off.

PHOTO CREDITS Copyright 2024, TDM Rights BV.
Photos: **A** Getty Images - Hulton Archive - Getty Images / **B** Shaun Botterill - GettyImages Sport - Getty Images / **C** James Keyser - The Chronicle Collection - Getty Images / **D** Imperial War Museum - **E** Watford - Mirrorpix - Getty Images / **F** Tim Graham Photo Library - Getty Images / **G** Jim James - PA Images - Getty Images / **H** Fiona Hanson - PA Images - Getty Images / **I** Charles Caratini - Sygma - Getty Images / **J** Francoise De Mulder - Roger Viollet - Getty Images / **K** Ira Wyman - Sygma - Getty Images / **L** Warner Bros - Moviepix - Getty Images / **M** David Jones - PA Images - Getty Images / **N** TV Times - Getty Images / **O** Ronald Grant Archive - Mary Evans / **P** Donald Maclellan - Hulton Archive - Getty Images / **Q** Ronald Grant Archive - Mary Evans / **R** AF Archive - Graham Whitby Boot - Mary Evans / **S** Lester Cohen - WireImage - Getty Images / **T** AF Archive - BBC - Mary Evans / **U** Mick Hutson - Redferns - Getty Images / **V** Universal History Images Groep - Getty Images / **W** Gutchie Kojima Shinko Music - Hulton Archive - Getty Images.

1993 — MY FIRST 18 YEARS

SPORT

Last BDO Championship
7th January 1993 The game of darts has been rising in stature and popularity since the early 1980s thanks to increased television exposure and the emergence of great personalities like Eric Bristow (photo) and his protégé Phil Taylor. As a split looms between the leading stars and darts administration body the British Darts Organisation (BDO), the very last BDO World Darts Championship sees all the big-name darts stars of the time - Bristow, Taylor, Dennis Priestley and Jocky Wilson included - knocked out before the final. The title is won by John Owen, who beats Alan Warriner 3-6.

National chaos
3rd April 1993 The Grand National at Aintree is cancelled after a chaotic false start in which 30 of the 39 horses keep running and seven even complete the course. Bookmakers are forced to repay the £75 million bets placed on the race. The official starter, Keith Brown, was taking charge of his last Grand National before retiring.

Seles stabbed
30th April 1993 World number one Monica Seles is stabbed between her shoulder blades by a spectator during a match in a World Tennis Association tournament in Hamburg. She will not play again for two years.

Giants of the game
British football mourns the loss of two giants of the game. Bobby Moore, the only player to captain England to World Cup victory, dies of cancer aged 53 on 24th February. Danny Blanchflower, whose death is announced on 9th December, was a Northern Ireland international who captained Tottenham Hotspur's famous double winning side in 1961 and later moved into journalism.

Ball of the century
4th June 1993 The England-Australia summer Test series sees the visitors retain the Ashes by winning four matches to England's one, with one match drawn. The most memorable moment comes on the second day of the first Test, when Australian spin bowler Shane Warne bowls out Mike Gatting with an extraordinary delivery that is soon named 'the ball of the century'.

World Cup misery
17th November 1993 England fail to qualify for the 1994 FIFA World Cup, in spite of beating San Marino 7-1 in their last qualification game. The damage was done in an earlier 2-0 defeat at the hands of the Netherlands. Manager Graham Taylor resigns eight days later. Wales also miss out on qualifying with a 2-1 defeat to Romania.

---

20 JAN 1993 — Bill Clinton is inaugurated as the 42nd US President.

6 FEB 1993 — Tennis superstar Arthur Ashe dies from HIV contracted through a blood transfusion.

12 MAR 1993 — 317 killed by bomb attacks in Bombay.

1993

DOMESTIC NEWS

Braer oil spill
5th January 1993 The Liberian oil tanker MV *Braer* hits rocks on the south coast of Shetland, causing a massive oil spill - 84,700 tonnes of crude oil - and threatening wildlife. The ship breaks up five days later during a ferocious North Atlantic storm. The upturned bow remains visible from the coast for years after.

Target Warrington
February - March 1993 Warrington in Cheshire becomes the new focus of Provisional IRA attacks on the British mainland. Bombs explode destroying gas holders while devices planted in the town centre kill three-year-old Jonathan Ball and twelve-year-old Timothy Parry. Attacks on the City of London resume on 24th April, when a truck bomb kills a photographer and causes huge damage to Bishopsgate and the Natwest Tower.

Stephen Lawrence
22nd April 1993 The murder of black teenager Stephen Lawrence at a bus shelter in Eltham, South London, has ramifications that are still being felt over 30 years later. Six suspects are arrested but not charged, leading to a private prosecution of the alleged perpetrators by Stephen's family that fails to achieve convictions. An enquiry into the handling of the case by the Metropolitan Police and the Criminal Prosecution Service delivers a damning report in 1998.

Virgin bites back
11th January 1993 British Airways apologises to Virgin Atlantic for undertaking a 'dirty tricks' campaign against the company to disrupt its commercial operations. Legal action by Virgin boss Richard Branson against BA results in an out of court settlement in his favour, leaving BA with a bill of over £3.5 million.

Bulger murder
12th February 1993 In one of the most distressing child murder cases in years, two-year-old James Bulger is abducted and killed by two ten-year-old boys in Bootle, Merseyside. At the end of their trial in November, the boys - Robert Thompson and Jon Venables - become the youngest convicted murderers in British legal history.

19 APR 1993
A 51-day stand-off at Waco, Texas, between FBI agents and Branch Davidian followers ends in 76 deaths.

17 MAY 1993
Rebecca Stephens is the first UK woman to reach the summit of Everest.

15 JUN 1993
James Hunt, 1976 Formula 1 World Drivers' Champion, dies of a heart attack at 45.

1993

Hotel collapse
4th June 1993 A huge coastal landslide at Scarborough, North Yorkshire, causes a large section of the Holbeck Hall Hotel to collapse into the sea. Some of the collapse is seen live on television during an edition of Yorkshire TV's *Calendar* news programme. Nobody is hurt and what remains of the building is demolished safely.

ROYALTY & POLITICS

Royal doors open
29th April 1993 In a new spirit of openness and accountability to the public, Buckingham Palace announces that the Queen will allow part of the building to be opened to visitors during the summer months.

Tunnel vision
20th June 1993 The first high-speed train journey through the Channel Tunnel takes place ahead of its official opening in 1994.

Equal status for Welsh
21st October 1993 The Welsh Language Act 1993 is passed into law, giving Welsh equal status with English in all aspects of public life in Wales. The most immediate impact is a visible one: all road signage in Wales will from now on be bilingual.

Lamont sacked
27th May 1993 In a reshuffle of his Cabinet prompted by his government's recent poor showing in the Newbury by-election, John Major sacks Norman Lamont and makes Kenneth Clarke his new Chancellor of the Exchequer. He refuses the offer of a lesser post as Secretary of State for the Environment and becomes a severe critic of Major's policies and a fierce Eurosceptic.

BNP takes council seat
17th September 1993 The right-wing anti-immigration British National Party (BNP) wins its first ever council seat, in Tower Hamlets in East London.

M40 minibus crash
18th November 1993 In what has been described as the UK's worst ever motorway accident, twelve children from Hagley Roman Catholic High School and their teacher Eleanor Fry are killed in a late-night minibus crash on the M40 near Warwick. They were returning home from a concert at the Royal Albert Hall.

---

4 JUL 1993
Pete Sampras beats fellow American Jim Courier in four sets, for his first of seven Wimbledon titles.

30 AUG 1993
The Eiffel Tower welcomes its 150 millionth paying visitor.

10 SEP 1993
Mystery sci-fi series *The X Files* debuts on US TV.

1993

Diana withdraws
3rd December 1993 Although there is still no sign of the Prince and Princess of Wales divorcing after their separation, Diana announces her intention to withdraw from public life in a speech at London's Hilton Hotel.

Downing Street Declaration
15th December 1993 A glimmer of hope for the peace process in Northern Ireland: Prime Minister John Major and Irish premier Albert Reynolds sign the Downing Street Declaration affirming the right of the people of Ireland to self-determination and that Northern Ireland would be transferred to the Republic of Ireland from the UK only if a majority of its population was in favour. It signifies a subtle but important change of policy and opens up the prospect of republican party Sinn Fein joining negotiations.

FOREIGN NEWS

Air Max
In the 1990s, the popularity of the Nike Air Max explodes. A true Air Max hunt spreads across the world and leads to bizarre scenes in stores. The shoe is popular with almost every subculture.

World Trade Center bombed
26th February 1993 A bomb explodes in a van parked below the north tower in the World Trade Center in New York, an attack by terrorists linked to Al-Qaeda. Their aim is to blow down the north tower against the south tower, so that the symbol of international trade disappears in one fell swoop. The attack kills six people and injures more than a thousand others, but it fails in its objective. The towers remain standing - at least for now.

1 OCT 1992
In defence of his heavyweight boxing title Lennox Lewis beats Frank Bruno by TKO in round 7.

30 NOV 1992
Toy giants Mattel and Fisher-Price complete a $15 million merger.

31 DEC 1992
Figures show there are now fifteen million users of the Internet and 623 websites.

1993

Spamming accident
31st March 1993 By mistake, software developer Richard Depew sends the same message two hundred times to a newsgroup on Usenet. The enormous amount of messages frustrates other users, who are turning to the newsgroup to discuss the progress of the web. One of the users, Joel Furr, is the first to give the message explosion a name: spam!

Srebrenica
16th April 1993 In Bosnia, the civil war is raging between Serbs and the Bosniaks and Croats. Tens of thousands of Muslim Bosnians who survived the massacres in their villages and towns are fleeing to enclaves where the Bosnian army has managed to hold back the Serbs. One of those enclaves is the city of Srebrenica, which is today declared a UN-protected 'safe area'.

Pablo Escobar
2nd December 1993 Colombian Pablo Escobar is the most feared drug baron in the world. The head of the infamous Medellín cartel controls about 80 per cent of the global cocaine trade, earning him more than $70 million a day in the best years. Escobar has a hand in thousands of murders to protect himself and his business, which makes him untouchable in Colombia and one of the richest yet also one of the most wanted people on earth. Escobar's fate is determined when, after several escapes from prison, the Colombian police investigation team trace him to his hideout in Medellín, where he is shot dead on the roof of his house.

Oslo Accords
13th September 1993 In the utmost secrecy, Israel and the PLO are negotiating a solution to their mutual conflict. In Oslo, out of sight of the cameras and international interference, an agreement is reached in which the Palestinians will be given self-government and can establish a Palestinian Authority. The formal signing by Prime Minister Yitzchak Rabin and PLO head Yasser Arafat will take place in Washington DC.

 ENTERTAINMENT

Morning motivation
Attired in eye-popping, multi-coloured lycra, Mr Motivator (real name Derrick Evans), becomes a regular on *GMTV* this year, encouraging the nation to get moving with his upbeat keep fit routines.

First browser
Mosaic becomes the first popular Internet browser. It is easy to install and for the first time images can be shown between the text on the web pages. In Mosaic you can also see which websites you have visited and save pages to view later.

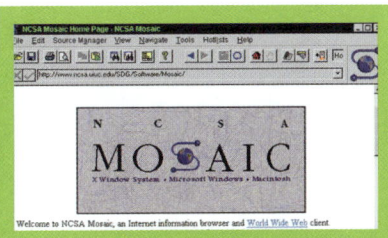

1993

Reservoir Dogs

Quentin Tarantino announces his arrival on the scene in 1992 when his heist-gone-wrong movie *Reservoir Dogs* is first shown at the Sundance Film Festival. The UK must wait until 15th January this year to see it, and then, due to a clamp down on film violence in the UK, another two and a half years before a VHS is available, during which time it firmly establishes itself as a cult classic. The film's poster, featuring the male cast in matching black suits and shades below a blood-spattered title, presages the unique blend of style and violence that will typify Tarantino's work. So too does the 1970s soundtrack, carefully curated by the director himself.

Thunderbirds are glued

After BBC2 repeats old episodes of *Thunderbirds* in 1992 there is a revival of interest in the retro puppet-led adventure show, and Matchbox Toys' Tracey Island playset sells out. But *Blue Peter* comes to the rescue on 7th January as presenter Anthea Turner shows viewers how to create their own Tracy Island out of cereal packets, drinking straws and sawdust. There are over 10,000 requests for the printed instructions published by the BBC.

DO YOU REMEMBER THIS?
VHS videocamera

Film according to French and Saunders

A highlight of comedy duo *French and Saunders*' sketch show is their regular film spoof segment. This year, Dawn becomes Hannibal Lecter and Jennifer, Clarice Starling in their own version of *Silence of the Lambs*. No films are safe from their clutches and *Thelma and Louise*, *Titanic* (Dawn plays Jack), *Gentlemen Prefer Blondes*, *Star Wars*, *Lord of the Rings* and *The Exorcist* all get the *French and Saunders* treatment over the years.

Wallace and Gromit - The Wrong Trousers

Aired on Boxing Day, Wensleydale cheese-loving inventor Wallace (voiced with gentle charm by Peter Sallis), his watchful dog Gromit and some robotic trousers get involved in foiling a diamond heist, masterminded by Wallace's new lodger, a dead-eyed criminal penguin, in this hilarious plasticine stop-motion animation adventure, created by 'claymation' genius, Nick Park.

Supermarket Sweep
Perma-tanned charmer Dale Winton hosts *Supermarket Sweep*, the ITV daytime quiz show where contestants answer questions and dash around a (mock-up) supermarket filling their trolleys and building up time or cash. The fun begins on 6th September.

Groundhog Day
Often cited as one of cinema's most perfect comedies, *Groundhog Day* has its UK release on 7th May. Bill Murray is bored, curmudgeonly weatherman Phil Connors, sent with his producer (Andie MacDowell) to the Pennsylvania town of Punxsutawney to report on the Groundhog Day ceremony (a genuine tradition in the US), only to then wake up on the same day, again, and again, and again... and again in a smart and mind-bending concept. Phil goes through confusion, delight, bitterness, and despair before eventually using his predicament for good and emerging a better human being.

Gone too soon?
The lives of two young actors are cut tragically short this year. Brandon Lee (photo), son of Bruce Lee, is shot in a freak accident on the set of *The Crow* on 31st March. On 31st October, River Phoenix dies of a drug-induced heart attack outside The Viper Room in Los Angeles. He is just 23 years old.

Monster movie
Steven Spielberg uses every visual effect trick in the book in what may well be the movie event of the decade - *Jurassic Park*. Seamlessly blending animatronics and live action with lightly applied computer-generated effects, audiences are transported to the ultimate theme park where eccentric millionaire John Hammond (Richard Attenborough) has brought dinosaurs back to life using DNA found in amber. Inevitably, things go badly wrong in this prehistoric paradise when a storm sets loose its most dangerous, and very hungry, inmates. Sam Neill, Laura Dern and Jeff Goldblum are among the specially selected group invited to preview the park and who go from cuddling herbivores to running for their lives from velociraptors and T-Rex. A terrifying, thrilling rollercoaster of a film.

Sleepless in Seattle
Tom Hanks and Meg Ryan star in Norah Ephron's whimsical long-distance love story, *Sleepless in Seattle*, released in the UK on 24th September. It's notable in that the two romantic leads, widower Sam and journalist Annie, spend just two minutes on screen together.

1993

Cracker
Robbie Coltrane plays one of TV's most charismatic characters in Jimmy McGovern's *Cracker*, which begins on ITV on 27th September. As Edward 'Fitz' Fitzgerald, he's a criminal psychologist, brought in to help profile suspects for Greater Manchester Police. Larger-than-life, Fitz is a flawed genius, admitting in one episode; 'I drink too much, I smoke too much, I gamble too much, I am too much.' Some scorching storylines and an assemblage of brilliant acting talent make *Cracker* a huge success. Among Coltrane's co-stars are Robert Carlyle and Christopher Eccleston, the DCI whose final scenes after being stabbed are seared into viewers' memories.

Lard questions
On 4th June, ex-Deputy Leader of the Labour Party Roy Hattersley fails to appear as a panellist on satirical news show *Have I Got News For You*. It is the third time Hattersley has cancelled at the last minute and the furious producers replace him with a tub of lard, stating that, 'they possessed the same qualities and were likely to give similar performances'. Despite his team-mate being The Rt. Hon. Tub of Lard, M.P., Paul Merton still wins the show.

Eurotrash
The 1990s appetite for outrageous and titillating entertainment shows no sign of dimming and so *Eurotrash*, which begins on Channel 4 on 24th September, fits right in. Presented by the suave Antoine de Caunes, and the enfant terrible of French fashion, Jean Paul Gaultier, *Eurotrash* feeds us with a smorgasbord of film clips offering snapshots of strange and bizarre behaviour from our European neighbours. Lily Savage enjoying the delights of a male naked cleaning service in Berlin, or Michael Winner visiting a Paris restaurant staffed by drag queens is all standard fare in the world of *Eurotrash*.

MUSIC

Bill bows out
7th January 1993 Bill Wyman confirms his departure from the Rolling Stones. He has not played or recorded with the band since 1990.

Mick is 50
26th July 1993 The unthinkable has happened. Mick Jagger is 50. He and 300 guests celebrate at a fancy dress birthday bash on a French Revolution theme.

Suede make the grade
10th April 1993 Formed in Haywards Heath in 1990 and now releasing their self-titled debut album, Suede are a new critics' favourite. Sporting a provocative cover picture of a gender-undefined couple kissing, the glam-rock influenced set enters the chart at No. 1 and wins the 1993 Mercury Prize.

1993

Ronson is dead
29th April 1993 Mick Ronson, David Bowie's ever-reliable Spider from Mars throughout his Ziggy Stardust period, dies of cancer aged 46.

Prince changes his name
7th June 1993 Prince is 35 today. To mark the occasion he announces that he will no longer be known by that name but by a squiggle-like symbol. From now he is referred to as The Artist Formerly Known as Prince. The move isn't quite as eccentric as it seems, as he and Warner Brothers are in dispute. The record label effectively owns the Prince name, so a new identity is a clever ruse to challenge his contract and gain greater control over his releases.

Goodbye Bruce
28th August 1993 Heavy metal aristocrats Iron Maiden say goodbye to singer Bruce Dickinson at their final gig together, a BBC show at Pinewood Studios. His replacement is Blaze Bayley from Wolfsbane. Dickinson rejoins in 1999.

Jackson abuse allegations
14th September 1993 A civil law suit is filed against Michael Jackson by the parents of thirteen-year-old Jordan Chandler alleging abuse. Jackson refutes the claims in a public statement issued in December.

Slivers of reggae
Two chart toppers prove that reggae is still a force. In March, Jamaican-born Shaggy matches a 1950s ska tune to a sample from Henry Mancini's film theme Peter Gunn and creates *Oh Carolina*. Three months later, UB40 (photo) add a reggae rhythm to the Elvis classic *Can't Help Falling in Love with You*. Both tracks are featured on the soundtrack of the Sharon Stone thriller *Sliver*.

Take That at the top
17th July 1993 Take That enjoy their first UK No. 1 with *Pray*. Becoming Britain's top boy band has not been a totally smooth ride, with their management's initial concentration on an older gay market rather than teenage girls now looking misplaced. After establishing themselves with two cover records - of Tavares' *It Only Takes a Minute* and Barry Manilow's *Could it be Magic* - they are now trusting the songwriting to Gary Barlow's Elton John-like facility for creating tunes to order.

1993

Meat Loaf is back
23rd October 1993 After the runaway success of *Bat Out of Hell* in the late 70s, Meat Loaf's career was derailed by poor health and legal problems. Now he's back working with songwriter Jim Steinman on a sequel, *Bat Out of Hell II: Back into Hell*, which they introduce with the chart topping *I'd Do Anything for Love (But I Won't Do That)*. It's like the last sixteen years had never happened.

MY FIRST 18 YEARS
TOP 10   1993

1. **Dreams** Gabrielle
2. **All That She Wants** Ace of Base
3. **Play Dead** Bjork
4. **Constant Craving** k. d. lang
5. **Pray** Take That
6. **The River of Dreams** Billy Joel
7. **Rubberband Girl** Kate Bush
8. **Fields of Gold** Sting
9. **Ordinary World** Duran Duran
10. **Moving On Up** M People

Open | Search | Scan

Rick retires
The polite, self-effacing and ever-spruce Rick Astley never looked comfortable with all the trappings of pop stardom. It's no real surprise, then, that he has chosen to retire from performing and recording at the grand old age of 27 after selling 40 million records worldwide. He stays true to his word for the next nine years.

Sugar-free Bjork
A national treasure in her native Iceland, Bjork has now left the Sugarcubes to release her solo album. The album *Debut* is a box of delights mixing trippy beats, new age atmospherics, Bond theme-like orchestral flourishes and even a looping Bollywood backing on the lovely *Venus as a Boy*. She has a voice that can go from a whisper to a roar in two seconds.

Zappa dies
4th December 1993 Frank Zappa, founder of the Mothers of Invention and one of rock music's great iconoclasts, dies of cancer aged 52. A favourite Zappa quote: 'Without deviation from the norm, progress is not possible.'

1994

MY FIRST 18 YEARS

SPORT

Bowing out with bronze
21st February 1994 Former gold medal winners Jayne Torvill and Christopher Dean announce their retirement from competition after taking bronze in the ice dancing at the Winter Olympics in Lillehammer.

Busby dies
8th January 1994 Former Manchester United manager Sir Matt Busby, who survived the 1958 Munich air disaster to rebuild the team and guide them to winning the European Cup in 1968, dies aged 84. Appropriately, United end the season by winning the 'double' as Premier League and FA Cup champions – the first side to do so since Arsenal in 1971.

Lara's record
6th June 1994 Brian Lara scores an unbeaten 501 runs off 427 balls in 474 minutes batting for Warwickshire against Durham. It creates a new first class cricket record for a highest score that still stands 30 years later. This is unquestionably his year: he breaks the world Test batting record by scoring 375 for the West Indies versus England in April and helps to steer his county to a treble of trophies – County Championship, Benson & Hedges Cup and Sunday League.

World Cup 1994
17th June – 17th July 1994 The FIFA World Cup stirs temporary 'soccer' fever in host country the US, with well over three million people attending the matches. Brazil (photo) beat Italy on penalties in the final after the game ends 0–0, with poster boy player Roberto Baggio missing his deciding spot kick. With none of the UK nations participating, most home interest centres on Ireland, managed by ex-England international Jack Charlton. The Irish cause a sensation in their first group match by beating Italy 1–0. A real tragedy of the tournament is the fate of Colombia's Andres Escobar, who is shot dead on 2nd July in his home city of Medellín in apparent revenge for scoring an own goal.

17 JAN 1994
Yahoo!, the world's first search engine, is launched.

8 FEB 1994
With 432 Test wickets to his name, India's Kapil Dev sets a new world record.

16 MAR 1994
American figure skater Tonya Harding pleads guilty to attacking former Olympic teammate Nancy Kerrigan.

1994

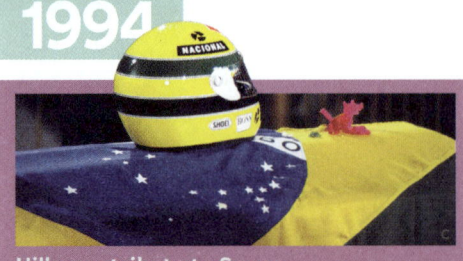

Hill pays tribute to Senna
11th December 1994 British driver Damon Hill is voted BBC Sports Personality of the Year at the end of a tumultuous year in motor racing. Hill had the responsibility of taking over as head driver of the Williams team after the death of Brazil's Ayrton Senna in the San Marino Grand Prix in May. In his acceptance speech at the BBC awards, Hill pays warm tribute to his former teammate. Hill's award is recognition for his triumph in the British Grand Prix at Silverstone, his six out of sixteen Formula One wins and his second place in the drivers' championship behind Michael Schumacher.

South Africa tour again
21st July - 21st August 1994 After 21 years in the wilderness, unable to compete internationally because of the country's apartheid policy, South Africa continue their return to Test match cricket with a series against England. The team is led by veteran Kepler Wessels, who during the long hiatus played 24 Tests for Australia. The series is drawn 1-1 but marred by accusations of ball tampering against England captain Michael Atherton.

Beeper

DOMESTIC NEWS

Rover sold
31st January 1994 BMW's acquisition of British Aerospace's 80 per cent stake in Rover leaves the UK without its own independent high-volume car manufacturer. Three weeks later, Honda sells its twenty per cent stake in Rover to BMW, giving the latter full ownership. The new Rover Group becomes the seventh largest carmaker in Europe.

Porn cinema fire
26th February 1994 An arson attack on an unlicensed adult cinema in Clerkenwell, London, kills eleven men. A homeless man nicknamed 'Deaf Dave' who had been refused entry is convicted after giving himself in to police. Four firefighters receive awards for their life-saving actions.

Cromwell Street murders
28th February 1994 Soon to be revealed as one of the UK's most notorious serial killers, Fred West is charged with murdering his daughter Heather and eighteen-year-old Shirley Robinson. Excavations at his house at 25 Cromwell Street, Gloucester, lead to discoveries of multiple bodies and the arrest of his wife Rose on 20th April. The couple are brought before Gloucester magistrates court on 30th June and charged with twelve murders.

22 APR 1994 Former US President Richard Nixon dies at 81.

19 MAY 1994 Death of Jacqueline Onassis, former US First Lady.

14 JUN 1994 UK holiday company Sunseeker Leisure collapses.

1994

Heathrow attacks
9th - 13th March 1994 The IRA delivers a series of mortar attacks on Heathrow Airport, causing heavy disruption to flights but no casualties.

Bottled up
4th August 1994 Famous for such slogans as 'drinka pinta milka day' and 'milk has got a lotta bottle', the Milk Marketing Board is set for closure after 61 years following deregulation of the UK's milk market under the new Agriculture Act.

Channel Tunnel opens
6th May 1994 The 35-mile-long Channel Tunnel is officially opened by the Queen and President Mitterrand after six years of construction. Linking the UK and France, it is the longest undersea tunnel in the world. The new five-platform terminus for Eurostar services to Paris and Brussels via the Channel Tunnel opens at London's Waterloo Station on 14th November.

Changes to criminal law
3rd November 1994 The Criminal Justice and Public Order Act becomes law, increasing police powers to stop and search suspects, criminalising some civil offences, tightening the obscenity laws and lowering the age of consent for homosexual acts to 18.

Tattoos and piercings
As body art becomes increasingly popular, tattoos are no longer reserved for rough sailors but are increasingly seen decorating arms, backs, shoulders and legs. First seen in the punk era of the late 70s, piercings are now a fashion item. In the music video for Aerosmith's *Cryin'*, teen idol Alicia Silverstone has a belly button piercing as well as a tattoo! Many teenage girls follow her example and show off their navel piercings under a short shirt. Ears, lips, tongues, noses, eyebrows and nipples are fair game, too. Some even get a piercing in more intimate places, to provide extra stimulation during sex.

Equipped for the streets
20th June 1994 As part of a far-reaching series of changes to UK policing, the traditional police truncheon is replaced with a US-style baton. Over the next few years, the 'bobby on the beat' virtually disappears, police community support officers (PCSOs) take over non-arresting duties, Tasers are introduced and police uniforms evolve into something straight out of Robocop. Many forces withdraw the century-old 'custodian helmet' in favour of peaked caps, though the Metropolitan Police retains the old school headwear for ceremonial duties.

2 JUL 1994
Mass trespass by anti-road activists at Twyford Down motorway construction site.

1 AUG 1994
Jordan and Israel end a 46-year-long state of war.

3 SEP 1994
Former England and Wolves captain Billy Wright dies aged 70.

1994

IRA ceasefire
31st August 1994 The IRA announces a ceasefire, which the UK government greets with scepticism. As a gesture of good faith, the government ends the long-time broadcasting ban on Sinn Fein and exclusion orders on the party's leaders, Gerry Adams and Martin McGuinness. In October, the Combined Loyalist Military Command (CLMC), representing all Loyalist paramilitary organisations, declares its own ceasefire.

'Release the balls!'
19th November 1994 The first National Lottery draw takes place on live television, during a show presented by Noel Edmonds who gives the famous instruction to 'Release the balls!' The lottery is operated by the Camelot Group under franchise, with proceeds going towards approved charitable and heritage projects. Seven winners share the opening jackpot, each scooping a cool £839,254.

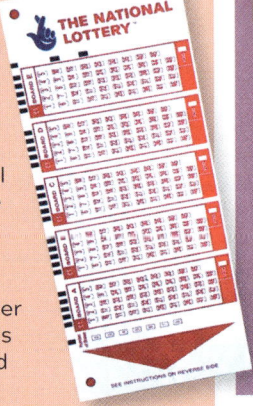

Labour leadership race
12th May 1994 Labour Party leader John Smith dies of a heart attack aged 55. His death triggers a leadership race won on 22nd July by Tony Blair, who beats John Prescott and Margaret Beckett. Prescott becomes Deputy Leader. Gordon Brown, seen by many as a contender himself, backs Blair's campaign, allegedly in return for a promise of becoming Chancellor of the Exchequer in a Labour Government and taking over from Blair as Prime Minister after ten years.

Cash for questions
20th October 1994 A major political scandal erupts after *The Guardian* alleges that Conservative MPs Neil Hamilton and Tim Smith have taken bribes from Harrods owner Mohamed Al-Fayed to ask questions on their behalf in Parliament. This follows a *Sunday Times* report in July that Conservative MPs Graham Riddick and David Treddinick had accepted payment for tabling a question, resulting in their suspension from Parliament. Smith resigns while Hamilton begins a libel action against *The Guardian*.

ROYALTY & POLITICS

MP's mystery death
7th February 1994 Conservative MP Stephen Milligan is found dead at his Chiswick home aged 45. Forensic tests later reveal that he died of asphyxiation during an auto-erotic act. The eventual inquest verdict is death by misadventure.

---

6 OKT 1994 The NHS launches a central register for potential organ donors to join.

28 NOV 1994 Norway follows Finland and Sweden in voting for European Union membership.

2 DEC 1994 Yitzhak Rabin, Shimon Peres and Yasser Arafat receive Nobel Peace Prize.

1994

Charles admits adultery
29th June 1994 As the war of words between Prince Charles and Princess Diana gathers momentum, Prince Charles is interviewed by his biographer Jonathan Dimbleby about the failure of his marriage. The programme is called *Charles: The Private Man, The Public Role*. Charles states that he was 'faithful and honourable' to Diana until the marriage broke down - a stark admittance of adultery. On the night of transmission and with the eyes of the world on her, Diana attends an event at the Serpentine Gallery in Kensington Gardens wearing what the press instantly dub her 'revenge' dress - a striking black off-the-shoulder number.

FOREIGN NEWS

Scream theft
12th February 1994 Edvard Munch's painting of *The Scream* is stolen from the National Gallery in Oslo. A ransom demand is made but the painting is recovered intact on 7th May during a sting operation. Four men are charged.

Rwandan genocide
6th April 1994 An attack on a plane that kills the Rwandan and Burundian Presidents is the starting signal for a gruesome genocide. Hutu militias slaughter about three-quarters of the Tutsi minority in a hundred days. Tutsis are beheaded with machetes, shot or killed with grenades. Exterminated villages are then razed to the ground with bulldozers and set on fire. About one million Tutsis and moderate Hutus die. Another two million Rwandans flee the country. In July, the Rwandan Patriotic Front force the interim government into Zaire and the genocide ends.

President Mandela
27th April 1994 The first free and racially unrestricted elections in South Africa yield a landslide victory for the African National Congress (ANC) led by 75-year-old Nelson Mandela, the man who was imprisoned for 27 years in the fight against apartheid. Mandela becomes the first black President of South Africa. South Africa rejoins the Commonwealth in June, having left in 1961.

Republican clean sweep
8th November 1994 In a mid-term congressional election triumph that has political commentators talking of a 'Republican revolution' in the US, the party takes control of both the House of Representatives and the Senate. In Texas, George W. Bush, son of the former President, is elected Governor.

Bezos founds Amazon
5th July 1994 Seattle-based science graduate Jeff Bezos starts an online book store from a rented garage in Bellevue, Washington. He initially calls the store Cadabra but soon changes the name to Amazon. Within three years, the company is ready to go public.

1994

Chasing O. J.
17th June 1994 Accused of murdering his ex-wife and one of her acquaintances five days before, American football star-turned-actor O. J. Simpson is the subject of a huge manhunt. Escaping as police arrive to question him, he is seen sitting in the back seat of a white Bronco with a gun to his head. Police give chase as the Bronco proceeds at low speed on Interstate 405, with every moment broadcast live to a television audience of millions. A whole hour passes before Simpson is finally arrested arriving at his home.

Estonia disaster
28th September 1994 The worst European shipping disaster since the Second World War occurs in the Baltic Sea between Estonia and Finland. The ferry *Estonia* sinks on its way to Stockholm when the car deck suddenly takes on water. 852 passengers die in the cold water. A hole in the hull found in the wreck points to a possible collision with a submarine.

Heaviest human
18th July 1994 According to her then boyfriend, Carol Yager weighed 727 kilos at her heaviest. This makes her the heaviest person who has ever lived. With that bizarre weight, health problems are obvious. Yager is hospitalised and loses 236 kilos within three months. She dies today from the effects of morbid obesity.

ENTERTAINMENT

Forrest Gump
7th October 1994 'Life is like a box of chocolates, you never know what you're gonna get'. So says the simple yet sage Forrest Gump, as he reflects on an extraordinary life. Tom Hanks perfects an innocent charm as Forrest, an idiot savant, who despite his shortcomings finds himself at the centre of American history, becoming a football star, meeting JFK and heroically saving the grumpy Lieutenant Dan during the Vietnam War. *Forrest Gump* wins six Oscars, including Best Picture and Best Actor for Hanks.

'Great Leader' is no more
8th July 1994 All North Koreans are crying, whether forced to or not. Their 'Great Leader' Kim Il-sung is no more. Kim Il-sung (photo left) is succeeded by his son Kim Jong-il (photo right).

1994

Schindler's List
18th February 1994 Steven Spielberg's *Schindler's List* is a harrowing, absorbing film about Oskar Schindler, the Nazi businessman who saved 1,200 Jews from concentration camps during the Holocaust by employing them in his factories. Liam Neesom is the charming Schindler while Ralph Fiennes is spectacularly unbalanced as sadistic camp commandant Amon Göth. Shot in black and white, *Schindler's List* is powerful, unflinching, and often horrifying, exposing the best and worst of humanity.

Sapphic moment
Brookside sets the nation talking when its 14th January episode features the first pre-watershed lesbian kiss on TV, between Beth Jordache (Anna Friel) and Margaret Clemence (Nicola Stephenson), a landmark LGBT moment in television history.

Pulp Fiction
Pulp Fiction, Quentin Tarantino's lurid patchwork of inter-locking crime stories, is released in the UK on 21st October. Inspired by a variety of film and pop culture references, from kung fu and film noir to *Saturday Night Fever*, it's kitsch, flamboyant and packed with attitude. John Travolta's role as a hitman, opposite Samuel L. Jackson, is career-reviving. He even slips on his dancing shoes for an iconic dance scene with Uma Thurman to Chuck Berry's *You Never Can Tell*.

Hello boys
Drivers crash their cars and pedestrians walk into lamp posts this year, all because of a distracting 48-sheet poster. Model Eva Herzigova stars in an advertising campaign for Playtex Wonderbra, where she marvels at the cleavage oomph achieved with a little bit of lingerie lift. Accompanied by the slogan, 'Hello boys', the advert is a sensation, Wonderbra sales soar and boobs are back, big time.

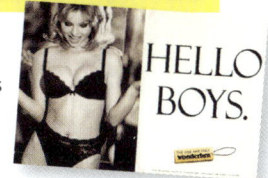

Mrs Doubtfire
Following in the stilettoes of other cross-dressing comedies such as *Some Like It Hot* and *Tootsie*, *Mrs Doubtfire* hits cinemas on 28th January, with Robin Williams on top form as a voice actor who, following his divorce, impersonates an elderly Scottish nanny in order to spend time with his kids. Williams sits for four hours in make-up every day to transform into an entirely plausible 60-year-old woman.

The X Files
19th September 1994 FBI super sleuths Fox Mulder (David Duchovny) and Dana Scully (Gillian Anderson), are given the mysterious cases nobody else can solve as each week they dive into the world of paranormal phenomena with the odd monster thrown in. *The X Files*, first shown on BBC2, is a sci-fi hit, partly due to the charismatic pairing of Duchovny and Anderson, and the dynamic of their characters, but also because the supernatural storylines are inventive, creepy, and often genuinely terrifying.

1994

Four weddings, a funeral and THAT dress
Everybody loves a wedding and this quirky British film has four, as well as a funeral to provide a poignant interlude amid the marriage mayhem. Hugh Grant is Charles, a seasoned, and occasionally jaded attendee of endless nuptials, who along with his posh pals, dashes around country lanes and Scottish castles, bumping into neurotic ex-girlfriends and amorous newlyweds. When sophisticated American fashion editor (Andie Macdowell) falls for his awkward, floppy-haired charm, it looks as if Charles may also be heading for the altar. Made for under £3 million, *Four Weddings and a Funeral* is an unexpected box office smash, making £245 million globally. It confirms Grant's A-list status, and when he attends the 11th May premiere in London with his girlfriend, Elizabeth Hurley, wearing a revealing Versace safety pin dress, his stock rises even higher.

Ready, Steady, Cook
Afternoons get gourmet from 24th October with the arrival of the fun cooking show, *Ready, Steady, Cook* on BBC1. Presented by Fern Britton, two professional chefs are provided with a bag of random ingredients valued at £5, from which they must concoct a delicious meal. After the dishes have been served up, audience members vote for either the red tomato or green pepper team. *Ready, Steady, Cook* not only offers culinary inspiration, but makes the participating chefs, including Ainsley Harriott, Anthony Worrall-Thompson and Nick Nairn, household names.

The Lion King
7th October 1994 *The Lion King* becomes an instant and much-loved classic. The story of Simba, the lion cub who witnesses the death of his father at the paws of his evil uncle Scar, is one of laughter and tragedy, terror and joy, with the African Savannah and its panoply of beasts brought wonderfully to life by Disney's animation team and a glorious soundtrack courtesy of Elton John and Tim Rice. Broadly appealing to young and old, it's the *Circle of Life* right there in front of us.

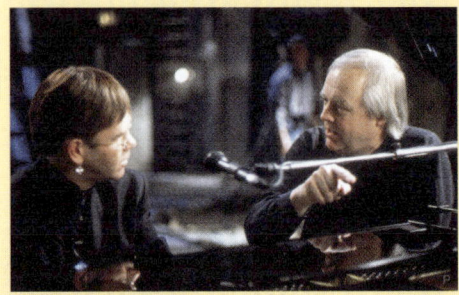

This week, I have been mostly watching *The Fast Show*
27th September 1994 Paul Whitehouse, Charlie Higson and crew launch their sketch show on BBC2, introducing a cast of vividly drawn, comic characters.

1994

MUSIC

Kurt Cobain
5th April 1994 Kurt Cobain of Nirvana shoots himself at his home in Seattle. His body is found three days later with a suicide note quoting a line from a Neil Young song, 'It's better to burn out than fade away.' He had been hospitalised a month earlier after an apparent suicide attempt and had been missing since walking out of a drug recovery centre in Los Angeles on 31st March. He was 27.

Riverdance at Eurovision
30th April 1994 Ireland hosts the Eurovision Song Contest and becomes the first country ever to win three years in a row, with *Rock'n'Roll Kids* by Paul Harrington and Charlie McGettigan. The show also launches the Riverdance phenomenon, when Michael Flatley and his dance company perform in the interlude before the votes are announced.

Michael and Lisa
26th May 1994 It is a romantic match that nobody could have predicted. Michael Jackson marries Lisa Marie Presley, daughter of Elvis and Priscilla, in the Dominican Republic. The marriage lasts two years.

Professional slavery
1st June 1994 George Michael's action against Sony Records concludes at the High Court in London. He loses the case and faces legal costs of up to four million pounds. Just as significant is the damage done to his career by putting all recording and releasing on hold.

Go Wets
4th June 1994 Wet Wet Wet begin a mammoth fifteen weeks at No. 1 with a revival of the Troggs' 1967 hit *Love is All Around*, recorded for the soundtrack of the rom-com movie *Four Weddings and a Funeral*. The band insist on the single's withdrawal from sale before it can top the chart for a further week and equal Bryan Adams' record for chart-topping longevity set in 1991.

Holiday hit
16th September 1994 European-made records often become hits in the UK after holidaymakers hear them in the discos and tavernas and seek them out back in Blighty. The latest is *Saturday Night* by Danish model-turned-singer Whigfield, which has shot to No. 1 in the UK its first week of release.

Money to burn
23rd August 1994 Stunt masters and music industry baiters the KLF are not done yet. Officially retired, they burn a million pounds in sterling on the Scottish island of Jura and video the event.

1994

Woodstock '94
12th - 14th August 1994 An attempt to re-create the spirit of Woodstock 1969 is made in upstate New York where thousands gather for Woodstock '94. Bad weather and gate crashers mark the occasion but performers include Aerosmith, Bob Dylan, Peter Gabriel, Red Hot Chili Peppers and the new stars of Irish rock, the Cranberries led by Dolores O'Riordan.

MY FIRST 18 YEARS — TOP 10 1994

1. Girls and Boys *Blur*
2. Kiss from a Rose *Seal*
3. Marvellous *The Lightning Seeds*
4. Linger *The Cranberries*
5. 7 Seconds *Youssou N'Dour, Neneh Cherry*
6. Patience of Angels *Eddi Reader*
7. All I Wanna Do *Sheryl Crow*
8. Think Twice *Celine Dion*
9. Cigarettes and Alcohol *Oasis*
10. Good as Gold *The Beautiful South*

M People
17th September 1994 Another surprise from the Mercury Music Prize panel. Although the hot favourites are Pulp and Blur, this year's award goes to *Elegant Slumming* by M People, a Manchester dance collective with the most soulful voice in current UK music – Heather Small.

Hello boyz
10th December 1994 There's a new name in the charts with a long career ahead of them. Boyzone are a five-piece boy band from Ireland fronted by Ronan Keating and Stephen Gateley. They debut with *Love Me for a Reason*, a cover of an Osmonds No. 1 from 1974. On the same day, a boy band with a much tougher attitude claims the top spot – East 17 (photo) with *Stay Another Day*. They're a foursome from Walthamstow whose image is everything that Boyzone's isn't – sullen, streetwise and dressed like rappers.

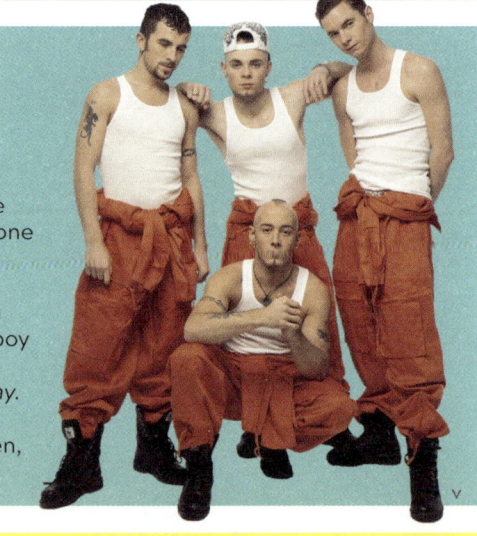

What a carry on
The biggest selling album of the year by a UK act is a surprise. It's *Carry On Up the Charts*, a collection of all the spiky domestic drama hits to date by the low-profile and decidedly unhip Beautiful South. Its million-plus sales make Paul Heaton and writing partner Dave Rotheray the UK's most successful songwriting partnership since Lennon and McCartney.

PHOTO CREDITS Copyright 2024, TDM Rights BV.
Photos: **A** Mirrorpix - Getty Images / **B** Mark Leech - Offside - Getty Images / **C** Pool Ribeiro Sassaki - Gamma-Rapho - Getty Images / **D** Tim Graham - Corbis Historical - Getty Images / **E** Christiane Zwerg - Moment Editorial - Getty Images / **F** PYMCA Avalon - Hulton Archive - Getty Images / **G** Michael Birt - Hulton Archive - Getty Images / **H** Tim Graham Photo Library - Getty Images / **I** Peter Turnley - Corbis Historical - Getty Images / **J** Sygma - Getty Images / **K** Sygma - Getty Images / **L** Sunset Boulevard - Corbis Historical - Getty Images / **M** AF Archive Universal - Mary Evans / **N** AF Archive - 20th Century Fox - Mary Evans / **O** Fred Duval - FilmMagic - Getty Images / **P** AF Archive - Walt Disney Pictures - Mary Evans / **Q** Ronald Grant Archive - Mary Evans / **R** Frank Micelotta Archive - Hulton Archive - Getty Images / **S** Tammie Arroyo - Hulton Archive - Getty Images / **T** Mirrorpix - Getty Images / **U** Marc Serota - Michael Ochs Archives - Getty Images / **V** Tim Roney - Hulton Archive - Getty Images.

1995

MY FIRST 18 YEARS

SPORT

Transfer records
A sign of the impact that the Premier League is making is the breaking of the UK transfer record three times in nine months, by Andy Cole (Newcastle to Manchester United, £7 million), Dennis Bergkamp (Inter Milan to Arsenal, £7.5 million) and Stan Collymore (Nottingham Forest to Liverpool, £8.5 million).

Perry dies
2nd February 1995 Tennis great Fred Perry, the last British player to win Wimbledon, dies following a fall in Melbourne, Australia, aged 85.

DO YOU REMEMBER THIS?

Scented pens

Phil powers to victory
2nd January 1995 Darts superstar Phil 'The Power' Taylor begins his domination of the World Darts Championship with a 6-2 victory in the final over Rod Harrington. He goes on to win eleven of the next twelve championship finals and countless other titles before his retirement in 2018.

Rugby goes professional
27th August 1995 Rugby Union will never be quite the same again as the International Rugby Football Board, meeting in Paris, votes to allow payment to players. The switch to professionalism comes under the threat of a breakaway competition funded by satellite television. It allows elite players to focus on training and playing rugby full-time, improving their skills and overall performance, and greatly increases the marketability of the sport.

Cantona's kick
25th January 1995 In an away game at Crystal Palace in January, Manchester United's enigmatic French forward Eric Cantona is sent off and literally kicks out kung fu-style at a spectator who abuses him verbally. He is given an eight-month ban by the FA, while police bring an assault charge that leaves him facing 120 hours of community service.

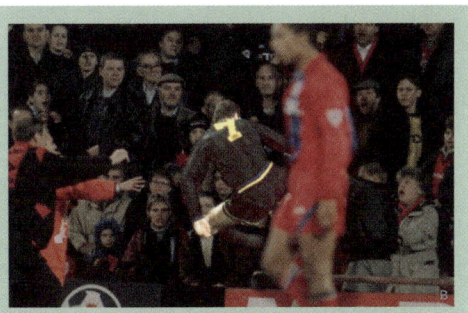

18 JAN 1995
Pope John Paul II begins his visit to Australia.

10 FEB 1995
£267 million compensation set for members of Maxwell pension fund.

5 MAR 1995
Graves of murdered Czar Nicholas and family found in St Petersburg.

1995

Champion Frank
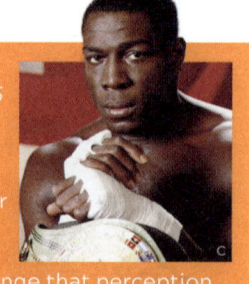
2nd September 1995 For decades, British heavyweight boxers have been regarded as cannon fodder for the all-conquering Americans. Lennox Lewis started to change that perception by becoming the World Boxing Council (WBC) champion in 1993. Now Frank Bruno has achieved what many thought was impossible by outpointing reigning champion Oliver McCall. Frank's reign as world's best is brief, ending with defeat to a resurgent Mike Tyson in 1996 and his retirement from the ring.

Rugby League World Cup
28th October 1995 The eleventh Rugby League World Cup climaxes at Wembley Stadium with a 16-8 victory for holders Australia versus England.

DOMESTIC NEWS

M3 completed
1st January 1995 The M3 motorway between London and Southampton is now fully open following the completion of the Twyford Down section that was the focus of so many environmental protests during its construction. Six lanes of traffic now cut through what was once one of Hampshire's most scenic areas of downland.

Rumbelows closes
7th February 1995 A familiar high street name since the 1950s and now part of Thorn Electrical Industries, electrical chain store Rumbelows closes all its 311 outlets due to dwindling sales.

MG brand revived
17th February 1995 The Rover Group announces the revival of the MG sports car, due for re-launch in September.

Barings Bank fails
26th February 1995 The UK's oldest merchant bank, Barings, collapses. The blame is levelled at a derivatives trader in the bank's Singapore office named Nick Leeson, who accumulated $140 million of losses. Leeson flees but is later arrested in Frankfurt and extradited for trial. In December he is convicted of fraud by a Singapore court and sentenced to six years in prison.

Damon Hill fined for speeding
1st March 1995 Formula One star Damon Hill is convicted of speeding at over 100 mph on the M40 in Oxfordshire. Admitting the charge, he is banned from driving for seven days by Bicester magistrates, fined £350 and ordered to pay court costs.

Fred West suicide
1st January 1995 Accused of twelve murders, the Gloucester builder Fred West is found hanged in his cell at Winson Green Prison in Birmingham. His wife Rose stands trial for ten murders in October and is found guilty on all counts. She is sentenced to life imprisonment without parole.

4 APR 1995
Radio and TV personality Kenny Everett dies at 50 of an AIDS-related illness.

20 MAY 1995
Kevin Moran of Manchester United is first player sent off in an FA Cup Final.

27 JUN 1995
Chechen rebels seize hundreds of hostages in Russian hospital.

1995

Ronnie Kray is dead
17th March 1995 Ronnie Kray, who with his brother Reggie led a notorious East London crime operation in the 1960s, dies of a heart attack aged 61. He had been a Category A prisoner at Broadmoor since being committed in 1979.

50 years since VE Day
8th May 1995 The May Day bank holiday is moved from the first Monday in May to a Friday for the first time to allow UK citizens to mark the 50th anniversary of the end of the Second World War in Europe. Services, commemorations, festivals, fetes and air displays are held up and down the country.

Campaign against ecstasy
9th October 1995 Teenager Leah Betts dies four days after taking the recreational drug MDMA ('ecstasy') and drinking seven litres of water. Her death triggers a high-profile media campaign against the tablets and their suppliers led by Leah's family.

Over the sea to Skye
16th October 1995 The arch-shaped Skye Bridge one and a half miles in length is opened, linking the Isle of Skye to the Scottish mainland at Kyle of Lochalsh. It remains a toll bridge until 2004, when it is purchased by the Scottish government and becomes toll-free.

Hirst wins the Turner Prize
29th November 1995 Controversial artist Damien Hirst reinforces his growing reputation and notoriety by winning the Turner Prize with *Mother and Child, Divided*, a sculpture made up of four glass tanks containing the two halves of a cow and calf preserved in formaldehyde.

Headteacher murdered
8th December 1995 Headteacher Philip Lawrence is fatally stabbed outside his school, St George's Roman Catholic Secondary School, while trying to protect a pupil from an attack by a gang from a neighbouring school. He is posthumously awarded the Queen's Gallantry Medal in 1997.

10 JUL 1995
Imprisoned Burmese opposition leader Aung San Suu Kyi released.

17 AUG 1995
Alison Hargreaves, who climbed Everest without oxygen in May, is killed in avalanche on K2.

8 SEP 1995
David Trimble voted new leader of Ulster Unionists.

1995

ROYALTY & POLITICS

Kinnock leaves Parliament
16th February 1995 Former Labour leader Neil Kinnock resigns his Islwyn seat as an MP to become a European Commissioner and sparks a by-election which his party wins comfortably.

The Queen in Armagh
9th March 1995 With the IRA ceasefire in place but amid high security, the Queen and the Duke of Edinburgh make a rare one-day visit to Northern Ireland to open the City of Armagh High School and meet Cardinal Cathal Daly.

South African visit
19th - 25th March 1995 The Queen and the Duke of Edinburgh make their first visit to South Africa for nearly 50 years as guests of President Nelson Mandela.

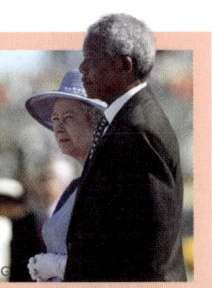

Major challenges his doubters
22nd June 1995 Fed up with criticism from his own MPs and even from within the Cabinet, John Major tells them it is time 'to put up or shut up' and resigns as leader of the Conservatives to stand again in a leadership ballot. The only senior MP prepared to take him on is Secretary of State for Wales John Redwood, who is defeated on 4th July by 89 votes to Major's 218.

Diana states her case
20th November 1995 Princess Diana gives an astonishingly frank interview to BBC reporter Martin Bashir in which she discusses her marriage to Prince Charles, her own adultery and depression, and her struggles with bulimia. A month after the interview, the Queen writes to Charles and Diana advising them to seek a divorce.

FOREIGN NEWS

Oklahoma City bombing
19th April 1995 A total of 168 people including 19 children are killed by a huge truck bomb left outside the Alfred P. Murrah Federal Building in Oklahoma City. The worst terrorist atrocity ever committed on US soil to this point, it is the work of anti-government extremists Timothy McVeigh, a Gulf War veteran, and Terry Nichols.

---

18 OCT 1995
Death of legendary horse Red Rum, winner of three Grand Nationals.

19 NOV 1995
Lech Walesa defeated in Polish presidential election.

29 DEC 1995
Emma Nicolson is second Tory MP this year to defect to opposition benches.

1995

Agreement in Dayton
July - December 1995 More than 8,000 Bosnian Muslims are massacred by Bosnian Serbs when they overrun the UN's 'safe haven' of Srebrenica. In August, after Bosnian Serb forces refuse to move weaponry out of Sarajevo, NATO begins a bombing campaign against Serb positions in Bosnia-Herzegovina. Negotiations between all parties involved to end the conflict finally begin in Dayton, Ohio, in November and are concluded on 14th December. Signed by the leaders of Bosnia, Serbia and Croatia, the agreement recognises Bosnia-Herzegovina as a complete state, fixes new boundaries and sets elections for 1996.

That's rich
17th July 1995 Forbes magazine names Microsoft co-founder Bill Gates as the world's richest man with a net worth of $12.9 billion.

eBay
3rd September 1995 In California's Silicon Valley, French-born Iranian American Pierre Omidyar (photo left) offers a broken laser pointer for sale through his own website. To his own surprise, a collector wants to buy it for almost fifteen dollars. It gives Omidyar an idea. He builds the first website on which people can bid on other people's items: AuctionWeb. The auction site soon changes its name to eBay and grows into the largest trading site in the world.

PlayStation launches
9th September 1995 Sony's PlayStation is launched in the US and Europe after a trial launch in Japan a year earlier. The PS1 is, literally, a game-changer, spawning over 7,900 individual games and selling over 100 million units and 960 million games over time.

Simpson on trial
3rd October 1995 The exhaustively televised trial of O. J. Simpson for the murders of his wife Nicole Brown Simpson and her friend Ronald Goldman puts American life on hold for months and concludes on its 133rd day with his acquittal on both counts.

Rabin murdered
4th November 1995 Israeli Prime Minister Yitzhak Rabin is assassinated in Tel Aviv. Not by a Palestinian or Arab terrorist, but by a Jewish extremist appalled by the Oslo Accords between Israel and Palestine. Conservative Benjamin Netanyahu wins the next elections. Peace between Israel and the Arab world seems further away than ever.

1995

Saquinivar approved
6th December 1995
On the day that President Clinton hosts the first White House conference on HIV/AIDS, the US Food and Drug Administration gives approval to Saquinavir, the first inhibitor medication to treat the disease. Figures released two years later show a decrease in the number of deaths from AIDS from 50,000 to around 18,000.

ENTERTAINMENT

The Shawshank Redemption
17th February 1995 When *The Shawshank Redemption* is first released in the USA it makes a paltry $16 million at the box office, but seven Academy Award nominations and word of mouth soon change its fortunes. Tim Robbins is Andy, the accountant serving a life sentence for the alleged murder of his wife and her lover, whose financial skills are exploited by corrupt prison management for money laundering purposes. Morgan Freeman is Red, the sagacious inmate, doing time for contraband smuggling, who befriends him. A tough watch in places, the definitions of good and evil are intentionally skewed but hope prevails with Andy and Red finding the redemption promised in the film's title, while retribution awaits those who abuse their power.

Making *Friends*
22nd April 1995 UK viewers first meet Ross, Phoebe, Monica, Rachel, Chandler and Joey, aka *Friends*, when Channel 4 airs the pilot episode. Hailed as the defining sitcom of the '90s, these twenty-something New Yorkers quickly charm us as we invest in Ross and Rachel's on-off romance, sing along to Phoebe's *Smelly Cat* song, wonder if Chandler could be any more adorable and swoon at Joey asking, 'How are you doin?' *Friends* is a phenomenon and an addiction; it even launches the hairdo of the decade as every woman requests the swingy, shaggy Rachel cut, as worn by Jennifer Aniston.

ER
US medical drama *ER* begins on Channel 4 on 1st February, socking it to British viewers who struggle to keep up with the frenetic pace as they watch patients shocked back to life by doctors who speak unintelligible rapid-fire medicalese. Writing in *The Times*, Libby Purves opines, 'It makes our own dear *Casualty* look like a wistful mood piece by Alan Bennett.' But as the show's characters begin to fully form, we acclimatise and can't wait for our next appointment. Compulsive viewing, *ER* is the shot in the arm we all need.

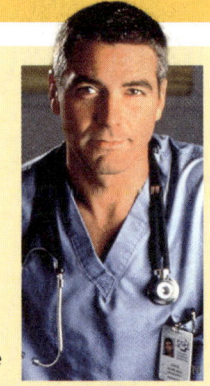

Hollyoaks
Hollyoaks, a new Chester-set soap opera conceived by Phil Redmond and aimed at a youthful audience, begins on Channel 4 on 23rd October.

1995

Shallow Grave
Made in just one month on a shoestring budget, Danny Boyle's directorial debut *Shallow Grave* stars Christopher Eccleston, Ewan McGregor and Kerry Fox as Edinburgh flatmates who find their just-moved-in fourth housemate (Keith Allen) mysteriously dead and conspire to dismember and dispose of his body to keep the huge stash of cash found in his room. Paranoia and suspicion send their plan spiralling out of control in a blacker-than-black comedy that becomes the most successful British-made film of 1995 and establishes Boyle as a name to watch.

They'll never take our freedom!
8th September 1995 Mel Gibson has a habit of making films that emphasise the perfidious English as invaders, conquerors and occupiers, and *Braveheart* is no exception. Still, it's impossible not to root for him as he daubs on the woad, twirls in his kilt and gives some rousing pre-battle pep talks as William Wallace, the Scottish freedom fighter who is ultimately betrayed. It's passionate, swashbuckling, and stunning to look at with a cast of sword-wielding thousands expertly choreographed in thrilling - and often gory - battle scenes.

Pocahontas
8th September 1995 Disney's *Pocahontas* is an idealised retelling of the relationship between the Native American princess and English settler Captain John Smith. Glen Keane, the animator responsible for drawing Ariel in *The Little Mermaid,* is drafted in to create the face of Pocahontas and uses two of her descendants as blueprints with further inspiration provided by supermodels such as Naomi Campbell and Kate Moss.

Goldeneye
It's all change at MI6 when, after a six-year hiatus, Bond is back in *Goldeneye*, a suave, silly but enormously successful rebooted Bond for the '90s. Donning the well-worn tuxedo for the first time is the devilishly handsome Pierce Brosnan, who many believe revives Sean Connery's lethal charm. Judi Dench becomes the first woman in the role of M, and Samantha Bond is Miss Moneypenny although veteran cast member Desmond Llewelyn returns as gadget boffin, Q. In its first week, *Goldeneye* becomes the third most successful film in UK box office history.

Don't Forget Your Toothbrush
The final episode of Chris Evans' audacious, high-energy entertainment show *Don't Forget Your Toothbrush* airs on Channel 4, and, determined to go out on a high, studio contestants can play a game to win either a Ferrari 308 or a fish finger. Over two series, the show has a reputation for big prizes and memorable stunts. Celebrity guests from Cher to Tony ('We love you madly') Hadley take part in a head-to-head quiz about themselves with a selected superfan, and usually come out the loser.

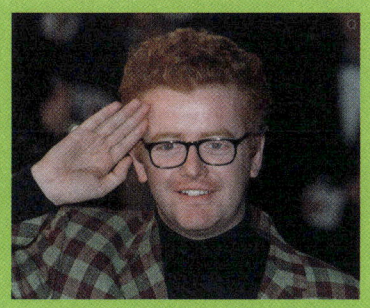

1995

Austen power
24th September heralds the beginning of BBC1's flagship costume drama, *Pride and Prejudice*, written by Andrew Davies. This new version is replete with gorgeous Regency frocks, stunning locations and a cast that includes Jennifer Ehle as Elizabeth Bennett and Colin Firth as the brooding Mr. Darcy. But what might Jane Austen have thought of the scene in episode 3 where Elizabeth bumps into Mr. Darcy just as he emerges from a quick swim in the lake at his country pile, Pemberley? With his dark locks dripping and wet shirt clinging to his well-defined torso, the nation's ladies collectively reach for the smelling salts, lest they be overcome.

Brad obsession
America's most-read magazine, *People* magazine (readership around 45 million) puts Brad Pitt, star of *Se7en* and *Twelve Monkeys* this year, on the cover of its 30th January issue with the headline 'The Sexiest Man Alive!' Who are we to argue?

Babe
15th December 1995 Co-producer and writer George Miller first fell in love with Dick King-Smith's delightful children's book, *The Sheep-Pig* back in the mid-1980s, but finally brings *Babe* to the screen this year, at a point when animatronics and other magical special effects are sufficiently developed to leave audiences almost believing they are truly watching animals talk. *Babe*, the tale of the little piglet with the tuft of hair who becomes a champion sheep herder is simply enchanting and leads many to contemplate vegetarianism as they leave the cinema.

Father Ted
Set on the fictional Craggy Island off the west coast of Ireland, sitcom *Father Ted* is sweet, surreal, and occasionally wicked, as three Roman Catholic priests, banished to this remote outpost for various misdemeanours, entertain us with their scrapes and misadventures. There is the titular Ted (Dermot Morgan), perpetually in deep water and frustrated by his idiotic housemates; wide-eyed innocent Father Dougal (Ardal O'Hanlon); and unrepentant alcoholic Father Jack (Frank Kelly), not forgetting their attentive housekeeper, Mrs Doyle (Pauline McLynn), compulsive feeder and server of tea, urging guests at the parochial home to, 'go on, go on, go on'. *Father Ted* goes on to inspire an annual Ted Fest festival in Ireland, and even a set of Irish stamps.

MUSIC

Richey Edwards disappears
1st February 1995 Richey Edwards of Welsh rock band Manic Street Preachers goes missing. His car is found abandoned two weeks later at a motorway services close to the Severn Bridge. His body is never found.

1995

REM's bad luck tour
1st January 1995 REM's very first world tour seems cursed. The misfortune begins in Lausanne, Switzerland, when drummer Bill Berry is forced to leave the stage with what he thinks is a severe migraine. Two days later he has major surgery to treat a brain aneurysm. In July, bassist Mike Mills has an emergency operation to remove an intestinal tumour, while two teenagers drown in the River Boyne while trying to reach the band's concert at Slane Castle. In August, Michael Stipe has hernia surgery prior to performing in Prague.

Jagged Little Pill
13th June 1995 A hallmark album for the 90s is released – Alanis Morisette's *Jagged Little Pill*. Bracketed with Tori Amos and Sheryl Crow, 21-year-old Alanis writes brutally frank material with a streak of venom. Topping the US charts in October, it becomes the third best selling album of the 90s at fifteen million sales, just behind Metallica's *Metallica* and Shania Twain's *Come On Over*.

Pulp faction
24th June 1995 Replacing the Stone Roses as headliners, Sheffield band Pulp light up Glastonbury with one of the festival's classic performances. Fronted by Jarvis Cocker, they've been together since 1983 without making much progress. With Britpop dawning, their blend of smart, acerbic lyrics and an updated glam rock sound is showcased brilliantly on their Mercury Prize-winning *Different Class* album.

Tommy Lee weds Baywatch star
14th February 1995 Tommy Lee of US hard rock band Motley Crüe marries actress Pamela Anderson of *Baywatch* fame on a Mexican beach.

Robson and Jerome
20th May 1995 Riding high with the first of three consecutive No. 1s are Robson Green and Jerome Flynn, stars of the ITV drama *Soldier, Soldier*. A young executive at RCA named Simon Cowell spotted them singing *Unchained Melody* in the show and offered them a recording deal, with Mike Stock and Matt Aitken. All three of their subsequent double-sided hits are songs at least 30 years old.

Robbie sacked
17th July 1995 Distraught Take That fans take in the news that youngest member Robbie Williams is leaving the band. His behaviour is starting to cause friction within the group and manager Nigel Martin-Smith has had enough. The group's latest No. 1 single *Never Forget* - produced by Jim Steinman - shows they can do perfectly well without him, while general opinion is that Robbie will struggle on his own. But is there a goodbye message to the fans in the song? How long can the Take That juggernaut last?

1995

Breaking Windows
24th August 1995 The Rolling Stones are paid a reported twelve million dollars by Microsoft for the use of *Start Me Up* in television ads promoting the new Windows 95 software.

Oh what a Knight
25th October 1995 Cliff Richard is knighted by the Queen at Buckingham Palace. He is the first figure from the British pop world to be so honoured.

MY FIRST 18 YEARS TOP 10 — 1995
1. **Wonderwall** *Oasis*
2. **Missing** *Everything but the Girl*
3. **Love Can Build a Bridge** *Cher, Chrissie Hynde ...*
4. **Back for Good** *Take That*
5. **Wake Up Boo** *The Boo Radleys*
6. **A Girl Like You** *Edwyn Collins*
7. **Boombastic** *Shaggy*
8. **Gangsta's Paradise** *Coolio*
9. **Disco 2000** *Pulp*
10. **Waterfalls** *TLC*

Which side are you on?
26th August 1995 The battle lines are drawn. On one side are Blur, Essex boys whose *Parklife* album is the last word in chirpy, knowing art school pop in the tradition of the Small Faces and the Kinks. On the other are Oasis, swaggering Manchester lads with chips on their shoulders whose songs on *Definitely Maybe* are anthemic and Beatle-like. Months of mutual sniping lead to the equivalent of a shoot-out at dawn: Blur issue *Country House* in the same week that Oasis release *Roll with It*. Blur's track goes straight in at No. 1 while *Roll with It* enters at No. 2. In the long term Oasis have the last laugh: *What's the Story, Morning Glory*, released in October, becomes the third best selling album of all time.

Beatles reunited
10th December 1995 At the end of a year that sees the release of *The Beatles Anthology* containing numerous unreleased studio and radio recordings, a tape of an unfinished John Lennon song, *Free as a Bird*, is completed by Paul, Ringo and George and reaches No. 2 in the UK.

Death of Dino
25th December 1995 Dean Martin dies at his home in Beverly Hills aged 78. His last years have been tough, burdened by divorce, poor health, the death of his son and a falling out with Frank Sinatra when he left a Rat Pack reunion tour. Though he disliked rock, Dean's easy-going, effortless vocal style was a model for Elvis, while his top-rated television show gave Americans their first glimpse of the Rolling Stones in 1964.

PHOTO CREDITS Copyright 2024, TDM Rights BV.
Photos: A John Gichigi - Getty Images / B Steve Morton Empics - PA Images - Getty Images / C John Gichigi - Getty Images / D Heritage Images - Hulton Archive - Getty Images / E Dave Benett - Hulton Archive - Getty Images / F European Community - / G Martin Keene - PA Images - Getty Images / H Tim Graham - Corbis Historical - Getty Images / I James D. Wilson - Hulton Archive - Getty Images / J Robert Lachman - Los Angeles Times - Getty Images / K Lee Celano - WireImage - Getty Images / L Archive Photos - Moviepix - Getty Images / M Hulton Archive - Getty Images / N Ronald Grant Archive - Mary Evans / O Ronald Grant Archive - Walt Disney - Mary Evans / P Sunset Boulevard - Corbis Historical - Getty Images / Q AF Archive - Graham Whitby Boot - Mary Evans / R Kennedy Miller Productions - Ronald Grant Archive - Mary Evans / S AF Archive - BBC - Mary Evans / T AF Archive - Channel 4 - Mary Evans / U Santiago Bueno - Sygma / V Steve Granitz - WireImage - Getty Images / W Tim Roney - Hulton Archive - Getty Images / X Avalon - Hulton Archive - Getty Images / Y Sunset Boulevard - Corbis Historical - Getty Images.

1996

MY FIRST 18 YEARS

SPORT

Super League launched
29th March 1996 A new era in rugby league begins with the first match in the Super League, a reconstituted elite league of England's top teams plus French side Paris Saint-Germain. With Sky Sports coverage and a switch from a winter to a summer season, the new league kicks off with all guns blazing as PSG beat Sheffield Eagles 30-24. St Helens finish the inaugural season as champions.

Germany on penalties - again
8th - 30th June 1996 The chant on every England fan's lips is 'football's coming home' as the 1996 European Championships - known as Euro 96 - are held for the first time in the country that gave football to the world. After an indifferent start, England's performances improve game on game, reaching a peak with a 4-1 demolition of the Netherlands. Negotiating a tricky quarter final with Spain, England and Germany play out a tense semi-final match. The match ends 1-1 but, once again, England suffer the heartbreak of a penalty shootout when Gareth Southgate misses his spot kick. Germany go on to win the tournament with a 2-1 victory over the Czech Republic.

United's double glory
11th May 1996 Manchester United's run of glory continues as they win the Premier League for the third time in four seasons and beat Liverpool 1-0 to win the FA Cup. In so doing they become the only team to date to win the famous 'double' of League title and FA Cup twice.

Dickie Bird retires
20th - 24th June 1996 The much loved Dickie Bird umpires his last Test match before retirement - England v India at Lord's - and receives a guard of honour from the players as he takes to the pitch.

Atlanta Olympics
19th July - 2nd August 1996 The Olympic Games in Atlanta, Georgia, produce a modest return for British athletes, the only gold coming in the men's coxless pairs for Matthew Pinsent and Steve Redgrave. Linford Christie's attempt to retain the 100 metres Olympic crown he won four years earlier is ruined by two false starts and disqualification in the final. The home star of the Games is Michael Johnson, winner of the 200 metres and 400 metres and Carl Lewis winning his fourth gold on the long jump. As expected, the US tops the medal table with 101 in total.

3 JAN 1996
The Motorola StarTAC goes on sale - the world's first flip mobile phone.

15 FEB 1996
Pembrokeshire beaches are heavily polluted after oil tanker runs aground.

21 MAR 1996
Death of Rev. Wilbert Awdry, creator of *Thomas the Tank Engine*.

1996

Frankie's magnificent seven
28th September 1996 UK-based Italian-born jockey Frankie Dettori - the reigning Champion Jockey - creates racing history by riding all seven winners in the British Festival of Racing at Ascot. Dettori's achievement is said to have lost the UK betting industry around £40 million.

Last *Titanic* passenger
14th February 1996 Eva Hart, the last living survivor of the *Titanic* maritime disaster in 1912, dies at the age of 91.

Dunblane massacre
13th March 1996 One-time Scout leader Thomas Hamilton enters a primary school in Dunblane near Stirling, Scotland, and shoots dead sixteen children and a teacher before turning one of his four guns on himself. The horrific events shock the world and lead to immediate calls to make possession of handguns illegal in the UK. It emerges that Hamilton had grievances against individuals and local organisations over rumours about his inappropriate behaviour towards young boys, and that he blamed them for the loss of his business in 1993. It also emerges that his guns were legally held.

Champion Hill
13th October 1996 In Formula One's 50th season, Damon Hill's win in the Japanese Grand Prix in Suzuka secures him his first and only Drivers' World Championship. In December he becomes the first sports star since Henry Cooper to win the BBC Sports Personality of the Year twice.

Bacardi Breezer

DOMESTIC NEWS

IRA breaks its ceasefire
9th February 1996 A huge truck bomb explodes in South Quays, Docklands, kills two and signals the end of the Provisional IRA ceasefire after seventeen months. Damage to the area is estimated at £150 million. Nine days later a bus bomb detonates prematurely and kills an IRA operative in Aldwych, London.

3 APR 1996
In the US Theodore Kaczynski the 'UnaBomber' is arrested.

18 MAY 1996
Dublin-born singer Aimear Quinn wins the 41st Eurovision Song Contest.

15 JUN 1996
Ella Fitzgerald, jazz vocalist and song interpreter supreme, dies at the age of 79.

1996

Legoland opens
17th March 1996 Legoland Windsor opens, becoming the second Legoland theme park in Europe.

Mad cow disease
20th March 1996 The crisis over 'mad cow disease' or bovine spongiform encephalopathy (BSE), which has been growing since the late 1980s, takes another turn as Secretary of State for Health Stephen Dorrell announces that eating BSE-infected beef can cause the fatal Creutzfeld-Jakobs disease (vCJD) in humans. The issue is linked to the practice of feeding meat and bone meal to cattle, which was widespread in UK farming prior to being banned in 1988. European Union, Japanese and US bans follow on importing UK beef. At home, beef sales drop by nearly a third. The cost to the UK economy of the whole crisis is estimated at approaching £4 billion.

Goodbye, Christopher Robin
20th - 23rd April 1996 Two major figures of children's literature pass away within days of each other - Christopher Robin Milne (76), the boy hero of his father's *Winnie the Pooh* books, and P. J. Travers (97), creator of *Mary Poppins*.

Dome site selected
19th June 1996 On the south side of the River Thames from the Isle of Dogs, the Greenwich peninsula is chosen as the site for the construction of the new Millennium Dome, set to open at the start of 2000. No specific use for the building has yet been determined.

Hello Dolly
5th July 1996 Although the news does not emerge until February 1997, the first mammal to be cloned from an adult cell is born at the Roslin Institute, a research department of Edinburgh University. The animal in question is a sheep named Dolly after singer Dolly Parton. Dolly began life as a single cell in a test tube from the mammary gland of a Finn Dorset sheep and an egg cell from a Scottish Blackface sheep. The embryo was then transferred to a surrogate mother. Dolly's birth represents a landmark on the road to producing genetically modified livestock. She lives for six years.

Severn wonder
5th June 1996 A second toll bridge over the River Severn is opened by Prince Charles, carrying the M4 motorway from England to Wales. Unlike the first Severn crossing, opened in 1966 and now part of the M48, it is a cable-stayed bridge rather than a suspension bridge and bears six lanes of traffic rather than four.

4 JUL 1996
Hotmail is launched as a free email service.

21 AUG 1996
The reconstructed Globe Theatre opens on the south bank of the Thames.

1 SEP 1996
David Beckham makes his England debut in World Cup qualifier versus Moldova.

1996

Ossie Clark murdered
6th August 1996 Fashion designer Ossie Clark is stabbed to death by his lover Diego Cogolato, who is later convicted of manslaughter and jailed for six years.

'House of horrors' torn down
12th October 1996 Amid tight security to deter souvenir hunters, the house of serial killers Fred and Rose West - 25 Cromwell Street, Gloucester - is demolished and all its contents destroyed.

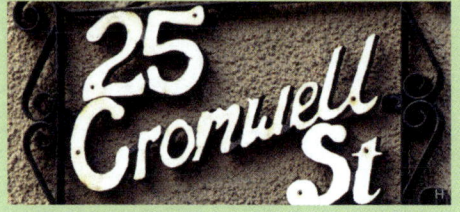

Charles and Diana divorce
28th August 1996 The divorce agreed between Prince Charles and Princess Diana is now final. Diana will continue to hold the title of Princess of Wales but will lose the title of Her Royal Highness. The divorce follows that of Charles's brother Andrew, Duke of York, from Sarah, Duchess of York, in May.

Education, education, education
1st October 1996 Labour leader Tony Blair makes one of the most memorable speeches of his political career, telling his party's conference at Blackpool that his three main priorities once elected will be 'education, education, education'.

McAlpine defects
6th October 1996 A former adviser to Margaret Thatcher, Conservative Party treasurer and a key party fundraiser, construction magnate Lord McAlpine, defects from the Tories to James Goldsmith's Referendum Party, which is campaigning for a referendum on the UK's continued membership of the European Union.

ROYALTY & POLITICS

Scargill's new party
13th January 1996 Appalled by the reformist tendencies of the Labour Party's new leadership, National Union of Miners leader Arthur Scargill announces the formation of a Socialist Labour Party to fight the next election on an unapologetically left-wing platform.

FOREIGN NEWS

Mitterrand dies
8th January 1996 Former President of France François Mitterrand dies of prostate cancer just six months after leaving office, aged 79.

22 OCT 1996
Chelsea FC executive Matthew Harding among five killed in helicopter crash.

5 NOV 1996
Bill Clinton re-elected as US President.

5 DEC 1996
NASA's first Mars Rover is launched.

1996

ANC in control
9th May 1996 In South Africa, the National Party withdraws from the coalition government it formed with the African National Congress, leaving the ANC to govern alone.

A gorilla's tenderness
16th August 1996 A three-year-old boy falls 24 feet into the gorilla enclosure at Brookfield Zoo, Chicago. Astonished visitors watch as a female gorilla named Binti Jua sits and tends to the unconscious boy until he is rescued.

Tasmanian devil
28th April 1996 The deadliest massacre in Australian history occurs in the tourist centre of Port Arthur, Tasmania, where Martin Bryant kills 35 people and wounds 23 others in a shooting spree with two semi-automatic rifles. The murders lead to an instant tightening of Australian gun laws.

Olympic Games attack
27th July 1996 A pipe bomb attack on visitors gathering at the Centennial Olympic Park in Atlanta, Georgia, kills one and injures over a hundred others. The park was being evacuated when the bomb exploded. When the perpetrator, anti-government activist Michael udolph, is arrested in 2003 he is charged with the Atlanta bombing and three subsequent bomb attacks.

Whitewater fraud
28th May 1996 James and Susan McDougal and Arkansas Governor Jim Guy Tucker are convicted of fraud relating to a $200,000 housing development near the Whitewater

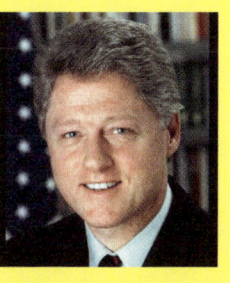

rapids in Arkansas. Public and media interest in the case centers on the investment made in the project by the current US President Bill Clinton during his own spell as Arkansas Governor. Although they are never prosecuted, the doggedness of lawyer Kenneth Starr in pursuing the Clintons will lead to revelations about a much more damaging affair - the President's dalliance or otherwise with White House intern Monica Lewinsky.

Yeltsin re-elected
3rd July 1996 Despite a series of health scares and an undisclosed heart attack that leaves him very close to death, Boris Yeltsin defeats his Communist Party challenger Gennady Zyuganov and is re-elected as President of Russia.

1996

Taliban takeover

27th September 1996 Radical Islamic group the Taliban reinforce their hold on Afghanistan by ousting President Burhanuddin Rabbani, executing former leader Mohammad Najibullah and capturing the capital city of Kabul. They are also giving refuge to members of the Al-Qaeda terrorist network, notably Osama Bin Laden, who just weeks before had issued a chilling declaration of Jihad 'on the Americans occupying the Country of the Two Sacred Places', meaning the US military presence in his homeland of Saudi Arabia.

O. J. back in court

23rd October 1996 O. J. Simpson enters court in California accused of the 'wrongful death' of his wife Nicole and her friend Ron Goldman. Although cleared of the charges in 1995 (photo), he is now the subject of a civil suit brought by her parents and Goldman's father. The trial lasts until February 1997.

Toy Story

The world's first computer-generated animation, *Toy Story*, opens at British cinemas on 22 March. Created by Pixar Animations and directed by John Lasseter, his first Pixar short, *Tin Toy*, which won an Oscar in 1988, caught the attention of Disney, who eventually asked Pixar to make a feature-length film on the subject of toys. The result is a film that is perfect in almost every way, with undeniable cross-generational appeal. Puppet cowboy Woody (voiced by Tom Hanks) and Buzz Lightyear (Tim Allen), the space toy who usurps Woody in his owner's affection, soon take their place among the ranks of much-loved cartoon characters, kicking off a franchise which is one of the most successful in cinema history. Animation will never be the same again.

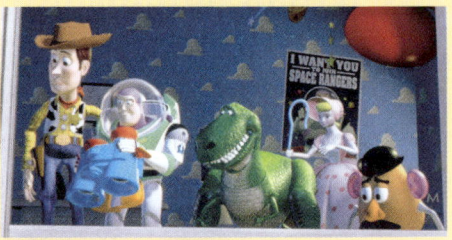

Our Friends in the North

Landmark dramas don't get much better than *Our Friends in the North*, which begins on BBC2 on 15th January. Peter Flannery's sprawling, state-of-the-nation saga (originating from his play for the RSC) traces the lives of four friends from the north-east through thirty years from 1964 to the present day, with major, real-life events such as the miners' strike punctuating their personal stories. The four leads - Mark Strong, Gina McKee, Christopher Eccleston, and a certain Daniel Craig - all go on to become major TV and feature film stars.

Ballykissangel

The arrival of a Manchester priest in a small, rural Irish community is the premise for *Ballykissangel*, which begins on 11th February on BBC1. Starring Stephen Tomkinson as Father Peter Clifford and Dervla Kirwan as pub landlady Assumpta Fitzgerald, *Ballykissangel* runs for five series and is watched by ten million at the peak of its popularity.

1996

Sense and Sensibility

23rd February 1996 The 1990s taste for all things Jane Austen continues with this film adaptation of her 1811 novel, *Sense and Sensibility*. Emma Thompson writes the screenplay and stars as Elinor Dashwood, elder sister to Kate Winslet's passionate Marianne, while their male co-stars are Hugh Grant, Greg Wise as the dashing yet despicable Willoughby and Alan Rickman, playing the wise and loyal Colonel Brandon. A delight from beginning to end, *Sense and Sensibility* is a box office success and wins Thompson an Oscar for Best Adapted Screenplay.

Trainspotting

Brutal, squalid, and boisterously funny, Danny Boyle's film version of Irvine Welsh's 1993 novel *Trainspotting* opens at cinemas on 26th February. Skilfully treading a fine line between the glorification and condemnation of heroin use, drugs may be the running thread through *Trainspotting*, but it's the characters that are etched into cinematic legend. Ewan McGregor loses two stone to play addict Renton and even considers (but decides against) trying heroin to better understand the character. Robert Carlyle is uncertain he has the right physique to play psychopathic loose cannon Begbie. Joining them are Ewen Bremner as likeable loser Spud, Jonny Lee Miller as Sick Boy and Kelly McDonald (in her first role) as schoolgirl seductress Diane. All leer out of the iconic posters plastered around the UK, a rogues' gallery of misfits from one of Britain's finest, era-defining films.

Ladette culture

As the decade's lad culture reaches its pinnacle, 1990s women refuse to take a back seat and the 'ladette' is born. *The Girlie Show* and its four rookie presenters, including Sara Cox in her first TV role, takes the ladette concept and runs with it in a programme first shown on 26th January on Channel 4. *The Girlie Show* follows in the edgy tradition of *The Word*, doing its best to court controversy with segments like 'Wanker of the Week' and 'Naked Apes' featuring a group of Sunderland lads, getting up to various lager-fuelled stunts. *The Girlie Show* feels amateurish and often cringeworthy but captures a moment and is notable for an early TV appearance of a group of females who really can be said to represent Girl Power - the Spice Girls.

TFI Friday

Court jester Chris Evans seems unstoppable and after skipping from *The Big Breakfast* to *Don't Forget Your Toothbrush*, his next project is *TFI Friday*, made by his own company, Ginger Productions. Its matey vibe, in-jokes and who's who of music special guests tap into the Cool Britannia zeitgeist. The audience spend most of the time in the studio bar where celebs also hang out in between performing or chatting to Chris. Habitual swearing by guests lands the show in trouble. But a little notoriety goes a long way, and *TFI Friday* with its Britpop tunes and laddish high jinks makes every night in feel like a night out.

1996

The English Patient
15th November 1996 The English Patient is an epic wartime romance adapted from the novel by Michael Ondaatje. Ralph Fiennes is the patient of the title, an air crash survivor burned beyond recognition and nursed by Nina (Juliette Binoche) as he slowly pieces together the story of his doomed love affair with Katharine Clifton (Kristin Scott Thomas). *The English Patient* is a triumph, both critically and commercially, and dominates the 1997 Oscars by winning nine awards in total.

Changing Rooms
Stippling, stencilling, and other paint effect terms all become part of daily parlance after *Changing Rooms* begins on BBC2 on 4th September. Friends or neighbours swap homes for a couple of days and with the help of a top interior designer and ever-helpful chippy, 'Handy' Andy, give a room a complete makeover, hoping the transformation will delight rather than displease. It's edge of your seat stuff.

MUSIC

Body count
We begin to spend more time in morgues than is probably acceptable when *Silent Witness* begins on BBC1 on 21st February. Differing from usual crime dramas, it follows forensic pathologist Dr Sam Ryan (Amanda Burton) and her team who are the key to solving cases. Dr Ryan's manner is calm and unruffled as she goes about carving up cadavers hoping they'll spill the beans along with their brains and intestines.

Take That split
12th February 1996 Confirmed today is the news that Take That are disbanding. For their last single they choose the Bee Gees' *How Deep is Your Love*, which duly tops the UK chart during March. Their parting gift to their fans is a *Greatest Hits* album.

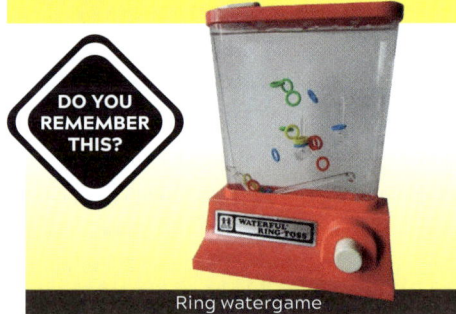

Ring watergame

Fargo
Kidnaps rarely go to plan in films, but none go quite as horribly wrong as the one in *Fargo*, Joel and Ethan Coen's wickedly funny story of deception fraud, and murder in snow-covered Minnesota. Mild-mannered car salesman Jerry Lundergaard (William H. Macey) attempts to clear his debts by arranging the abduction of his wife by two thugs and it's the town's heavily pregnant police chief, Marge Gunderson (Frances McDormand) who has to sort out the mess.

1996

All spice
When 1996 dawns, the Spice Girls are virtually unknown and are yet to have a single released. Seven months later they are not just a pop phenomenon but a national obsession, thanks not only to clever marketing and media management but also to a genuinely new and assertive spirit emerging in the UK. With their distinct personalities, images and nicknames, Geri, Victoria, Emma, Mel B and Mel C represent a cross-section of young British womanhood that female fans respond to. And the music's not bad, either: mostly self-written soul-based tracks geared to the dance floor. For the moment, this really is a Spice World and the rest of us just happen to live in it.

Jarvis objects
19th February 1996 Notorious for moments of unscheduled chaos, the 1996 BRIT Awards produce another. Enraged by Jackson's self-depiction as a Christ-like figure while performing *Earth Song*, Jarvis Cocker of Pulp jumps on to the stage to protest. Much of the incident is missed by the television cameras.

Collins leaves Genesis
28th March 1996 Phil Collins leaves Genesis to prioritise his solo career. Mike Rutherford and Tony Banks decide to continue but wait a whole year before announcing his replacement, Ray Wilson from Stiltskin.

Flint makes fire
30th March 1996 At No. 1 is the most disturbing single of the year, *Firestarter* by Essex rap band the Prodigy. Filmed in a disused tube tunnel, its video features Keith Flint dancing and snarling at the camera and sends the tabloid press into fits of rage for supposedly encouraging arson.

Pumpkin deaths
11th May 1996 Chicago rock band Smashing Pumpkins abandon their UK and Irish tour when a seventeen-year-old fan, Bernadette O'Brien, is fatally crushed during a crowd surfing incident at a Dublin concert. More tragedy follows in July when keyboard player Jonathan Melvoin dies from a heroin overdose.

Older and wiser
13th May 1996 Smarting from his ill-fated legal action against Sony, George Michael releases *Older*, his first album for Virgin. The clue is in the title: this is George as a mature and explorative artist, tackling big emotional themes and newly influenced by Brazilian music. Although he has not yet come out as gay, the hints are there in the two No. 1 singles extracted from the album, *Fastlove* and *Jesus to a Child*.

1996

Football's coming home
8th June 1996 As UEFA's Euro '96 tournament begins on home soil, England's hopes of progress are high. But it's not the official theme song, *We're in this Together* by Simply Red, that helps sweep the team to the semi-final. The song that captures the nation's mood is *Three Lions* by comedians Frank Skinner and David Baddiel and Ian Broudie of the Lightning Seeds. Though England's run ends in defeat to eventual winners Germany, the song reaches No. 1 and will be revived during every subsequent Euros and World Cup, as England's 'thirty years of hurt' without a trophy extends to 56 and counting.

Oasis at Knebworth
10th August 1996 Oasis fever reaches a new high point as the band play two outdoor concerts to over 350,000 at Knebworth House in Hertfordshire. A further two million apply for tickets but are disappointed.

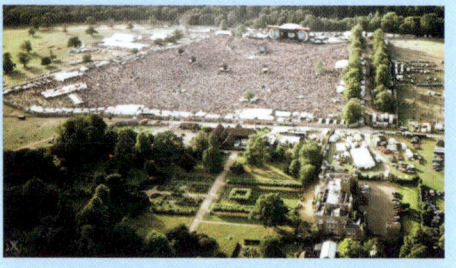

MY FIRST 18 YEARS — TOP 10 — 1996
1. **Don't Look Back in Anger** Oasis
2. **A Design for Life** Manic Street Preachers
3. **Killing Me Softly** The Fugees
4. **Macarena** Los Del Rio
5. **Stupid Girl** Garbage
6. **Virtual Insanity** Jamiroquai
7. **Lifted** Lighthouse Family
8. **How Bizarre** OMC
9. **Say You'll Be There** The Spice Girls
10. **You're Gorgeous** Babybird

Tupac murdered
7th September 1996 Leading rapper Tupac Shakur is shot in a drive-by shooting in Las Vegas. He dies six days later. No arrest is made until 2023.

Last of the Roses?
29th October 1996 Two bands suffer personnel upheavals on the same day. In the US, guitarist Slash departs Guns N' Roses via a fax message to MTV. In the UK, Ian Brown and Gary Mounfield leave the Stone Roses, effectively dissolving the band altogether.

A knight to remember
12th November 1996 Long-time Beatles producer George Martin is knighted for services to the music industry at a Buckingham Palace investiture.

1997

MY FIRST 18 YEARS

SPORT

FA Cup near miss, United glory
In the FA Cup, Division Two club Chesterfield make it all the way to the semi-final before losing to Middlesbrough 3-0. Chelsea, managed by ex-Netherlands star Ruud Gullit, beat Middlesbrough 2-0 to win the club's first trophy for a quarter of a century. Other major football stories of 1997 include Harrods boss Mohamed Al Fayed's purchase of Fulham, Eric Cantona's surprise retirement at 31, and an unforgettably close finish to the season as Manchester United peg back Newcastle's seemingly unstoppable race to the title and Toon manager Kevin Keegan loses his cool in an after-match rant against Alex Ferguson. Meanwhile, Scotland's top football clubs vote to create an elite league on the English model, to be called the Scottish Premier League and set to start in 1998.

Denis Compton RIP
23rd April 1997 A hero of English cricket's great post-war era, the debonair Denis Compton dies aged 78. He spent his whole club career with Middlesex and played in 78 Test matches, achieving a batting average of just over 50 per innings. He also played professionally for Arsenal, winning the league title with them in 1948 and the FA Cup in 1950.

A bout with bite
1st July 1997 In the aftermath of Evander Holyfield's defeat of Mike Tyson in June, in which Tyson was disqualified for biting each of Holyfield's ears, the Nevada Athletic Commission suspends Tyson, withholds his $20 million fee and fines him $3 million.

Grand National abandoned
5th April 1997 The showcase Grand National meeting at Aintree is abandoned after credible bomb threats are received just an hour before the race is due to be run. For the first time ever, the race is run on the following Monday. The winner is Lord Gyllene ridden by Tony Dobbin.

Breaking new grounds
30th July 1997 Sunderland FC's new home, the Stadium of Light, is the first of several new stadia opened in time for the new football season. It is built on the site of Monkwearmouth Colliery, which closed in 1993. Derby County's new ground at Pride Park opens on 14th August, the same day that Sir Stanley Matthews opens Stoke City's new ground, the Britannia Stadium, and the Deputy Prime Minister declares Bolton Wanderers' new Reebok Stadium open for business.

9 JAN 1997
Volkswagen settle lawsuit brought by General Motors over alleged espionage.

19 FEB 1997
Death of Chinese leader Deng Xiaoping aged 92.

26 MAR 1997
Mass suicide in San Diego by 39 members of religious cult Heaven's Gate.

1997

Villeneuve is champion
26th October 1997 Jacques Villeneuve becomes the first Canadian to win the Formula One championship with Williams, securing the title in the last race of the season in Spain while rival Michael Schumacher is penalised for deliberately ramming Villeneuve's car.

UUP agree to talks
17th September 1997 A breakthrough comes in the peace process in Northern Ireland. The Ulster Unionists, representing a large swathe of loyalist opinion, agree to take part in talks that include Sinn Fein.

Louise Woodward case
31st October 1997 After a high-profile trial that makes headlines all around the world, eighteen-year-old British au pair Louise Woodward is convicted by a Massachusetts court of murdering Matthew Eappen, an eight-month-old boy she was caring for. Two weeks later her conviction is reduced on appeal to manslaughter, and she is released having served nearly a year in prison.

DOMESTIC NEWS

Channel 5 launches
30th March 1997 Channel 5 is launched, the fifth terrestrial television channel in the UK. The first programme on air is *Family Affairs*, a new soap opera.

Hague marries
19th December 1997 New Conservative Party leader William Hague marries Ffion Jenkins, whom he met while serving as Secretary of State for Wales.

Wild about Harry
26th June 1997 Harry Potter and the Philosopher's Stone by unknown children's author J. K. Rowling is published by Bloomsbury with an initial print run of just 500 copies in hardback. The book's reputation grows steadily through word of mouth, positive reviews and winning the Smarties Book Prize.

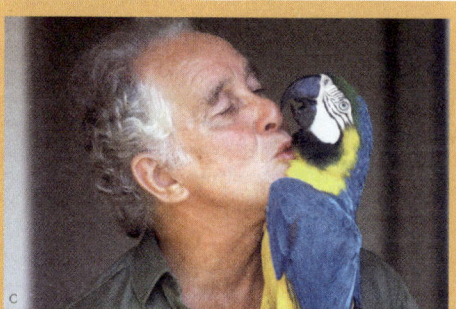

Biggs stays in Brazil
12th November 1997 The Supreme Court in Brazil refuses the UK's request to extradite the Great Train Robber Ronnie Biggs, who escaped from Wandsworth Prison in 1965. He has been living in Brazil since 1970.

Halifax makes history
2nd June 1997 The UK's biggest building society, the Halifax, is floated on the London Stock Exchange. Now officially a bank, its 7.5 million account holders become shareholders.

---

7 APR 1997
Steve Irwin's *The Crocodile Hunter* premieres.

27 MAY 1997
NATO-Russian co-operation charter signed in Paris.

10 JUN 1997
Pol Pot orders murder of his defence minister and eleven family members.

1997

Britannia leaves the waves
11th December 1997 The Royal Yacht *Britannia* is formally decommissioned in a moving ceremony that brings the Queen to tears. Having transported the royal family to events and on tours since 1954, the yacht is now ageing and is too expensive to refit. Soon after coming to power, the new Labour government decides that a replacement yacht will not be provided out of the public purse.

Labour landslide
1st May 1997 Although Tony Blair's victory in the General Election is widely expected, its scale is stunning. The Labour Party win 418 seats, giving it a majority of 179, while the number of Conservative held seats reduces from 343 to 165. After eighteen years in government, the Conservatives lose seats in constituencies that have been 'true blue' for decades, including those of seven former Cabinet ministers and the man tipped to take over from John Major, Michael Portillo. The Conservatives lose all their seats in Scotland and Wales, while the Liberal Democrats increase their tally in the Commons from 28 seats to 46. The next day, John Major resigns as Conservative Party leader while Tony Blair enters 10 Downing Street as Prime Minister.

ROYALTY & POLITICS

Labour's first measures
2nd July 1997 The new Labour government's first budget, presented to the House of Commons by Chancellor of the Exchequer Gordon Brown, focuses on boosting funding for education, healthcare and getting the long-term unemployed back into work.

Wales says 'yes' (just)
18th September 1997 A referendum in Wales on devolution produces a much closer result than that achieved by the 'yes' campaign in Scotland. Just over 50 per cent of those voting opt for the creation of a Welsh Assembly - enough to regard the 'yes' vote as carried. The Wales Act 1998 is introduced to prepare the way for elections to the new Assembly in 1999.

Scotland says 'yes'
11th September 1997 A referendum in Scotland on devolution of some powers from Westminster to a Scottish Parliament delivers a firm 'yes' vote. The final figures are 74.29 per cent for yes, 25.71 per cent for no. A second question on whether such a Parliament should have tax-raising powers is backed by a 63.48 per cent 'yes' vote.

---

2 JUL 1997 All-American movie great James Stewart dies aged 89.

29 AUG 1997 Netflix is founded as an online DVD rental service in California.

17 SEP 1997 A draft international landmines treaty is rejected by the US.

1997

Diana is dead
31st August 1997 The UK wakes to news of the deaths of Diana, Princess of Wales, and her companion Dodi Fayed in a high-speed car accident in a road tunnel in Paris. The focus of much media attention after their relationship blossomed during the summer, the couple were escaping photographers on scooters after leaving the Ritz in a car driven by chauffeur Henri Paul, who is also killed. Prince Charles flies to France to bring Diana's body home and normal life in the UK seems to come to a halt. An extraordinary week follows, as the flowers mount at Kensington Palace and along the Mall and criticism of the royal family's response to Diana's death grows. Guided by advice from Tony Blair and his media team, the Queen returns from Balmoral to Buckingham Palace and makes a live television tribute to Diana on the evening of 5th September.

'Goodbye, England's rose'
6th September 1997 Diana, Princess of Wales, is given a state funeral in all but name with a service at Westminster Abbey. Prince Charles, Prince Philip and Diana's brother Charles Spencer join Princes William and Harry in following the coffin on foot from Buckingham Palace to the Abbey. Charles Spencer delivers a powerful eulogy that includes a scorching rebuke of her treatment by the royal family and the media which provokes a wave of applause in the Abbey that spreads to the thousands in the streets and parks of central London. Thousands more line the route as the funeral cortege makes its way to Northamptonshire and a private burial at Althorp, the Spencers' childhood home.

 FOREIGN NEWS

Looted art
27th January 1997 Research published today shows that museums in France own almost two thousand works of art stolen by the Nazis, mostly from Jewish owners, during the German Occupation. Some are even thought to be on display in the Louvre. The question of rightful ownership and the right to restitution becomes a huge issue within the international art world during the year.

Hong Kong handover
1st July 1997 After several years of negotiations and an attempt by Governor Chris Patten to strengthen democracy in Hong Kong, control of the colony is passed from the UK to the People's Republic of China. The handover of sovereignty is completed with due ceremony after the end of the 99-year lease.

7 OCT 1997
All-party talks on Northern Ireland begin.

1 NOV 1997
Titanic receives its world premiere at the Tokyo International Film Festival.

11 DEC 1997
Kyoto Protocol commits signatory nations to limiting greenhouse gases.

1997

Comet Hale-Bopp
1st March 1997 Anyone looking at the starry sky in the spring will see a large and remarkably bright comet with the naked eye. Hale-Bopp, named after its two discoverers, measures 40 kilometers in diameter and provides quite a spectacle at night.

Che is buried
13th July 1997 The remains of revolutionary leader Che Guevara are returned to Cuba from Bolivia, where he was executed in 1967, for burial with full military honours. A mausoleum has been built for him in Santa Clara, where he led his forces to victory during the Cuban revolution in 1958.

Versace murdered
15th July 1997 The great Italian fashion designer Gianni Versace is shot dead outside his home in Miami Beach, Florida. He was 50 years old. His killer Andrew Cunanan commits suicide before police find him. Versace's funeral is held at Milan Cathedral on 22nd July and attended by over 2,000 people including his close friends Elton John and Diana, Princess of Wales.

O. J. trial decision
5th February 1997 The civil law case against O. J. Simpson over the 'wrongful death' of his wife Nicole Brown Simpson and Ronald Goldman, who were murdered in 1994, is finally concluded. The jury finds Simpson responsible for both deaths and awards the families of the victims $33.5 million in damages.

Land mine treaty
3rd December 1997 A treaty agreeing the prohibition of the manufacture and use of anti-personnel land mines is signed by 121 countries at a conference in the Canadian capital of Ottawa. Notable omissions from the list of signatories are the US, China, Russia and South Korea. The campaign against land mines was a cause especially close to the heart of the late Diana, Princess of Wales, who did much to bring it to international attention.

1997

Google registered
15th September 1997 In 1996, Stanford students Larry Page and Sergey Brin devise a system to make searching the Internet easier. You enter a search term on their website, after which servers scour the Internet looking for web pages that match your search query. The results then appear neatly arranged, one below the other, on the screen. On this day, Page and Brin register the domain name google.com for their search engine, after the word 'googol' for a number composed of one followed by 100 zeros.

Kyoto Treaty
11th December 1997 In the Japanese city of Kyoto, 84 countries conclude a major climate agreement. The Kyoto Treaty stipulates that industrialised countries will significantly reduce emissions of harmful greenhouse gases that contribute to global warming.

ENTERTAINMENT

Scream
Slasher movie *Scream*, directed by Wes Craven, is released on 31st January. Unusually for a horror film it features several well-known stars including Courtney Cox and Drew Barrymore, which help to make it a screaming success and to revive what many thought a dying genre. Six *Scream* films follow this original.

Spicegirls in a Spiceworld
A year and a half after they burst onto the music scene with *Wannabe*, the Spice Girls star in their own movie, the comic romp *Spiceworld*, which opens on Boxing Day.

Show me the money
When slick sports agent Jerry McGuire has an existential crisis and writes a polemic to his colleagues about the exploitative nature of the business, he finds himself fired and left with just one client: a washed-up footballer (Cuba Gooding Junior) with an inflated ego whose pay demands outweigh his current form. Only a lone member of staff, single mother Dorothy (Renee Zellweger) agrees to join him in setting up his own venture. Cruise is at his best in a role that requires him to fit in but break free of the machismo of sports management, while Zellweger, who nobody has heard of before, is charming as his love interest, especially as she's given that killer line, 'You had me at hello.' Jonathan Lipnicki is cute as a button as her son Ray and Gooding Junior wins an Oscar for Best Supporting Actor as Rod Stillwell. A hugely likeable and heartwarming film, even if American football leaves you cold.

1997

This Life
This Life, the BBC2 drama about four law graduates sharing a London house (and each other's beds) first aired in 1996 yet passed largely under the radar. But a new series this year warrants a repeat of the first, beginning 2nd January, and suddenly, the antics of Miles, Egg, Millie, Anna and co have us hooked. *This Life* reflects twentysomething life in the big smoke in all its messy, messed-up glamour and grunginess. They sleep around, have massive hangovers, and take ecstasy or cocaine in between arguing over the phone bill and losing the house keys - all part and parcel of 'this life'. Soundtracked with music from Blur, Oasis and Elastica, this is water cooler TV for the Cool Britannia brigade.

Mrs Brown
5th September 1997 Judi Dench takes on the role of the grieving, reclusive Queen Victoria in *Mrs Brown*, her first lead film role, despite decades of television and stage credits. Comedian Billy Connolly is cast as John Brown, her Highland ghillie, aggressively loyal to his mistress with a brusqueness that makes him enemies among courtiers, royal family members and the press. Dench receives a Best Actress Oscar nomination and wins a BAFTA and Golden Globe for her subtle portrayal of the imperious yet vulnerable monarch.

L.A. Confidential
31st October 1997 A stylish homage to film noir, *L.A. Confidential* is a sizzling tale of bent cops, mobsters, and classy dames. Director Curtis Hanson chooses two relatively unknown Australians - Guy Pearce and Russell Crowe - to star in this adaptation of James Ellroy's 1990 novel, alongside Kevin Spacey and Kim Basinger.

Eh-oh! It's the Teletubbies
31st March 1997 Tinky-Winky, Dipsy, Laa-laa and Po, aka the *Teletubbies*, wave at us from Teletubbieland on BBC2. There has never been anything quite like them. Four brightly coloured, human-sized, toddler-shaped creatures with antennae and a liking for pink custard, they speak in gibberish, have screens in their bellies and clean up any mess with the help of a vacuum cleaner called Noo-noo. Teletubbieland is a tranquil green land of rolling hillocks where rabbits hop around peacefully, as the Teletubbies potter. Dipsy has a hat, Po a scooter, Laa-Laa an orange ball, and the metrosexual Tiny-Winky has a handbag. All their antics take place under a shining sun with the face of a delighted, chuckling baby. The *Teletubbies* are HUGE and soft toys are in short supply this Christmas when everybody wants one to help them go 'Tubby-bye-bye'.

Yeh, baby!
Shamelessly lampooning the spy thrillers of the 1960s, Mike Myers is *Austin Powers, International Man of Mystery*, a toothy secret agent and serial lothario, who, cryogenically frozen, brings swinging London to the present day as he tries to save the world from his arch-nemesis, Dr Evil (also Myers). Myers created Powers in tribute to his late, British-born father, who he says introduced him to 'James Bond, Peter Sellers, The Beatles, The Goodies, Peter Cook and Dudley Moore'.

1997

Liam and Patsy wed
7th April 1997 Liam Gallagher marries actress Patsy Kensit at Westminster Register Office.

Ground Force
19th September 1997 After the success of home makeover show *Changing Rooms*, BBC2 executives figure that garden make-overs might prove just as popular. And they do, with *Ground Force* deploying a crack team of gardening wizards who descend on a house for the weekend, while the unsuspecting owner is bundled away for the duration. The result? Tears of gratitude and gasps of appreciation at the end of the show, as cracked patios give way to smart decking, and weed-choked beds are transformed into blooming beautiful borders.

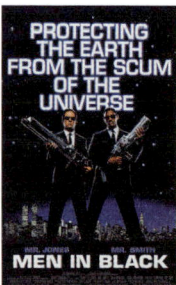

Men in Black
1st August 1997 Agent J and Agent K (Will Smith and a deadpan Tommy Lee Jones), dressed in shades and sharp suits, are the *Men in Black*, part of an ultra-secret government organisation responsible for hunting down earth-dwelling aliens. Aliens employ all kinds of trickery to disguise their true selves, but if the public do witness extra-terrestrial activity, the MIB deploy neutralisers to wipe their memory instantly. Accompanied by a hit single courtesy of Smith, *Men in Black* is the megahit of the summer.

Gotcha Tamagotchi
Tamagotchi, little egg-shaped digital pets, are the latest fad from Japan and become the best-selling toy this Christmas. Requiring some responsibility on the part of the owner, it's important to keep an eye on your Tamagotchi's health, food, activities and behaviour to ensure it thrives. Whether or not a Tamagotchi survives until next Christmas is an excellent litmus test to see if your offspring really will look after that puppy they've been pleading for.

Titanic
James Cameron's film about the sinking of the *Titanic* cost a whopping $200 million and is filmmaking on an epic scale. The result is a movie layered with romance, drama, tragedy, stunning period details and awesome special effects. The pairing of Leonardo di Caprio and Kate Winslet as Jack and Rose, the couple who find love across the class divide, creates some of cinema's most memorable moments and by the end, we're so carried away with the story, as Jack slips into the icy depths of the Atlantic we want to reach across and pull him back out again.

MUSIC

Harvey sacked
18th February 1997 Brian Harvey is sacked from East 17 after defending the drug ecstasy in a radio interview. With their chart fortunes faltering, he is invited back during 1998 when the group relaunches itself as E-17.

1997

The Full Monty
In 1996, *Brassed Off*, a film about a Yorkshire colliery band, took the decline of the mining industry as its backdrop. This year's *The Full Monty*, released 29th August, has as its setting Sheffield steel. On the dole, and losing hope, ex-steel worker Gaz (Robert Carlyle) has a money-making idea and auditions a motley assortment of male hopefuls to form a striptease act, which promises to go 'the full monty'. As jolly as it is, the film also explores several more serious issues including depression and fathers' rights, but the male protagonists come through the process with a renewed sense of purpose and self-esteem restored. Feelgood is an overused term in the world of film, but *The Full Monty* IS guaranteed to leave you with a smile on your face.

Knight fever
11th March 1997 Paul McCartney is knighted by the Queen at Buckingham Palace.

Bitter sweet Verve
13th September 1997 Wigan five-piece the Verve have endured one disbandment and a reconciliation before finally coming good with the *Urban Hymns* album. However, legal action over the sampling of the Rolling Stones' *The Last Time* on *Bitter Sweet Symphony* accounts for most of the profits. A second track from the album, *The Drugs Don't Work* - which, contrary to tabloid reports, concerns medical drugs, not the recreational kind - reaches No. 1. Another break-up follows as gifted but prickly front man Richard Ashcroft begins a solo career.

Radiohead rules OK
21st May 1997 Critics' favourites Radiohead make their big leap towards Pink Floyd-type sanctity with the multi-award winning *OK Computer*, an experimental album triggered by Miles Davis' *Bitches Brew* and blending ambient and electronic elements with lyrics about a dystopian future. An appearance at Glastonbury boosts their live reputation. They also become one of the first bands in the UK to start a website.

UK wins Eurovision
3rd May 1997 The UK entry wins the Eurovision Song Contest for only the fifth time, though Katrina Leskanich of Katrina and the Waves is actually American. *Love Shine a Light* is written by band member Kimberley Rew.

Another rap murder
9th March 1997 It's another bleak day for the US rap scene as gang violence claims another victim. Chris Wallace aka Biggie Smalls aka Notorious B.I.G. is shot dead in Los Angeles. Fellow rapper Puff Daddy records a tribute to him, *I'll Be Missing You*, with Notorious B.I.G.'s widow Faith Evans. The track is a reworking of *Every Breath You Take* by the Police and tops the US and UK listings in June.

1997

Elton's tribute
6th September 1997 Following the shocking death of Diana, Princess of Wales in a car crash in Paris, Elton John is asked to sing a tribute at her funeral in Westminster Abbey. In front of a television audience estimated at over two billion people, he performs his song *Candle in the Wind*, with lyrics revised for the occasion by Bernie Taupin. Released as a single, it becomes the biggest global seller ever - eclipsing even Bing Crosby's *White Christmas* - at 33 million, with proceeds going to the Memorial Fund.

MY FIRST 18 YEARS TOP 10 — 1997

1. Song 2 *Blur*
2. Say What You Want *Texas*
3. Brimful of Asha *Cornershop*
4. Men in Black *Will Smith*
5. Never Ever *All Saints*
6. Don't Speak *No Doubt*
7. Tubthumping *Chumbawamba*
8. Where Have All the Cowboys Gone? *Paula Cole*
9. Torn *Natalie Umbruglia*
10. Stand By Me *Oasis*

Denver dies
12th October 1997 Singer-songwriter John Denver, best known for *Annie's Song*, *Leavin' on a Jet Plane* and *Take Me Home Country Roads*, is killed when the aircraft he is piloting crashes into Monterey Bay in California.

Barbie barbs
1st November 1997 Danish band Aqua, currently at No. 1 in the UK with the satirical *Barbie Girl*, are threatened with a law suit by Barbie doll manufacturer Mattel. Agreement is eventually reached to include a sticker on the single making clear that it is not a Mattel-endorsed product.

Hutchence suicide
22nd November 1997 INXS singer Michael Hutchence commits suicide at a hotel in Sydney. He had never fully recovered from a fist fight with a taxi driver in 1992 that left him without a sense of taste or smell. Alcohol and drug problems followed, worsened by a decline in the band's popularity and the fallout from his relationship with Paula Yates, with whom he had a daughter, Tiger Lily. The final straw seems to have been the custody battle between Yates and husband Bob Geldof, which prevented Tiger Lily from coming to Australia.

Bee Gees storm off
30th October 1997 The Bee Gees walk out of a television interview with chat show host Clive Anderson when he calls them 'tossers'. Nobody had told them that insulting his guests is a big part of Anderson's style.

1998

MY FIRST 18 YEARS

SPORT

Rugby League's biggest upset
2nd May 1998 Wembley Stadium is the stage for the biggest upset in the history of the Rugby League Challenge Cup. In just their fifteenth season since formation, Sheffield Eagles beat overwhelming favourites Wigan Warriors - whose team includes Jason Robinson and Andy Farrell - 17-8.

Fashanu suicide
2nd May 1998 Former Norwich City and Nottingham Forest footballer Justin Fashanu - scorer of *Match of the Day*'s goal of the season in 1980 - hangs himself in a lock-up garage in East London. He was 37 and the first UK footballer to come out as gay. He had just returned from the US where he had been charged with assaulting a seventeen-year-old man.

BBC loses Test cricket
15th October 1998 The England and Wales Cricket Board accepts a bid worth £103 million from Channel 4 and satellite broadcaster BskyB for the televising of Test match cricket. The agreement brings to an end five decades of live Test cricket coverage on BBC TV.

World Cup in France
10th June - 12th July 1998 After a memorable football season in which Arsène Wenger's Arsenal win the rare 'double' of Premier League and FA Cup, attention turns to the FIFA World Cup in France, for which England and Scotland both qualify. Scotland fail at the group stage while England progress despite defeat against Romania but lose on penalties after a 2-2 draw with Argentina in which eighteen-year-old Michael Owen scores a spectacular opening goal. After scoring against Colombia, England's David Beckham turns from hero to villain when he receives a red card for a petulant kick against Diego Simeone in the Argentina game and effectively costs his side the match. In the final, Zinedine Zidane leads France to a 3-0 demolition of the favourites Brazil. The French achievement is even more remarkable given the sending off of Marcel Desailly in the 68th minute.

1 JAN 1998
Vanity Fair describes Leonardo DiCaprio as 'the world's biggest heartthrob.'

28 FEB 1998
Massacre in Likoshane triggers conflict in Kosovo.

9 MAR 1998
Dr. Dre signs then unknown rapper Eminem.

1998

Team games at the Commonwealths
11th - 21st September 1998 Team sports are added to the Commonwealth Games for the first time at the tournament in Kuala Lumpur, Malaysia. Hockey, netball, and rugby sevens are included with the latter making a particularly popular debut. In the final of the sevens, New Zealand beat Fiji 21-12 in the gold medal match thanks to a man of the match performance from Jonah Lomu, who is now returning to his best form after being out for a year with illness. England enjoy a strong Games overall, finishing second in the medal table behind Australia.

DOMESTIC NEWS

Angel of the North
15th February 1998 Antony Gormley's iconic sculpture *Angel of the North* is completed. Constructed in weathering steel and installed close to the A1 on the outskirts of Gateshead, it is over 60 feet tall with a wingspan of 177 feet and can be seen from miles around.

DVD launched in UK
6th June 1998 Successfully launched in Japan and the US, the DVD format debuts in the UK with the release of *Jumanji*. The format takes off slowly as a higher quality, more user friendly and virtually unbreakable alternative to VHS.

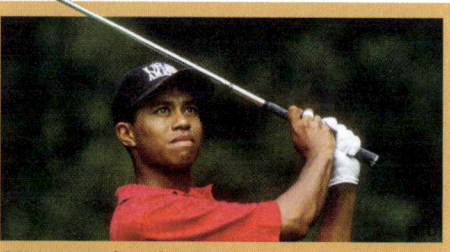

O'Meara wins the Open
19th July 1998 A blustery and chilly British Open Championship, held this year at Royal Birkdale in Southport, sees American Mark O'Meara win his second championship of the year in a play-off with Brian Watts. The veteran steals the spotlight from the rising superstar everyone is talking about, Tiger Woods, who won the Masters in 1997 at the age of 21. Woods finishes third.

Derek Bentley pardoned
30th July 1998 Ever since he was hanged in 1953 as an accessory to, but not the perpetrator of the murder of a Croydon policeman, the family of Derek Bentley has campaigned resolutely to have his name pardoned. Now, one day after a pardon is granted, the Court of Appeal confirms that the conviction is quashed.

Death of 'Flo-Jo'
21st September 1998 The athletics world is stunned by the sudden death at 38 of US track and field star Florence Griffith-Joyner, winner of three Olympic golds and two silvers, after an epileptic seizure.

23 APR 1998
With eleven Oscars, *Titanic* is the big winner at the Academy Awards.

20 MAY 1998
3,000th episode of *Neighbours* broadcast on BBC TV.

1 JUN 1998
The European Central Bank is founded.

1998

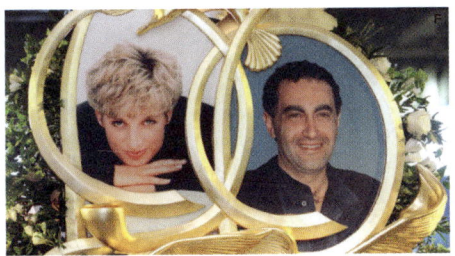

Al Fayed accuses
12th February 1998 The fallout from Princess Diana's death continues. Mohamed Al Fayed, father of Dodi Fayed, now claims that the deaths of Diana and his son were not accidental. Reports suggest he will even attempt to sue the royal family and Prime Minister Tony Blair for their supposed part in their demise. He insists that Dodi - a Muslim - was intending to ask Diana to marry him, which neither the royals nor the government could have countenanced.

Omagh bombing
15th August 1998 The worst single terrorist bombing in Northern Ireland's history occurs in Omagh, County Tyrone. A car bomb explodes on the town's high street, killing a total of 29 people and two unborn children. Planted by a nationalist splinter group called the Real Irish Republican Army as a response to the Good Friday Agreement secured in April, the bombing causes revulsion across both Protestant and Catholic communities. It has the opposite effect to that intended by the bombers by giving a fresh impetus to the peace process.

Rolls-Royce to Germany
31st March 1998 The quintessentially British Rolls-Royce brand name and world-famous logo is licensed to German car manufacturer BMW for £40 million.

Trafford Centre opens
10th September 1998 The massive indoor Trafford Centre shopping destination opens in Manchester. Constructed in three years at a cost of £600 million, it is the third largest UK retail park and a new departure in shopping mall planning. Its stores are enclosed in a sumptuous and highly decorated setting at a time when retail parks are associated with plain, neutral and antiseptic design.

Last waltz for *Come Dancing*
29th December 1998 BBC TV's *Come Dancing* celebrates its 50th anniversary with a special show from the Royal Albert Hall. Although not billed as such, it is the last ever edition of a programme that has brought ballroom dancing to the nation's living rooms since 1948. The programme will resurface in a very different format as *Strictly Come Dancing* in 2004.

ROYALTY & POLITICS

Enoch Powell dies
8th February 1998 Enoch Powell dies in London aged 85. The former Conservative Minister of Health turned race and immigration into a major political issue with his infamous 'rivers of blood' speech in 1968.

17 JUL 1998 Terms for a new International Criminal Court are established.

3 AUG 1998 Boyzone release their best-selling single *No Matter What*.

24 SEP 1998 Iran's President Khatami retracts fatwa against author Salman Rushdie.

1998

Land mines banned
12th February 1998 The government announces a complete ban on the use of land mines - a cause championed by the late Diana, Princess of Wales - by the UK armed forces.

William and Harry in Canada
24th March 1998 Prince Charles takes Prince William and Prince Harry with him on a working holiday to Vancouver and Whistler. It is one of their first public appearances anywhere since the funeral of their mother, Princess Diana. Canadian newspapers coin the phrase 'Willsmania' to describe William's effect on the many teenage girls who flock to see him.

Ron Davies resigns
27th October 1998 Just a year after guiding Wales to a 'yes' vote in the devolution referendum, Secretary of State for Wales Ron Davies resigns from the government. Having been mugged at knifepoint in a known gay meeting place on Clapham Common, his attempts to explain himself have made him a target for gossip and insinuations.

FOREIGN NEWS

Apple
7th May 1998 'iMac comes from the marriage between the excitement of the Internet with the simplicity of Macintosh.' With these words, Apple director Steve Jobs proudly presents the first iMac consumer-targeted computer. The 'i' of the iMac mainly stands for the Internet but also for 'individual, instruct, inform and inspire'. From now on, the 'i' will return in the name of almost all Apple products. The iMac has a remarkably large screen, is lightning fast and very beautifully designed. The first iMac costs around $1,300.

Good Friday Agreement
10th April 1998 Momentous all-party talks on the future of Northern Ireland conclude with what comes to be called 'the Good Friday Agreement'. Under its terms, self-government is restored to Northern Ireland on the principle of power sharing, a commitment to civil and political rights, reforms to the police service and the disbanding of paramilitary organisations. The agreement is endorsed by the people of Ireland, north and south, in referendums held on 22nd May, the results of which show clear majority support. It is possibly the most significant achievement of Tony Blair's tenure as Prime Minister.

27 OCT 1998
German Chancellor Helmut Kohl leaves office after sixteen years.

1 NOV 1998
European Court of Human Rights is established.

1 DEC 1998
Exxon buys Mobil in £73.7 billion deal, creating largest global company.

1998

Lewinsky affair
26th January 1998 'I did not have sexual relations with that woman, Miss Lewinsky.' With these words, 49-year-old US President Bill Clinton refutes allegations that he had an affair with the 22-year-old intern and Pentagon employee. For her part, Monica Lewinsky claims she had sexual contact with the President at least nine times between 1995 and 1997. It's all a bit more complicated than Clinton makes it seem. Due to the strict definition of the term 'sexual contact', oral sex 'receiving' does not fall under that heading, while oral sex 'giving' does. In August he admits that he had 'inappropriate physical contact' with her. On 19th December the scandal leads to Clinton's impeachment - only the second such procedure against a serving President.

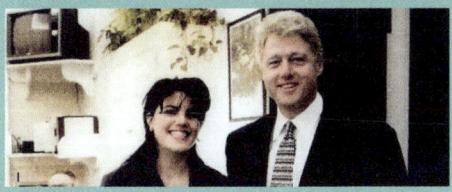

Ford Focus launches
5th March 1998 The new Ford Focus is launched at the Geneva Motor Show. It replaces the ageing Ford Escort in the small family car range and sells well in the US, where Ford traditionally has dificulty selling European models. It helps halt the decline in Ford's market share in Europe and wins Car of the Year in 1999.

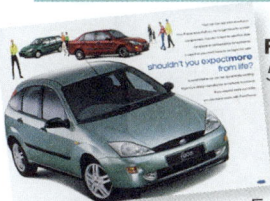

Bluetooth
7th May 1998 A new technology connects devices wirelessly at a short distance. 'Bluetooth' is named after Viking leader Harald 'Blauwtooth' I of Denmark and was invented by the Dutch electrical engineer Jaap Haartsen and developed by his employer Ericsson from Sweden.

Windows 98
25th June 1998 Microsoft launches its latest computer operating system. Windows 98 allows the user to connect USB devices to a PC while Internet Explorer is integrated into the system for the first time. New software also allows the use of multiple screens and external DVD players.

Bin Laden blamed
7th August 1998 Co-ordinated bombings at US embassies in Dar es Salaam, Tanzania, and the Kenyan capital Nairobi kill a total of 224 and injure thousands. The blame is attributed to Osama bin Laden and his increasingly active Al-Qaeda terrorist cells.

Space station
20th November 1998 The first module of the International Space Station (ISS) takes off from the Cosmodrome in Baikonur, Kazakhstan. This permanently manned space station is intended to serve as a work, transport and maintenance site for future missions to the moon, Mars and other planets.

Pinochet indicted
10th October 1998 Former Chilean dictator General Augusto Pinochet is indicted for human rights violations that he is accused of having committed during his 1973-1990 rule. While visiting the UK for medical treatment, he is placed under house arrest by British police. There he stays until March 2000, when he is released on medical grounds on the orders of Home Secretary Jack Straw.

1998

ENTERTAINMENT

Furby love
Disconcertingly reminiscent of Gizmo in *The Gremlins* movies, Furby toys are launched this year. A fluffy, colourful robot which moves its eyes and ears and progresses from speaking Furbish to picking up English (or several other languages), the toy is a bestseller, shifting 1.8 million this year and a staggering 14 million in 1999.

Boogie Nights
16th January 1998 A curveball among the decade's mainstream movies, *Boogie Nights* lifts the lid on the 1970s porn industry with a wry, funny, and compassionate story that centres on Mark Wahlberg as the exceptionally well-endowed teenager who goes on to become porn sensation Dirk Diggler. *Boogie Nights* is brimming with spot-on seventies style and a terrific cast including Julianne Moore, Phillip Seymour Hoffmann and Burt Reynolds, as filmmaker and pornographer-in-chief.

Ally McBeal
The hit American comedy *Ally McBeal*, starring Calista Flockhart, begins on Channel 4 on 3rd June. Ally is a Boston lawyer with a fertile imagination, a chequered love life and a wardrobe of very short skirts. The partners at her law firm seem to spend more time having sing-songs in the bar or performing dance routines in their unisex toilets. It's gleefully quirky and bursting with A-list special guests.

Afterbirth amuse bouche
4th February 1998 Hugh Fearnley-Whittingstall, host of *TV Dinners*, pushes culinary boundaries (and possibly boundaries of good taste) when he cooks a woman's afterbirth with onion and garlic, creating a paté to serve to guests at a celebration event for the arrival of the new baby. The Broadcasting Standards Authority comments that the show 'would have been disagreeable to many' and there are 21 complaints to the Independent Television.

'I do' in Dibley
The Vicar of Dibley with Dawn French in the titular role has given us many side-splitting moments. There's the time Geraldine falls in a puddle while trying to impress her boyfriend, and the Christmas Day when, for the sake of politeness, she is forced to visit several parishioners' homes and consume multiple Christmas dinners. Then on 22nd January, we tune in to see Alice (Emma Chambers) get married to Hugo in what is possibly the best TV wedding ever. The rings are Hula Hoops and Alice's bridesmaids are dressed as Laa-Laa and Po from the *Teletubbies*!

Goodness, Gracious, Me
Beginning as a radio show in 1996, comedy sketch show *Goodness Gracious Me* transfers to TV screens for the first time on 12th January. Featuring Sanjeev Baskhar, Meera Syal, Kulvinder Ghir and Nina Wadia it's the first comedy TV series to explore British Asian culture, with many parodies of Asian stereotypes. It's clever, insightful, and downright funny, whatever your heritage.

1998

Saving Private Ryan
11th September 1998 The first 23 minutes of Steven Spielberg's Second World War epic *Saving Private Ryan* might just be the most intense, harrowing movie opening we've seen; a recreation of the Normandy landings on Omaha beach with American landing craft disgorging soldiers, many mown down by German machine guns before they are even out of the water. It's a relentless, gut-wrenching reminder of the horror and heroism of 6th June 1944, and underpinning all this is a more sentimental story in which a group of soldiers go searching for a paratrooper behind the lines whose brothers have all been killed in action. A visceral and groundbreaking depiction of war.

The Truman Show
9th October 1998 'We accept the reality we're presented with.' *The Truman Show* casts Jim Carrey as Truman Burbank, adopted by a television studio at birth and since then, the unwitting star of a show in which he inhabits an artificially created world in which all the inhabitants are actors, and 5,000 cameras a day are trained on his every movement. Truman is the only one unaware of this enormous deception until strange occurences begin to arouse his suspicions.

Armageddon
7th August 1998 What would America do without Bruce Willis? He's saved the good old USA so many times and he's at it once again, this time as seasoned deep core driller who assembles a team of experts to fly to an asteroid hurtling towards Earth and drill a hole deep enough to detonate a nuclear device and destroy it before it does its worst. *Armageddon* is bloated, bombastic, an assault on the eyes and ears. But it's also an undeniably gripping piece of entertainment.

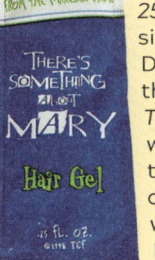

There's Something About Mary
25th September 1998 The irresistible and dazzling Cameron Diaz takes on the title role in the Farrelly brothers' comedy, *There's Something About Mary*, which has four male suitors trying to double cross and outwit each other in a bid to win Mary's heart. A thread of Farrelly puerility runs through the film, most famously, in a scene where Mary accidentally borrows some 'hair gel' hanging from her date's ear.

Matchmaker McCall
Dating show *Streetmate* begins on Channel 4 on 30th October. With the energy of a Duracell bunny, Davina McCall is on a mission, to find romance on Britain's high streets, and play matchmaker to unsuspecting passers-by who she accosts and asks if they'll go on a date with someone who is looking for love.

1998

SM:tv Live
29th August 1998 SM:tv Live is the latest kids' Saturday morning show from ITV. Wrapped around various cartoons and children's drama series, SM:tv has Ant McPartlin and Declan Donnelly solidifying their on-screen partnership as 'Ant & Dec' with Cat Deeley on board too. Together they host a long-running quiz, 'Wonkey Donkey', challenge celebrities to score a goal against Ant in 'Eat My Goal' and act up in Friends spoof, 'Chums'. In addition, there are the usual celebrity guests, pop bands and practical jokes.

The Royle Family
14th September 1998 We're invited into the living room of the Royle Family for the first time on. Rarely moving from the sofa are Barbara, Jim and their kids Denise and Antony. They don't do much but watch the telly, smoke, gossip, bicker, and generally pass the time of day. There's Nana too and Denise's fiancée, Dave, with a few others dropping round. There's no music, and no canned laughter which all adds to the authentic atmosphere. Sheer brilliance and a trailblazer for future fly-on-the-wall style comedies.

Carl Wilson
6th February 1998 Carl Wilson of the Beach Boys, Brian's brother and the angelic voice on Good Vibrations and God Only Knows, dies at the age of 51 after a long struggle with lung cancer. Other notable departures this year include rockabilly king and Blue Suede Shoes creator Carl Perkins, aged 65, and Sonny Bono of Sonny and Cher fame, who is killed in a skiing accident aged 62.

MUSIC

Women in control
Has there ever been a better time for women in music? Madonna's long run may be starting to stall but she is ringing the changes yet again by working with UK producer William Orbit. Mariah Carey has broken with her mentor and husband Tommy Mottola to take a new path. Country music's new shining star is Canadian singer Shania Twain, whose career moves up several notches in 1998 with the world-conquering Come on Over album. The Spice Girls' success has spawned a flurry of all-girl groups including All Saints and Irish trio B*Witched, while TLC and Destiny's Child (featuring a certain Beyoncé Knowles) have brought a tough, sassy streak back to rhythm and blues. This year also sees Christina Aguilera launch with Reflection from Disney's Mulan and the release of a breakthrough record by one Britney Spears. The music business may still be a man's world - but there's no question that female performers are increasingly calling the tune.

1998

Frank's final curtain
14th May 1997 Frank Sinatra is dead. Second only to Bing Crosby as the voice of the century, 'ol' blue eyes' faces his final curtain at the Cedars-Sinai Medical Center in Los Angeles following a heart attack. A singer of immaculate taste and the greatest interpreter of the 'great American songbook' created by Gershwin, Cole Porter, Rodgers and Hart and their contemporaries, he was also one of the great figures of Hollywood's golden age.

Bring on the Knight
24th February 1998 Accompanied at Buckingham Palace by his partner David Furnish, Elton John is knighted by the Queen for services to music.

Titanic ballad
23rd March 1998 The Academy Award for Best Song goes to *My Heart Goes On* from James Cameron's *Titanic*, about the most famous shipwreck in history. It's just one of eleven Academy Awards earned by the biggest box office movie in years. Celine Dion sings it at the very end of the film, as the credits roll over a dark screen.

George goes outside
7th April 1998 George Michael is arrested in Beverly Hills, California, for engaging in 'a lewd act' in a public restroom. Sentenced to 80 hours of community service, George accuses the LA police of hounding gays and opens up about his homosexuality. *Outside* - a hit almost everywhere except the US - is his humorous take on the whole incident.

Mick takes on Liam
8th June 1998 Two Mancunian musicians have a difference of opinion at London's Metropolitan Hotel. Simply Red's Mick Hucknall is berated by Liam for saying Oasis are an embarrassment to Manchester. Reports suggest that Mick comes out best in the resulting brawl.

Geri exits
31st May 1998 Geri Halliwell - Ginger Spice - announces that she has left the Spice Girls. It follows the sacking of manager Simon Fuller and rumours of squabbles within the group, but ticket sales for their forthcoming world tour are strong and the year ends with another No. 1 - *Goodbye*, widely assumed to be a 'so long and thanks' message to Geri.

1998

Song of *Angels*
Ever since the demise of Take That, the smart money has been on Gary Barlow becoming a fully fledged solo superstar. He has had hits and even a No. 1, but it's his old nemesis Robbie Williams who is set to go stratospheric. Partly it's down to Robbie's charisma and naughty-boy charm, but it also has much to do with the songs he is writing with the experienced Guy Chambers. In particular, *Angels* is touching people in unexpected ways. Although only a No. 4, it sticks around for ages and in a short time becomes a popular choice at weddings and funerals. In 2005, it will be voted the UK's best song of the previous 25 years.

MY FIRST 18 YEARS — TOP 10 — 1998

1. **You Make Me Wanna** Usher
2. **C'est la Vie** B*Witched
3. **Millennium** Robbie Williams
4. **You Get What You Give** New Radicals
5. **Truly Madly Deeply** Savage Garden
6. **One Week** Barenaked Ladies
7. **Never Ever** All Saints
8. **Dance the Night Away** The Mavericks
9. **Save Tonight** Eagle Eye Cherry
10. **Here's Where the Story Ends** Tin Tin Out

Rocking the valleys
5th September 1998 Welsh rock is resurgent as Manic Street Preachers take *If You Tolerate This Your Children Will Be Next* - inspired by a Spanish Civil War poster - to No. 1. Another trio, Stereophonics from Abercynon, are making waves with finely observed songs lifted from valley life like *Local Boy in the Photograph*.

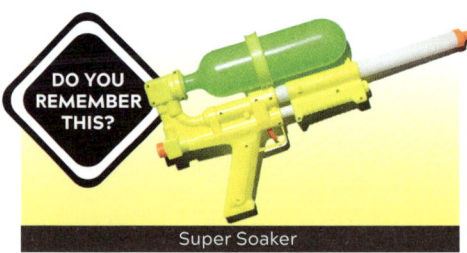

Do you remember this? Super Soaker

Just believe…
31st October 1998 A regular hitmaker since 1965, Cher's ability to reinvent herself both image-wise and musically has been astonishing. Now in her 50s, she's back at No. 1 with *Believe*, with which she becomes the oldest female solo singer ever to achieve a No. 1. It is also the first hit record to employ the audio processing software Auto Tune, which alters pitch and ensures vocals are perfectly tuned.

PHOTO CREDITS Copyright 2024, TDM Rights BV.
Photos: **A** Mike Hewitt - Getty Images Europe - Getty Images / **B** Tony Marshall Empics - PA Images - Getty Images / **C** Slu Forster - Getty Images Europe - Getty Images / **D** J.D. Cuban - Getty Images North America - Getty Images / **E** Ronald Reagan Library - / **F** Sion Touhig - Sygma - Getty Images / **G** Tim Graham Photo Library - Getty Images / **H** John Stillwell - PA Images - Getty Images / **I** Hulton Archive - Getty Images / **J** Jeff Christensen - Hutlon Archive - Getty Images / **K** Ghoulardi Film Co - Ronald Grant Archive - Mary Evans / **L** Ronald Grant Archive - Mary Evans / **M** Hulton Archive - Getty Images / **N** Stefan Rousseau - PA Images - Getty Images / **O** Archive Photos - Moviepix - Getty Images / **P** Archive Photos - Moviepix - Getty Images / **Q** Rob Verhorst - Redferns - Getty Images / **R** Michael Ochs Archives - Getty Images / **S** Ronald Grant Archive - Mary Evans / **T** Bettmann - Getty Images / **U** Kevin.Mazur - Wire Image - Getty Images / **V** Tim Roney - Hulton Archive - Getty Images / **W** Brian Rasic - Hulton Archive - Getty Images.

1999

MY FIRST 18 YEARS

SPORT

Manager merry-go-round
In a big year for England football managers past and present, current manager Glenn Hoddle is sacked over comments he made in an interview suggesting that disabled people are paying for sins committed in a former life. His replacement is ex-Newcastle and now Fulham manager Kevin Keegan. In September, current Newcastle manager Ruud Gullit is replaced by former England, Fulham and Ipswich manager Bobby Robson. Inarguably the most successful England manager of all, the World Cup-winning Sir Alf Ramsey passes away on 28th April aged 79.

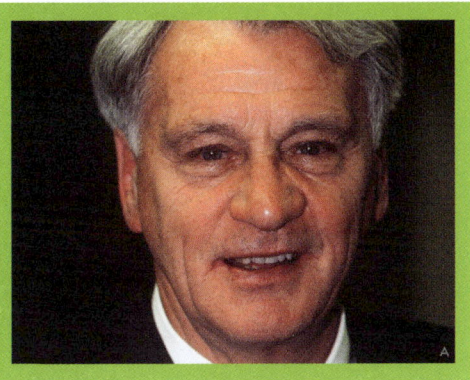

A Wales v England classic
11th April 1999 Although a memorable year in rugby union for World Cup final Australia's 35-12 defeat of France, the match of the year comes in the Five Nations. England go into their last match of the tournament needing to beat Wales to win the Grand Slam. Choosing to play at Wembley because Cardiff Arms Park was in the process of being rebuilt as the Millennium Stadium, Wales win 32-31 and deny arch enemies England not only the Grand Slam but a table-topping finish. Scotland win the Five Nations on points difference.

Gough's hat trick
2nd January 1999 It is one of those great moments in the history of the Ashes: having taken ten wickets in the first Test of the series, Yorkshire fast bowler Darren Gough (whose nickname is 'Dazzler') takes a hat trick of wickets in the fifth Test in Sydney - the first by any English bowler against Australia in almost a century. He finishes the series with 21 wickets to his name.

Man Utd win the treble
16th May 1999 Managed by the soon-to-be knighted Alex Ferguson, Manchester United snatch the Champions League title in the most dramatic fashion, scoring two late goals after Bayern Munich had led for much of the match. United thereby become the first club in history to win the 'treble' of league, FA Cup and Champions League in one season.

25 JAN 1999
Six International Olympic Committee members expelled in corruption crackdown.

7 FEB 1999
Prince Abdullah is crowned King of Jordan after the death of King Hussein.

29 MAR 1999
Microsoft begins rollout of office suite Word 2000.

1999

DOMESTIC NEWS

Minimum wage
1st April 1999 A national minimum wage is introduced across the UK, ensuring that workers over 21 receive an income of at least £3.60 an hour.

Hendry's seventh heaven
3rd May 1999 Stephen Hendry wins his seventh and last World Snooker Championship, defeating Mark Williams in the final 18-11 at the Crucible in Sheffield. The win caps an amazing decade and gives him a record number of Championship titles, beating the six won by Ray Reardon and Steve Davis. The record will stand until Ronnie O'Sullivan equals it in 2022. Hendry's semi-final match with O'Sullivan includes eight century breaks, the most ever in a single match at the Championships.

Stephen Lawrence inquiry
24th February 1999 The Macpherson Inquiry into the handling of the murder in 1993 of black teenager Stephen Lawrence labels London's Metropolitan Police 'institutionally racist' and accuses officers of incompetence and making 'fundamental errors' in their investigation of the crime.

Red card madness
16th October 1999 Any normal Saturday in the football seasons would see a handful of players sent off. Today that total is an incredible 26 across the Premier League and Football League - a new record.

Jill Dando murdered
26th April 1999 The television presenter Jill Dando is shot dead on the doorstep of her home in Fulham, West London. Police are baffled regarding the motive behind the murder. A local man, Barry George, is eventually charged and convicted but is released from prison after eight years and a retrial ordered. He is acquitted in 2008. As of 2024, the murder remains unsolved.

---

20 APR 1999
Twelve killed in mass shooting at Columbine High School, Colorado.

26 MAY 1999
Two-month war begins in Kashmir between India and Pakistan.

14 JUN 1999
George W. Bush announces he will seek Republican nomination for President.

1999

Nail bomb attacks
17th - 30th April 1999
A string of nail bombings hits London on successive weekends, targeting the black community in Brixton, the Bengali community of Brick Lane In East London and the heart of the gay community in Soho. The last attack on a gay pub close to Leicester Square kills a pregnant woman and two friends. Within hours, 22-year-old former British National Party member David Copeland from Farnborough is charged with carrying out the attacks.

Burglar shot dead
2nd August 1999 Norfolk farmer Tony Martin is charged with the murder of a sixteen-year-old burglar found shot dead at his home and the wounding of a 29-year-old intruder. He is subsequently found guilty of murder and serves three years of a five-year sentence.

Midland Bank rebranded
27th September 1999 Just as the Royal Bank of Scotland bids to take over the National Westminster Bank - successfully, as it transpires - the Midland Bank changes its branding and is renamed HSBC after its Hong Kong-based owner.

Ladbroke Grove train crash
5th October 1999 A collision between two trains at Ladbroke Grove on the Reading to Paddington line kills 31 people, both drivers included, and injures 417. In the aftermath and at the subsequent inquiry, concerns are raised about the safety of UK railways following privatisation and especially the decision taken on cost grounds not to roll out a new automatic train protection system.

Tracey's bed
19th October 1999 Artist Tracey Emin provokes a media storm when her artwork *My Bed* goes on display at the Tate Gallery. The work is exactly what its title suggests: Tracey's own unmade bed, with stained bed sheets, empty cigarette packets and discarded clothes.

London Eye
31st December 1999 As the nation prepares to celebrate a new millennium, Prime Minister Tony Blair opens the London Eye observation wheel on London's South Bank. Intended as a temporary attraction, it proves so popular that it becomes permanent.

Dr Death trial begins
5th October 1999 The trial opens at Preston Crown Court of Hyde GP Dr Harold Shipman, who is charged with the murders of fifteen elderly patients between 1995 and 1998.

16 JUL 1999
John F. Kennedy Jr., and two others are killed in a plane crash.

3 AUG 1999
Arsenal signes Thierry Henry for a bargain £10 million from Juventus.

11 SEP 1999
Serena Williams wins the US Open - her first Grand Slam title.

1999

ROYALTY & POLITICS

Northern Ireland Assembly
2nd December 1999 After elections in June 1998, power now officially devolves from Westminster to the new Northern Ireland Assembly set up as part of the Good Friday Agreement. Decommissioning of weapons by paramilitary groups is expected to start immediately.

Millennium Dome
On the same day, the controversial Millennium Dome in Greenwich - hugely expensive to build and lacking a clear purpose or future - is opened by the Queen. Tony Blair causes some consternation by taking her hand during the singing of Auld Lang Syne as midnight strikes.

FOREIGN NEWS

Millennium bug
Computer scientists fear the end of the millennium. When storing data in computers, only the last two digits of the year are used. Because the computer does not recognise the first two digits, experts predict that systems will interpret '1-1-'00' as the first day of 1900 and not 2000. Banks may refuse debit cards with an expiry date after 2000. Worse, financial markets, distribution centres and airports will come to a standstill due to the so-called 'millennium bug'. But all fears are unfounded: the world moves from one millennium into another without any issue. Was it all just a storm in a teacup?

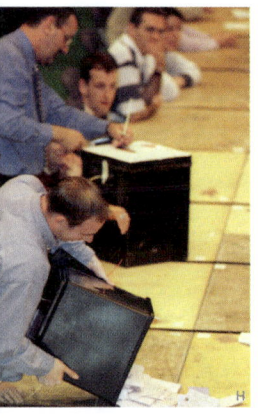

Elections in Scotland and Wales
6th May 1999 Following the 1998 referendums on devolution, voting takes place in the first elections for the new Scottish Parliament and Welsh Assembly (Senedd in Welsh). In Scotland and Wales, the same scenario develops as Labour and the Liberal Democrats form a coalition.

Kennedy elected Lib Dem leader
9th August 1999 Charles Kennedy, MP for Ross, Skye and Lochaber, is elected leader of the Liberal Democrats following the retirement of Paddy Ashdown.

31 OCT 1999
McLaren driver Mika Häkkinen wins his second straight F1 World Drivers Championship.

8 NOV 1999
Nineteenth James Bond film *The World is Not Enough* premieres.

3 DEC 1999
NASA loses radio contact with the Mars Polar Lander.

1999

Hello Euro
1st January 1999 A historic day for Europe as eleven European countries switch to the euro and age-old currencies such as the Austrian schilling, the French franc, the German mark and the Dutch guilder pass into history. On the European financial markets, all prices are now indicated in euros. The European single currency is three years away.

Six billion people
19th July 1999 According to the UN, the six billionth person on the planet is born on this day. A baby in Sarajevo is given the symbolic honour of being designated the world's six billionth citizen.

Australia says no
6th November 1999 In a national referendum to decide whether Australia should become a republic and replace the Queen and Governor General with a President, 54.87 per cent of Australians unexpectedly vote no. The issue is laid to rest for another generation.

Clinton survives
12th February 1999 Following the Monica Lewinsky affair that monopolised political life in the US for much of 1998, the House of Representatives votes to impeach President Clinton on two of four articles of impeachment. He is acquitted by the US Senate on one of them and voting is split evenly on the other, so the President survives. Although he does not resign, Clinton's last years as President - not to mention his reputation and legacy - are forever tarnished.

Putin for Yeltsin
31st December 1999 Boris Yeltsin resigns unexpectedly as President of Russia. Yeltsin hands power to his Prime Minister Vladimir Putin. A former head of the FSB security service and a formidable political manipulator, Putin becomes acting President ahead of elections that will see him take over in 2000.

War in Kosovo
24th March 1999 The break-up of Yugoslavia has another bloody sequel when ethnic Albanians in the province of Kosovo in southern Serbia start a guerrilla war to free themselves from Serb domination. When the Serbs invade the region, NATO launches air strikes for the first time against a sovereign state. On 10th June, Serbian leader Slobodan Milošević agrees to a Serbian withdrawal.

Last day of the millennium
31st December 1999 The nations of the world mark the end of the millennium in different ways. New buildings and structures are named after it, such as the Millennium Dome in London and the Millennium Tower in Vienna.

Motorcycle wars
15th April 1999 Suzuki introduces the GSX1300R production motorcycle that breaks the magical limit of 300 km/h. The GSX1300R is nicknamed 'Hayabusa', Japanese for peregrine falcon, after the bird of prey that can reach the same top speed in its dives as the Suzuki.

1999

ENTERTAINMENT

Sex and the City
3rd February 1999 Based on the *New York Times* column by Candace Bushnell, HBO's *Sex and the City* brings some New York sass and glamour to Channel 4. Journalist, fashionista, shoeaholic and girl-about-town Carrie Bradshaw (Sarah Jessica Parker) negotiates the rocky dating terrain of Manhattan in her column, drawing on her own experiences and those of her three closest friends. They do lunch, go shopping, share sex secrets, and go through the trials and tribulations of life. Funny, fast-paced, and enjoyably risqué, 'SATC' is a huge hit.

Notting Hill
27th April 1999 Five years after *Four Weddings and a Funeral*, Hugh Grant turns on the bumbling, upper-class charm again for another Richard Curtis-penned smash hit - *Notting Hill*. This time, he is William Thacker, a Portobello Road bookseller who bumps into and begins an on-off romance with the world's biggest movie star, Anna Scott (Julia Roberts). With the bonus of Will's eccentric circle of friends, *Notting Hill* is full of charm and cheer, as we root for William to get his girl.

Wild Horses
The Guiness TV advertisement 'Surfer' is launched this year, setting a new standard for creative TV commercials. The black and white advert features a Polynesian surfer waiting patiently for the perfect wave, with the crashing surf transforming into galloping white horses (an image inspired by Walter Crane's 1893 painting, *Neptune's Horses*). 'Surfer' is a sensory experience and goes on to win multiple awards and accolades.

The Pony Club
14th March 1999 Fiona Allen, Sally Phillips and Doon Mackichan are the main trio in *Smack the Pony*, a female-orientated sketch show which begins on Channel 4. From the competitive singing match, where ordinary workers on a tea break try to outdo each other while singing along to songs on the radio, to female athletes competing in high heels, or the New Age healer, who pulls her patient by her eyebrows, *Smack the Pony* is hysterical and a little bit surreal.

The Matrix
11th June 1999 Written and directed by former comic book writers, brothers Andy and Larry Wachowski, stylish sci-fi blockbuster *The Matrix* stars Keanu Reeves as Neo, a hacker who is recruited to save the human race from being subjugated and controlled by AI machines. Laurence Fishburne and Carrie-Anne Moss co-star in a movie that sets new standards for its action sequences, with some balletic John Woo-style martial arts and slo-mo gunfights.

1999

There's nowt so queer as folk
23rd February 1999 Channel 4's *Queer as Folk* is an eight-part series about the lives and loves of three gay men in Manchester's Canal Street area. It's a drama in which gay characters - and gay culture - are introduced into mainstream television, and for many, represents a seismic shift in attitudes.

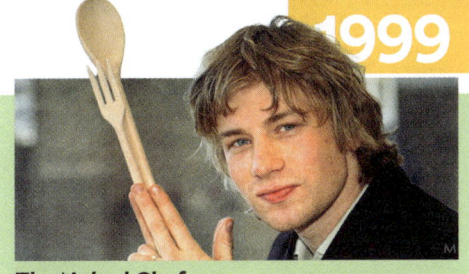

The Naked Chef
14th April 1999 Rustling up some 'pukka' grub in *The Naked Chef*, which begins on BBC2, is Jamie Oliver, a 23-year-old Essex lad who has cut his culinary teeth at Carluccio's and The River Café. With his blokey, relaxed approach and simple, fresh dishes, the show introduces a new kind of TV chef and gets men as well as younger people into the kitchen to bish, bash, bosh some proper big flavours onto the plate. Cookbooks, more shows, restaurant chains and campaigns are all in the future for this bright star of the culinary scene.

Daniel's Dickens debut
The BBC presents a new adaptation of Charles Dickens's novel *David Copperfield* on Christmas Day and Boxing Day this year. With an all-star cast featuring the cream of British acting talent, there is Bob Hoskins as the ever-optimistic Mr Micawber, Maggie Smith as Betsey Trotwood and Ian McKellen as Mr Creakle. Notably, making his acting debut as David Copperfield in boyhood is a certain Daniel Radcliffe, who two years later will take on the role of Harry Potter in the franchise based on J. K. Rowling's books.

Bob the Builder
12th April 1999 Can we fix it? Yes we can! The stop-motion animation children's series *Bob the Builder* begins on CBBC. Bob, together with Wendy and a line-up of helpful diggers and trucks, the builder who will never let you down. Bob the Builder becomes one of the BBC's most lucrative characters.

Fight Club

12th November 1999 'The first rule of Fight Club is that you don't talk about Fight Club. The second rule of Fight Club is that you don't talk about Fight Club.' David Fincher's compelling film serves up a tale of male dignity and self-worth restored through the violent process of organised punch-ups. Edward Norton stars as the disillusioned office worker who goes in search of fulfilment with the help of charismatic soap salesman Tyler Durden (Brad Pitt), an intriguing movie with a surprising, surreal twist at the end.

Farewell Rod Hull
On 17th March Rod Hull, whose Emu had caused such havoc on television during the 1970s and '80s, goes up on the roof of his bungalow to adjust the TV aerial while watching a football match between Inter Milan vs. Manchester United. He falls, sustaining fatal injuries and is declared dead on arrival in hospital.

1999

The Sopranos
The first episode of the acclaimed American crime drama, The Sopranos, is broadcast on Channel 4 on 15th July. The HBO series about North Jersey mobster Tony Soprano (James Gandolfini), whose conflicted priorities over business and family lead to panic attacks and reluctant visits to a therapist, goes on to be voted the best-written series of all time by the Writers Guild of America in 2013.

Crimewatch
Following the shocking murder of its presenter Jill Dando in April, the 18th May edition of Crimewatch stages a reconstruction of her final moments in an attempt to find the perpetrator. Nick Ross, Jill's co-presenter, introduces the programme by saying, 'Jill Dando was much more than a colleague, she was everyone's friend. Crimewatch is poorer without her. But, this programme was her passion. And now, as Jill helped others, we hope we can do the same for her.'

Walking with Dinosaurs
On 4th October, BBC1 travels 220 million years back in time to the Mesozoic period, when dinosaurs walked the earth. Narrated by Kenneth Branagh, utilising CGI and animatronics, Walking with Dinosaurs is the most expensive documentary ever made, costing £37,654 per minute. But it's also the BBC's most successful science programme, watched by over 15 million people.

Star Wars from the beginning
16th July 1999 Star Wars Episode 1: The Phantom Menace is released. Set 32 years before the original trilogy, in the time of the Galactic Republic, The Phantom Menace has Jedi Master Qui-Gon Jinn (Liam Neeson) and his apprentice Obi-Wan Kenobi (Ewan McGregor) joining forces with a slave child, Anakin Skywalker, to protect Queen Amidala of Naboo (Natalie Portman) and bring interplanetary peace, as the long-dormant Sith rise again to claim power. The special effects are breathtaking and The Phantom Menace, the first of Lucas's prequel trilogy, brings Star Wars to a new generation.

MUSIC

Five Grammys in one night
24th February 1999 Lauryn Hill wins a spectacular five solo Grammy awards at the annual industry bash in Los Angeles. She is the first ever artist to do so. It's a reflection of the impact of her album The Miseducation of Lauryn Hill over the previous year, following her time with hip hop trio the Fugees.

1999

Goodbye Saigon, hello Lion King
As one big show closes in the West End, another opens. On 30th October, *Miss Saigon* comes to an end after a successful ten-year run. Just two weeks earlier, on 16th October, *The Lion King* opens at the Lyceum Theatre. With its inventive use of masks, puppetry, and costume to recreate the animals of the African savannah, and with a predominantly black cast, Disney's 1996 hit film translates to the stage in an awe-inspiring production.

S Club 7
19th June 1999 Following the likes of B*Witched, 5ive and Billie Piper, another fresh-faced teenage UK act is at No. 1 with *Bring It All Back*. S Club 7 are an all-singing, all-dancing group put together by ex-Spice Girls manager Simon Fuller and boasting a television series of their own. More hits follow and even an offshoot group, *S Club Juniors*, in 2001.

Napster launches
1st June 1999 The MP3 file-sharing application Napster is launched, facilitating the sharing of music between consumers and (its detractors say) encouraging internet piracy. It attracts over 80 million users within a year.

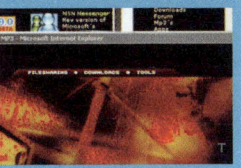

Britney's breakthrough
30th January 1999 The year belongs to the fetchingly childlike voice of Britney Spears. In the space of twelve months, her album *Baby One More Time* becomes the second best selling album of the decade while the single of the same name spends eight months in the US chart. Her UK debut follows in February as the single hits No. 1. A former member of US TV's *Mickey Mouse Club*, Britney followed the 'singing in a shopping mall' route that brought Tiffany and Debbie Gibson to attention a few years earlier, but it's a video showing an unsmiling Britney dancing down a corridor in high school uniform that clinches her breakthrough.

Wear sunscreen
12th June 1999 Anyone leaving university or high school in the summer of 1999 will always remember *Everybody's Free (To Wear Sunscreen)*, otherwise known as the *Sunscreen Song*. It's not a song as such but a recitation of advice, based on an actual graduation speech. The unusual recording has sample from the soundtrack of the 1996 film *Romeo + Juliet*. The narration is by Lee Perry, an Australian who adopted an American accent.

Musica latina
17th July 1999 Latin music is enjoying a huge surge in the US as artists from Puerto Rico, Cuba and South America cross over to the mainstream with English language records. Ricky Martin sets the pace with *Livin' La Vida Loca*, now No. 1 in the UK, just as Jennifer Lopez and Enrique Iglesias build on their huge Hispanic following and just two months before German-born Lou Bega revives the Perez Prado hit *Mambo No. 5*.

1999

Van's the man
1st September 1999 The Irish Music Hall of Fame opens in Dublin to honour Ireland's proud musical tradition. The first musician to be inducted is Van Morrison, now in his 35th year as a performer.

MY FIRST 18 YEARS — TOP 10 — 1999

1. *Maria* Blondie
2. *Genie in a Bottle* Christina Aguilera
3. *Tragedy* Steps
4. *No Scrubs* TLC
5. *Livin' la Vida Loca* Riccky Martin
6. *My Name Is* Eminem
7. *Runaway* The Corrs
8. *Sweet Like Chocolate* Shanks & Bigfoot
9. *Kiss Me* Sixpence None the Richer
10. *Smooth* Santana featuring Rob Thomas

Fatboy weds Ball
21st August 1999 Fatboy Slim - formerly Norman Cook of the Housemartins - marries Radio 1 breakfast presenter Zoe Ball at Babington House, Somerset. Fatboy is now an ace dance music producer and remixer whose *Praise You* is a prime example of the art of sampling. A No. 1 in January, it samples a little known Camille Yarborough gospel track from 1975.

Dame Shirley
31st December 1999 The New Year honours list is published. Shirley Bassey is made a Dame Commander of the Order of the British Empire (DBE) for services to entertainment.

Glitter disgrace
12th November 1999 Gary Glitter is sentenced to four months in prison after he admits downloading pornographic images of children. Police were alerted when he took his computer to PC World for repair. It is the first of a series of prison terms that he will serve for sexual offences.

Living their Westlife
25th December 1999 The very last UK No. 1 of the second millennium is the fourth chart-topper of the year for new Irish pop sensations Westlife, co-managed by Ronan Keating of Boyzone. Rather curiously it combines Abba's upbeat, optimistic *I Have a Dream* with a Jacques Brel song about suicide, *Seasons in the Sun*, that was a No. 1 for Terry Jacks back in 1974.

George attacked
30th December 1999 George Harrison and his wife are attacked in their home by an intruder. Both survive but George is left with a punctured lung and head injuries.

PHOTO CREDITS Copyright 2024, TDM Rights BV.
Photos: A Marcus Brandt - Bongarts - Getty Images / B Peter Jordan - PA Images - Getty Images / C Phil Cole - Getty Images Europe - Getty Images / D John Stillwell - PA Images - Getty Images / E Colin Davey - Hulton Archive - Getty Images / F Sean Dempsey - PA Images - Getty Images / G PA Images - Getty Images / H David Cheskin - PA Images - Getty Images / I Cynthia Johnson - Hulton Archive - Getty Images / J AF Archive - HBO - Mary Evans / K Archive Photos - Moviepix - Getty Images / L Ronald Grant Archive - Mary Evans / M Michael Walters - PA Images - / N Getty Images North Americ - Getty Images / O Central Press - Hulton Archive - Getty Images / P Bobby Bank - WireImage - Getty Images / Q AF Archive - BBC - Mary Evans / R Sunset Boulevard - Corbis Historical - Getty Images / S Jim Smeal - Ron Galella Collection - Getty Images / T Bruno Vincent - Getty Images / U Picture Alliance - Getty Images / V Brian Rasic - Hulton Archive - Getty Images / W Gie Knaeps - Hulton Archive - Getty Images / X Gareth Davies - Hulton Archive - Getty Images / Y Picture Alliance - Getty Images.

2000

MY FIRST 18 YEARS

SPORT

Sporting legends
2000 sees the passing of three truly iconic figures in UK sport: England and Kent cricket captain Colin Cowdrey (68) and footballers Stanley Matthews (85) and Wilf Mannion (81). Matthews played for Blackpool, Stoke City and England during one of the longest playing careers in world football, retiring at the age of 50 with a knighthood. Mannion spent much of his career at Middlesbrough and was capped for England 26 times.

Euro 2000
12th - 20th June 2000 England is the only UK home nation represented at Euro 2000, which is hosted jointly by Belgium and the Netherlands. A morale-boosting win against Germany is followed by elimination at the group stage. World Cup holders France defeat Italy 2-1 in the final. In September, England lose their last game at the old Wembley Stadium 1-0 to Germany in a World Cup qualifier, after which Kevin Keegan resigns as manager. A month later, the FA signs Swedish coach Sven-Goran Eriksson as his replacement.

Olympics in Sydney
15th September - 1st October 2000 The first Olympic Games of the new millennium opens in Sydney. An outstanding Games from a UK perspective, its highlights include Steve Redgrave's fifth rowing gold medal, Denise Lewis's gold in the women's pentathlon, Jonathan Edwards' spectacular triple jump gold and Jason Queally's gold in the cycling. Equally encouraging are the performances of young athletes on the cusp of still greater Olympic achievement - Kelly Holmes, Chris Hoy and Bradley Wiggins included. The tally of eleven golds, ten silvers and seven bronze medals is Great Britain's highest since 1920. The undoubted star of the Games overall is Australian swimmer Ian Thorpe, who wins an astonishing five medals - three gold, two silver - at the age of seventeen.

Goodbye, Wembley
7th October 2000 Wembley Stadium is closed ahead of a rebuilding programme expected to take three years, during which the famous twin towers will be demolished and the capacity increased to 90,000 spectators.

13 JAN 2000
Microsoft chairman Bill Gates steps aside as chief executive.

4 FEB 2000
The Sims video game is released.

30 MAR 2000
Richard Branson awarded knighthood.

2000

Cricket under floodlights
3rd August 2000 A piece of cricket history is made – though not to the liking of traditionalists – when a match between West Indies and Zimbabwe is the first one day international to be played in England under floodlights. The venue is Gloucestershire's cricket ground at Bristol. Over 7,000 attend.

Easy, Tiger!
23rd July 2000 In a magnificent year in which he also wins the PGA Championship and the US Open, Tiger Woods wins the British Open at St Andrews at the age of 24. He becomes only the fifth player to complete a career Grand Slam and his six consecutive wins on the PGA Tour add up to the longest winning run since Ben Hogan in 1948.

Shipman is guilty
31st January 2000 At the trial of Dr Harold Shipman, the GP is found guilty of murdering fifteen patients in his care and sentenced to life imprisonment. A subsequent inquiry into the circumstances behind the murders suggests that his victims may number over 200. He hangs himself in prison in January 2004.

Trams return to London
11th May 2000 With the official opening of Croydon Tramlink, trams return to London for the first time since the tramlines were taken up in 1952.

DOMESTIC NEWS

Tony Blair v. the WI
7th June 2000 Rarely one to seem fazed by anything, Tony Blair is completely bemused by the hostile reception he gets at the annual conference of the Women's Institute. Breaking the convention that speeches to the assembly should not be political, he is heckled and slow handclapped by the wholly female audience.

May Day protests
1st May 2000 Rioting breaks out during protests in London by anti-capitalist groups. The Cenotaph in Whitehall and the Winston Churchill statue in Parliament Square are among landmarks defaced or attacked, while a McDonalds restaurant in Whitehall is ransacked. Controversial police counter-tactics include penning in thousands including passers-by in streets or squares. Ninety-five protestors are arrested and nine police and nine civilians injured.

People smuggling tragedy
18 June 2000 In Dover, a total of 58 Chinese illegal immigrants are found suffocated to death in a lorry that had just crossed the Channel by ferry from France. Two survivors are hospitalised. The Dutch driver, Perry Wacker, is arrested and convicted of manslaughter in April 2000. He receives fourteen years, imprisonment.

---

22 APR 2000
Telephone dialling codes change across the UK.

12 MAY 2000
Tate Modern art gallery opens at the inconverted Bankside Power Station.

10 JUN 2000
London's Millennium Footbridge sways precariously and closes days after opening.

2000

Victoria, Sarah and Damilola
The names of three murdered children, all ten years old or younger, dominate the headlines in 2000. In February, Victoria Climbie dies after neglect and torture by her guardians, leading to a report severely criticising the social services responsible for her protection and recommending major changes to protocols. In July, the abduction and murder of Sarah Payne by a known child sex offender leads to long-term changes to the law regarding disclosure of offences. In December, the fatal stabbing of Nigerian-born Damilola Taylor on his way home from school in Peckham, London, raises deep and lasting disquiet concerning juvenile knife crime.

Reggie Kray dies
1st October 2000 East End gangster Reggie Kray dies from cancer aged 66, five years after the death of his brother Ronnie following a heart attack in Parkhurst Prison.

Attack on M16
20th September 2000 A rocket launcher attack around 10pm by Irish republican dissident group the Real IRA causes superficial damage to the eighth floor of the M16 building in Vauxhall, South London.

ROYALTY & POLITICS

Fuel protests
8th September 2000 The UK is struck by a series of well-organised protests by road haulage operators and their drivers, who are angry at rising fuel prices and demand a reduction in fuel duty. The protests include picketing oil refineries and forming slow-moving convoys of lorries on motorways. Their action leads to panic buying, fuel shortages and temporary closure of petrol stations.

Fatal attack at constituency surgery
29th January 2000 Cheltenham's Liberal Democrat MP Nigel Jones is attacked with a samurai sword at his weekly surgery for constituents. Local councillor Andrew Pennington rushes to his aid but is stabbed three times and dies in hospital.

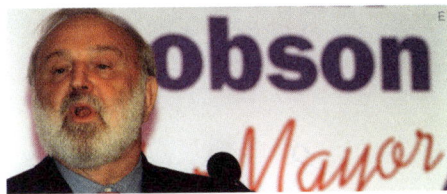

Mayor of London
4th May 2000 In London's first mayoral election, Tony Blair faces embarrassment as Labour's candidate Frank Dobson comes third in the ballot and Ken Livingstone, the Brent East MP who was rejected by Blair but opted to stand as an independent, takes the prize. Conservative Steven Norris comes second.

---

28 JUL 2000 — Last 80 prisoners leave Maze Prison in Northern Ireland.

18 AUG 2000 — Mile-wide stretch of ice-free water in Arctic raises fresh global warming fears.

28 SEP 2000 — Death of former Canadian Prime Minister Pierre Trudeau aged 80.

2000

End of Day
6th August 2000 UK broadcasting's most incisive political interviewer, Sir Robin Day, dies in London aged 77. His television career began with ITN in 1957 but reached its zenith in the 1960s with the BBC. His large-framed spectacles, bow tie and perpetually sceptical demeanour were an impressionist's dream.

Donald Dewar dies
10th October 2000 Having devoted the last two years to making a Scottish Parliament a reality, First Minister Donald Dewar dies after a fall outside his official residence in Edinburgh. He had only been in office for eighteen months.

Queen Mother is 100
19th July 2000 Prior to celebrating her hundredth birthday on 4th August, Queen Elizabeth the Queen Mother is honoured by a birthday pageant on Horse Guards Parade. Back in Buckingham Palace, she and daughters Elizabeth and Margaret acknowledge a 40,000-strong crowd from the balcony.

FOREIGN NEWS

Kursk sinks
12th August 2000 The Russian submarine *Kursk* sinks in the Barents Sea during exercises. Unable to rescue the sub and unwilling to ask for western help, the Russian authorities face criticism at home and abroad for their handling of the emergency. The entire crew of 118 is lost.

Biggest ever merger
11th January 2000 America Online (AOL) purchases Time Warner in a deal worth $162 billion. It is the largest ever corporate merger with the combined value of the two companies estimated at $360 billion. Within three years, however, the name AOL is dropped from the company's title. By 2010, CEO Jeff Bewkes is moved to call the merger 'the biggest mistake in corporate history'.

Concorde crashes
25th July 2000 An Air France Concorde en route to New York crashes soon after take-off from Charles de Gaulle Airport in Paris. All 109 passengers and crew are killed together with four people in the hotel it crashes into. It is the first and only fatal accident in Concorde's history and instantly grounds the Air France and British Airways fleets. Having undermined the supersonic airliner's long-held reputation for safety, it brings its long-term future into question.

The Nokia brick
1st September 2000 Released today, the Nokia 3310 acquires cult status very quickly. Over 126 million are eventually sold. The small mobile phone - usually with a characteristic dark blue front and gray push buttons - is almost impossible to break. Countless internet videos show people trying to demolish the 'Nokia brick', usually without success.

---

4 OCT 2000 Production of the Mini ends at Longbridge, Birmingham, after four decades.

30 NOV 2000 Freedom of Information Act creates right of access to info held by public authorities.

31 DEC 2000 Closure of the Millennium Dome.

2000

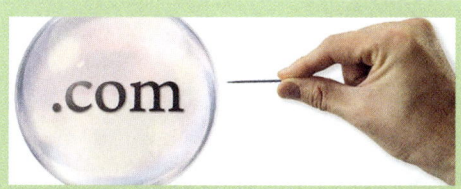

Internet bubble bursts
17th March 2000 World Online is set to become Europe's largest internet provider worth twelve billion euros. But the hype turns out to be short-lived. Major shareholders sell their shares the same day. While the internet is booming like never before and dotcom companies are springing up everywhere, there is speculation about the 'new economy' that runs on online services. The over-enthusiasm drives shares of internet companies to record highs and pimply young internet entrepreneurs become paper billionaires in no time. But the start-up capital of many companies is running out and suddenly real money has to be made. In the meantime, news of the first dotcom scandals are filtering through, and the stock markets plummet so dizzyingly that investors, losses are estimated at around 4 to 4.5 trillion pounds.

Al-Qaeda – again
12th October 2000 In Aden, Yemen, the destroyer USS *Cole* is attacked by Al-Qaeda suicide bombers in an explosives-laden boat. Seventeen of the crew are killed.

Space Station
2nd November 2000 American William Shepherd and Russians Yuri Gidzenko and Sergei Krikalev reach the International Space Station (ISS) after a journey of more than two days on Soyuz TM-31.

PlayStation 2
24th November 2000 Sony launches its new PlayStation 2 console in Europe as an answer to the Sega Dreamcast, released two years earlier. Over 1.5 billion will be sold during its lifetime.

Closest election ever?
7th November 2000 The US Presidential election race is one of the tightest in history. Neither Republican George W. Bush nor Democrat Al Gore is a clear winner, and the outcome is only decided more than a month later after re-counts of the ballots in the key deciding state of Florida. Bush is finally declared the victorious candidate on 12th December, winning the electoral college with 271 votes to Gore's 266 but losing the popular vote by over half a million votes.

ENTERTAINMENT

An unexpected delivery
The patter of tiny feet is heard in Albert Square on 26th October when Sonia Jackson gives birth to a baby unexpectedly. Poor Sonia didn't even know she was pregnant, but actress Natalie Cassidy acts her socks off in an episode that has *Eastenders* fans glued to their TV screens. Despite Sonia being in a relationship with Jamie Mitchell, the baby's father turns out to be Martin Fowler.

2000

Toy Story 2

After the phenomenal success of 1995's *Toy Story*, Pixar give Woody, Buzz and chums a second outing in a sequel that is generally agreed to be even better than the first. This time, Woody accidentally ends up at a yard sale and is bought by a greedy toy collector who realises he's found a bargain. At his new home, Woody meets Jesse the cowgirl who, along with Bullseye the Horse and Stinky Pete the Prospector are all toy characters from the 1950s series, *Woody's Round-Up*. But Woody soon realises that as a collectable piece of toy history, he's destined for a museum in Japan. Thankfully, Buzz and the rest of the *Toy Story* squad are on a mission to rescue him from a life behind glass. *Toy Story 2* is released in UK cinemas on 11th February.

Billy Elliot

29th September 2000 There could not be a more incongruous backdrop to the story of a boy who wants to be a ballet dancer, than a pit village in County Durham during the 1984 miners' strike. Billy Elliot is a boy who discovers he prefers dance over boxing classes. But with his widowed dad and older brother both on the picket line and struggling financially, not to mention prejudiced about boys and ballet, it's up to jaded dance teacher Sandra (Julie Walters) to be his coach and cheerleader. Jamie Bell, who plays eleven-year-old Billy with gauche abandon, was picked for the role out of 2,000 boys, and goes on to win an Oscar, aged fourteen, for Best Supporting Actor. It's a film with great warmth and heart, and with an ending that will have you crying happy tears.

Blue Peter Time Capsule

On *7th June 1971*, *Blue Peter* presenters John Noakes, Valerie Singleton and Peter Purves buried a time capsule in front of BBC Television Centre, intended to be opened in the future, specifically the year 2000. On 7th January, one week into the new millennium, they join the current presenters to open the box. The contents, which include a Blue Peter annual and a set of decimal coins, have suffered some water damage but are mostly well preserved. Doesn't time fly?

Gladiator

12th May 2000 About 30 years have passed since Hollywood last released a Roman epic, but Ridley Scott's stunning film, *Gladiator*, is worth waiting for, earning five Oscars including Best Picture and Best Actor for Russell Crowe as Maximus, the exiled general turned gladiator. Crowe shed the pounds and hit the gym so that he would look the part in the gladiatorial arena. Joaquin Phoenix is appropriately cruel and callous as Maximus's villainous adversary, the Roman Emperor Commodus, while the film is also notable for the final performance of Oliver Reed, as the gruff gladiator trainer Antonius Proximo. After Reed's sudden death halfway through filming, Scott created his remaining scenes using CGI.

2000

Meet the Parents

12th November 2000 Robert de Niro may have a reputation as a Hollywood heavyweight, but he can also do comedy brilliantly. Exhibit A is *Meet the Parents* in which de Niro plays Jack, a paranoid ex-CIA agent who is fiercely protective of his family and such a control freak he trains his pet cat to use the toilet. He's the future father-in-law to Ben Stiller's Gaylord 'Greg' Focker, a well-meaning Jewish nurse, who wants to ask girlfriend Pam to marry him but he realises he must meet her parents first. As Greg attempts to fit into Jack's regimented lifestyle, it seems that everything he does turns into a disaster, from breaking Pam's sister's nose during a water volleyball match to accidentally causing a major sewage leak. You'll cringe and you'll cry with laughter; *Meet the Parents* is a gem of a comedy and leads to an equally brilliant sequel, *Meet the Fockers*, in 2004.

Pottermania

Harry Potter and the Goblet of Fire, the fourth instalment in J. K. Rowling's Harry Potter novels, is published on 8th July in both the UK and USA, and on a Saturday so that young fans can get their paws on a copy early without any worry about school. A special Hogwarts Express train is commissioned by publisher Bloomsbury, which begins at Platform 1 (renamed Platform 9 ¾) at King's Cross, with Rowling signing copies before it proceeds northward to Perth in Scotland, making several stops en route. Some families camp outside bookshops overnight to be sure to secure their copy of the first million run when the doors open at 9am, and everywhere from airports to Little Chef restaurants at service stations have stocked copies to help those who have missed out on buying the book through the traditional channels.

Erin Brockovich

7th April 2000 A legal drama about polluted water does not, on the surface, appear the most compelling of subjects for a movie, but *Erin Brockovich*, based on a true story, is much more than that. Julia Roberts stars as the title character, a single mother of three who discovers a cover-up by Pacific Gas and Electric Company, which has been paying the medical bills of the residents of Hinkley, California, after the town's groundwater was contaminated. Brockovich doggedly pieces together evidence, her research leading to PG&E paying out an unprecedented $333 million compensation to Hinkley's residents. Roberts is captivating as the gutsy, tenacious Brockovich, and wins an Oscar for her performance. The real Erin Brockovich continues as an environmental activist and legal campaigner to this day.

Star by his side

In 1999, Ian Moor from Willerby, Hull wins ITV's lookalike-soundalike contest *Stars in their Eyes*, with his rendition of Chris de Burgh's *Lady in Red*, On 20th May this year, as reigning champion, he returns to the programme's grand final to reprise his performance when, after one verse, the audience are delighted to witness the real Chris de Burgh arrive on stage to sing his smoochy smash hit with Moor. Moor later gives up singing and becomes a school science lab technician in east Yorkshire.

Scooting around

Scooters have been a fun way for kids to get around for a century, but this year sees a craze for folding scooters, aimed at both adults and children, with JD Bug the pioneer of this new form of whizzy wheels.

2000

A millionaire at last
Who Wants to be a Millionaire, the quiz show where brainy contestants can win big, has been on our screens since September 1998 but nobody has yet managed to win the jackpot £1,000,000 - until now. On 20th November, Judith Keppel, a garden designer from Fulham, appears on the show, and knows the answer to the final question - Eleanor of Aquitaine was married to Henry II. In a bizarre case of serendipity, she can actually trace her ancestry back to Plantagenet royalty Henry II and Eleanor of Aquitaine.

Castaway 2000
On *18th January*, BBC1 airs the first programme of *Castaway 2000*, a bold social experiment in which 36 people are left on the remote Scottish island of Taransay to build a community and develop self-sufficiency skills. It's the BBC's first true foray into reality TV, although with no tangible prize for the participants. Several of the castaways leave, but most remain until the bitter end (January 2001). Prominent among the group is 26-year-old Ben Fogle who goes on to become a presenter for the BBC.

The Weakest Link
'You are the weakest link. Goodbye.' Stony-faced Anne Robinson takes absolutely no prisoners as deadpan host of this quiz show which humiliates anyone who lets the side down. *The Weakest Link* first airs on BBC2 on 14th August with the game show format licensed around the world, though surely no other hosts can have such a store of withering putdowns as Ms Robinson?

We're all watching *Big Brother*
Taking its name from George Orwell's dystopian novel *1984*, the premise of *Big Brother* is to put a group of strangers in a house together, install cameras everywhere for 24-hour surveillance, then sit back and watch what happens. Taking place over 64 days this summer, *Big Brother* explores an entirely new type of television and becomes a phenomenal success as the nation is gripped by the doings inside the house. The winner, Craig Phillips, a Liverpudlian builder, promises to give his entire £70,000 prize money to a friend with Down Syndrome to pay for a heart and lung transplant.

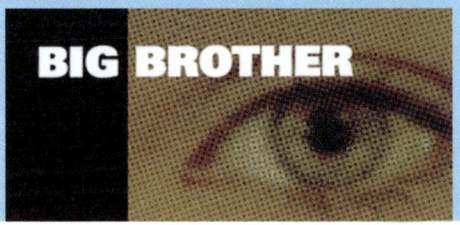

Clocking Off
23rd January 2000 The first series of *Clocking Off* drama about a Manchester factory and its workers, begins on BBC1. Outside of their mundane jobs, the lives of the Mackintosh Textiles' employees are anything but dull with infidelity, insurance fiddles, plastic surgery, arson and abscondment all tackled as each episode brings one character and their story to the fore. *Clocking Off* runs for four series, and gathers a cluster of BAFTAs along the way.

Monarch of the Glen
Scottish-set drama *Monarch of the Glen* begins on BBC1 on 27th February with Alastair Mackenzie as Archie Macdonald, a London restaurateur, called back to his Highland home Glenbogle House to become Laird. Based very loosely on the Highland novels of Compton Mackenzie, the show stars Richard Briers and Susan Hampshire as Archie's parents, and Julian Fellowes as Lord Kilwillie, *Monarch of the Glen* runs for seven series until 2005.

2000

MUSIC

Santana sweep the board
23rd February 2000 At the Grammys, the big winners of the evening are Santana who go home with eight separate awards - a stunning achievement for a band formed 35 years earlier.

Polar award
12th January 2000 Bob Dylan wins the Polar Music Prize, founded by ABBA manager and collaborator Stig Anderson in 1989 in recognition of greatness across all forms of music. Usually one to shun award ceremonies, he flies to Stockholm to accept the award.

Dury dies
27th March 2000 Ian Dury of *Sex, Drugs and Rock'n'Roll* fame dies of liver cancer aged 57.

One-hit wonders
7th May 2000 Irish boyband Westlife make an eye-catching US debut with their single *Swear It Again* at No. 1. Their failure to build on that success while sweeping all before them in the UK is one of the puzzles of early 21st-century pop. The band fails to register even one more US hit, while they rack up a total of 28 UK hits over the next nineteen years.

End of the squiggle
16th May 2000 Now no longer contracted to Warner Brothers, The Artist Formerly Known as Prince reverts to the name by which everybody knows him. The squiggle is banished forever.

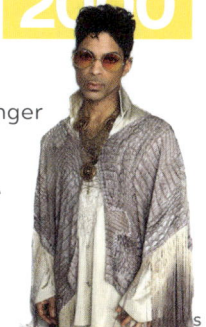

Meet Slim Shady
23rd May 2000 The release of *The Marshall Mathers* LP by Detroit-based Eminem follows up the previous year's *Slim Shady* LP and overturns the perception of white rap as something wholly imitative and commercially suspect. From a working-class background and a single-parent home, Eminem raps it like he sees it, with impressive rhyming and real musicality. Having created the character Slim Shady as a mask for satire and commentary, he closes out the year with *Stan*, told from the point of view of an unnervingly obsessive fan.

50 Cent shooting
24th May 2000 Rising rap star 50 Cent (Curtis Jackson) is shot nine times in a murder attempt in Queens, New York. Although the shooting puts his career on hold, he makes a full recovery.

2000

Bowie at Glasto
23rd June 2000 David Bowie is the closing act at the Glastonbury Festival, which he has not played since 1971. Festival co-organiser Emily Eavis describes his set as 'spellbinding' and one of the best in the festival's history. Witnessed by over a quarter of a million festival goers, the BBC TV recording of the event is only shown in its entirety after Bowie's death.

Festival disaster
30th June 2000 A crush during grunge band Pearl Jam's headlining set at the Roskilde Festival in Denmark kills nine fans and injures 26.

Coldplay debut
10th July 2000
A new band comprising former University College of London students is tipped for greatness. Led by Chris Martin (photo), Coldplay release their debut album, *Parachutes*.

Craig wins a MOBO
4th October 2000 The MOBO (Music of Black Origin) Awards have become a fixture on the music industry calendar since their inception in 1996. This year's Best Single winner is Southampton-born Craig David for *Fill Me In*. Just nineteen years old, he is fresh from topping the UK chart with *7 Days*, the tale of a week-long love affair told with classic soul and hip hop touches.

MY FIRST 18 YEARS — TOP 10 — 2000

1. **Dancing in the Moonlight** *Toploader*
2. **Don't Call Me Baby** *Madison Avenue*
3. **Oops! I Did it Again** *Britney Spears*
4. **Spinning Around** *Kylie Minogue*
5. **Groovejet** *Spiller with Sophie Ellis-Bextor*
6. **Yellow** *Coldplay*
7. **Who Let the Dogs Out** *Baha Men*
8. **Umbrella** *Rhianna*
9. **Babylon** *David Gray*
10. **I Try** *Macy Gray*

Yes he can!
23rd December 2000 The UK's Christmas No. 1 is *Can We Fix It?*, the theme song from *Bob the Builder*, the latest animated television show for children in the tradition of *Postman Pat* and *Fireman Sam*. Performing it is the show's narrator, actor Neil Morrissey.

Worthy Corrs
15th July 2000 A real musical hotspot at the start of the new millennium is Ireland. U2 maintain their unstoppable progress with *All That You Can Leave Behind* and the single *Beautiful Day* while the Riverdance influence has had a profound effect on Broadway and West End choreography. Holding their own are the Corrs, three sisters and a brother from Dundalk, who follow their BRIT Award for Best International Group with the album *In Blue* and its chart-topping single *Breathless*.

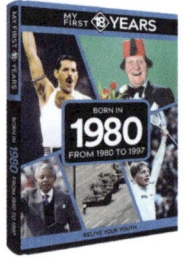